Nature Religion Today

Nature Religion Today

Paganism in the Modern World

Edited by
Joanne Pearson, Richard H. Roberts and
Geoffrey Samuel

Edinburgh University Press

© Edinburgh University Press, 1998

Edinburgh University Press
22 George Square, Edinburgh

Typeset in 11 on 13pt Goudy Old Style
by Hewer Text Ltd Edinburgh, and
printed and bound in Great Britain by
The Cromwell Press, Trowbridge, Wilts

A CIP record for this book is available from the British Library

ISBN 0 7486 1057 X

Contents

Part Three   Nature Religion in Practice

List of Contributors

Peter Beyer is Associate Professor of Religious Studies at the University of Ottawa, Canada. He is author of *Religion and Globalization* (Sage, 1994) and is currently exploring the possibility of analysing religion as a global social system. He has recently published articles on this subject in the journals *Numen*, *International Sociology* and *Social Compass*.

Vivianne Crowley lectures in the Psychology of Religion at King's College, University of London, and is Adjunct Professor at the Union Institute, Cincinnati, Ohio. She is author of *Wicca: The Old Religion in the New Millennium*, *Phoenix from the Flame: Living as a Pagan in the 21st Century*, *Principles of Paganism* and *Principles of Wicca* (all Thorsons/HarperCollins).

Susan Greenwood is a social anthropologist and teaches Gender Studies at the University of Kent at Canterbury. Her academic interests lie in gender, shamanism and magical philosophy. Recent publications include 'The British Occult Subculture: Beyond Good and Evil?' (1996), 'Feminist Witchcraft: A Transformatory Politics' (1996), and 'The Magical Will: Gender and Power in Magical Practices' (1996).

Wouter J. Hanegraaff is Research Associate at the University of Utrecht, the Netherlands. He specialises in the history of western esoteric traditions since the Renaissance and is currently working on a book on western concepts of 'magic'. He is author of *New Age Religion and Western Culture: Esotericism in the Mirror of Secular Thought* (Brill, 1996) and co-editor (with Roelof van den Broek) of *Gnosis and Hermeticism from Antiquity to Modern Times* (SUNY, 1998).

Ronald Hutton is Professor of History at the University of Bristol. His previous publications include *The Pagan Religions of the Ancient British Isles*, *The Rise and Fall of Merry England* and *Stations of the Sun*. His work on the history of modern Pagan witchcraft, *The Triumph of the Moon*, is due to be published by Oxford University Press in 1999.

Prudence Jones is a writer and researcher based in Cambridge. From 1979 to 1990 she ran the Pagan Federation, Europe's oldest Pagan association, and from 1985 to 1989 she also ran the Pagan Anti-Defamation League with Nigel Pennick. She is a trained psychotherapist and a philosophy supervisor at Cambridge University. Her latest book (with Nigel Pennick) is *A History of Pagan Europe* (Routledge, 1995).

Alastair McIntosh is a fellow of the now-independent green academic network, the Centre for Human Ecology. He developed its MSc and PhD teaching programme between 1990 and 1996 whilst the CHE was still within Edinburgh University. He is a founding trustee of the Isle of Eigg Trust which, in 1997, saw the Hebridean island restored to community ownership. In 1994 he led unprecedented theological opposition at the public inquiry into the proposed Isle of Harris super-quarry.

Joanne Pearson is researching a PhD in the Department of Religious Studies, Lancaster University, investigating contemporary British Wicca. She co-ordinated the international conference 'Nature Religion Today: Western Paganism, Shamanism and Esotericism in the 1990s' held in Ambleside in April 1996, and this collected volume is her first major publication.

Elizabeth Puttick is a sociologist of religion, specialising in new religions, shamanism, ecospirituality, gender issues and personal development. She has many years' personal and professional experience on these subjects, on which she has written and lectured widely. She teaches a course on MindBodySpirit at the City University, London. Her latest book is *Women in New Religions* (Macmillan, 1997).

Richard Roberts is Professor of Religious Studies at Lancaster University. His major interests include religion and social theory and the multidisciplinary analysis of contemporary religion, and he has published widely on contemporary religion, theology, rhetoric and the human sciences. His recent publications include the edited collection *Religion and the Transformations of Capitalism: Comparative Responses* (Routledge, 1995), and he convened the organising committee for the 'Nature Religion Today' conference held in Ambleside in April 1996.

Jone Salomonsen teaches Philosophy of Religion and Ethics at the University of Oslo, and has recently completed her PhD on feminist Wicca as an expression of women's religiosity in the contemporary USA. She has published a volume, in Norway, on Wicca, neo-shamanism and the men's movement, and is currently working on a book on modern ritual.

Geoffrey Samuel is Associate Professor of Sociology and Anthropology at the University of Newcastle, New South Wales, Australia, and Professor of Religious Studies at Lancaster University. He is a specialist in Tibetan Buddhism, shamanism and the scientific study of altered states of consciousness. His recent publications include *Civilized Shamans: Buddhism in Tibetan Societies* (Smithsonian, 1993) and he was also a member of the organising committee for the 'Nature Religion Today' conference held in Ambleside in April 1996.

Philip Shallcrass has been a Druid for over twenty years, and is joint chief, with Emma Restall Orr, of the British Druid Order, which he founded in 1979. Philip is currently working on two books on the Bardic tradition, as well as editing *The Druids'*

Voice: The Magazine of Contemporary Druidry. He is an artist, poet, musician and singer-songwriter, and gives lectures and workshops on various aspects of Druidry and Paganism.

Steven Sutcliffe has been researching a PhD in the history and sociology of the New Age in Britain in the Department of Religious Studies at the Open University. He is currently editing a forthcoming volume on alternative forms of religion in twentieth-century Britain for Edinburgh University Press.

Acknowledgements

The editors would like to express their thanks both to the many people who helped plan, took part in and otherwise supported the conference from which this collection draws its contributions, and to the staff of Charlotte Mason College in Ambleside, which proved an ideal location for the event, with its constant reminder of the inspiring presence of nature.

We would like to thank the British Academy for its financial support, and also Lancaster University's Research Committee which, despite the financial difficulties of the university at the time, matched the British Academy's contribution. Particular thanks are due to Marion Bowman, Charlotte Hardman and Graham Harvey, whose pioneering work on earlier conferences encouraged our efforts, and to Graham and Marion, who were especially supportive to Jo during the organisation of the conference.

Richard Roberts and Geoffrey Samuel wish to express their especial gratitude to Jo Pearson, who undertook the bulk of the editorial work in the preparation of the final text. Finally, all three of us would like to express our warm appreciation of the contributions made to the conference by all the participants, particularly those from outside the United Kingdom. Unfortunately, it has proved possible to publish only a selection of the many papers presented.

Jo Pearson, Richard Roberts and Geoffrey Samuel
Lancaster University, August 1997

Introduction

Contemporary Paganism, or Neo-Paganism (as explained below, we adopt the former usage in this book), is now a well-differentiated area of religious growth with important elective affinities with feminism, increasing ecological awareness, and other new social movements. This collection draws upon the work of a wide range of contributors who, as social scientists and/or practitioners, engage in critical exploration of what is now becoming a major religious development. Paganism is commanding increasing public attention at a time when traditional main-line religions, most notably Christianity and Judaism in Europe and North America, appear to be in decline and to be redifferentiating (along with other major world religions) into fundamentalisms with a weakening positive engagement with world issues other than a narrow range of intensely debated moral concerns, frequently associated with sexuality.

This volume of essays originated in the conference 'Nature Religion Today: Western Paganism, Shamanism and Esotericism in the 1990s', organised by the Department of Religious Studies at Lancaster University, and held at Ambleside, in the English Lake District, in April 1996. This conference, which followed a first, pioneering event held at Newcastle in 1994, sought to explore the innovations in practice and belief which constitute contemporary Paganism, and which appear to be part of a widespread cultural response to the decay of main-line religions and to a widely felt awareness of ecological crisis. The conference itself was a remarkable experience, drawing together on the academic side representatives not only of such disciplines as religious studies, sociology and anthropology, but also of dance and theatre studies, history, and women's and cultural studies. In addition, the conference was well supported by the Pagan community, and the many papers were supplemented by performance which enlivened a memorable event. Inevitably, as editors, we have had to make a selection from material that much exceeded the space available in this publication. Given the primarily academic character of the volume, we have focused upon a range of issues that together have coherence and, we hope, will help to drive forward the interpretation of this field of religious activity.

Readers, particularly those new to this field of study, may welcome some clarification of terminology. We use *Paganism* as a general and inclusive category for a range of specific traditions, all of which may in varying degrees be described as *nature religions* in the sense that they involve a reorientation towards, and a resacralisation of, both external nature and our own physical embodiment. 'Paganism' is the preferred term among practitioners, but many scholars, and some practitioners, especially in North America, prefer the usage 'Neo-Paganism'. We have chosen the simpler term, in large part because of the emphasis on continuity in much of the material in this collection.

Of the various Pagan traditions discussed in this book, *Wicca* came to public notice in the 1950s through the work of Gerald Gardner and his associates. Wicca, which presents itself as a contemporary version of a continuing Pagan tradition of witchcraft, now has many thousands of followers in the UK and elsewhere. *Feminist witchcraft* refers to a number of subsequent developments, mostly originating in the USA with the work of Starhawk, Z. Budapest and others from the late 1970s onwards. These groups also present themselves as practising witchcraft, but with a greater emphasis on the Goddess and frequently with explicit connections to feminist thought. The *Druid* revival dates to the eighteenth century, but specifically pagan Druid traditions such as that represented by Philip Shallcrass in this volume appeared in the UK and USA from the 1970s onwards.

The term *New Age* is used in the wider community, and by some analysts, as a general term under which contemporary Paganism may be subsumed (cf. Heelas 1996). As will become evident (see Joanne Pearson's chapter in particular), the appropriateness of describing contemporary Pagans as 'New Age' is open to question, and many Pagans strongly object to this description.

Nature Religion Today is organised in three parts. The first addresses the impact of a growing, yet differentiated, awareness of the earth as the basis of the spiritual life; the second examines the correlative consciousness of the Goddess as symbolic, ritual and mythic focal point of Pagan nature religion; and the third presents accounts of four significant examples of the cultural practice of contemporary nature religion. Before, however, reviewing the contents of the collection, we outline the context within which we view the developments described in this book.

Paganism and other forms of contemporary nature religion are important components in a religious resurgence which exists on a global scale and impinges increasingly upon many aspects of society and culture. This increased salience of religion has to be understood in the dual perspective provided by social theory of the world system as a whole (i.e. 'globalisation' theory) on the one hand, and localised processes of identity formation on the other. The intersection between global and local processes is, as Roland Robertson (Robertson 1992) and others have argued, the key zone of socio-scientific interpretation of cultural change. Nature religion intersects directly with a range of ecological concerns, but it is not a marginal or primarily rural phenomenon. Instead, it involves a general revaluation of the conditions of all human life. Most significantly, nature religion involves the re-ritualisation of the stages of human existence from birth, through growth and maturity, to death, which intersects with natural annual and cosmic cycles.

Paradoxically, the emphasis within nature religion upon female aspects of the human condition creates a tense and interesting relationship between a Pagan recovery and enactment of the reality of nature and the earth, and expressions of contemporary feminism which seek in their extreme forms to abrogate nature in order to enhance the biologically untrammelled empowerment of women. Thus from the standpoint of the newly emergent paradigms of globalisation theory and of differentiated feminisms, resurgent nature religion poses significant questions not simply for women but for humanity as a whole. In this collection, these issues are explored from a wide range of standpoints in ways which forge closer links between social and cultural theory and present-day religious change and development.

In the first part of the book, 'A Chthonic Imperative? Religion and Nature in the Modern World', we explore the rediscovery of the constitutive role of the earth, the *chthonos*, in contemporary forms of religiosity. The ascription 'chthonic' was first used as a technical term by the classicist and anthropologist Jane Harrison (Harrison 1908), and whilst her work was influential in academic circles, it is only with the explosion of interest in earth-related spirituality that this somewhat recondite conception is gaining a new role as an interpretative topos. The imperative within nature religion that humankind should not only respect and ascribe value to the natural world but seek out ultimacy in terms of ritual and symbolic interaction is open to a range of interpretations, and our contributors explore many of these.

Peter Beyer opens this part with a critical sociological examination of nature religion understood as an oppositional response to the process of globalisation. Beyer regards nature religion as a useful analytical abstraction which can be construed as an aspect of the localisation and intensification of particular identities that emerge in the face of the integrative and homogenising power of globalisation. Thus, unlike most of the contributors to this volume, Beyer does not move from the local to the global, but interprets religious particularities as reactions to changes in the world system. This contribution draws the substantive content of the collection into an informed dialogue with central aspects of current social theory.

Following the global perspective developed by Peter Beyer, Wouter Hanegraaff and Steven Sutcliffe examine some of the uses of nature religion within the widespread New Age movement. This movement is regarded by some leading nature religionists, for example Monica Sjöö, as dangerously divorced from serious ecological responsibility (Sjöö 1992). Hanegraaff argues that the New Age, despite its supposed 'resacralisation' of nature, is actually a kind of secular naturalism, with no room for the supernatural or for a reality subsisting, as it were, outside the laws of science. He uses a contrast between the characters Settembrini and Naphta in Thomas Mann's *The Magic Mountain* to illustrate the difference between this secular view of nature and an account which recognises and accepts the sacred as awe-inspiring, beyond human understanding, and not necessarily benevolent. Furthermore, Hanegraaff argues that the New Age can be understood as a product of the secularisation of nature, illustrating this through a comparison of Boehme's *Naturphilosophie* with New Age ideas. Hanegraaff's interpretation is similar in certain respects to that of Beyer, in that he provides an account which runs counter to the self-understanding of practitioners, who regard themselves as a revival of ancient esotericism.

Steven Sutcliffe investigates transformations of the concept of 'nature', again as this has been exploited in New Age. Sutcliffe argues that there is a marked parallel between the catastrophist apocalyptic traditions of Judaism and Christianity and New Age beliefs in the transvaluation of the material world. The dualistic and quasi-gnostic aspects of New Age are only in part countered by the esoteric, vitalistic experience of nature reported by key activists. On the basis of a wide-ranging review, in particular of the Findhorn Community, Sutcliffe suggests that examining the category of 'nature' can provide important insight into forms of New Age religiosity.

The question of whether Wicca can appropriately be subsumed under a general New Age category is then explored by Joanne Pearson, who argues against the common academic assumption that Wicca is to be regarded as part of the New Age. Many academic studies assume this, yet evidence from research in the field indicates that the great majority of Wiccans and Pagans do not regard themselves as 'New Age' and would wish to repudiate such an identification, choosing to see Wicca as a 'revived religion' rather than as a new religious movement assimilable into the category of New Age. On this basis, Pearson argues for the distinctiveness of Wicca in the context of contemporary religiosity, and for the existence of a Pagan alternative in the modern world.

In the concluding chapter of this section, Richard Roberts extends the examination of contextual factors in the interpretation of nature religion by focusing on the 'chthonic imperative'. This imperative is integral to both Paganism and the growing consciousness of the Goddess. Roberts regards these as complementary aspects of a new social movement and an 'imagined community' that is impelled by a revisionary account of human, in particular western, history and prehistory. The main theses of the chthonic imperative, the demand that we re-engage with the earth as source of primal meaning, are summarised in dialogue with Monica Sjöö and Barbara Mor's representative text, *The Great Cosmic Mother*. Roberts contrasts this project with the successive mediations central to the western Latin tradition of Christianity, and concludes that an immediate relationship of ultimacy with nature is attractive but not unproblematic.

The second part of the book, 'The Pagan Alternative: the Goddess and Nature', begins with a consideration of whether there is historical continuity between the ancient origins of Paganism and contemporary practice. Prudence Jones argues that classical Graeco-Roman religion was a 'nature religion' in several important ways, and that European folk custom successfully preserved significant fragments of ancient practice that can undergo contemporary revival. Jones proceeds to argue that Catherine Albanese's account of modern nature religion in North America as either 'traditional' or New Age (Albanese 1990) does not apply to European experience without substantial modification. She illustrates the great richness and diversity of the gods of the ancient world and shows how these have important affinities with current practices in Europe, Asia and North America. Jones argues that there is sufficient continuity in European Pagan traditions to resist the charge that contemporary Paganism depends upon the inappropriate assimilation of the cultural inheritance of indigenous peoples.

Ronald Hutton explores the process by which the modern western world came to have its most common image of the Goddess. Hutton suggests that the assimilation of a range of images of the Goddess into a composite figure was heavily influenced in early modernity by the rise of western science and, in a more positive way, by

Romanticism. The exaltation of nature and the discovery of the beauties of wilderness went hand in hand with poetic and musical representations of the affinities of female divinity with aspects of the natural world. Central to Hutton's argument is a tension between changing sensibility and the desire to claim a historical continuity of dedication to the Goddess. This desire for historical continuity led to a persuasive stretching of archaeological evidence. Ronald Hutton shows how interpretation of the role of the Goddess aroused acute controversy and even polarisation within the archaeological community, and notes the different paths taken in reinterpreting the material in recent times in the UK and USA.

Ronald Hutton's reflections on the 'discovery of the modern Goddess' provide an informed context for Susan Greenwood's examination of the nature of the Goddess in modern witchcraft, particularly with regard to the issues of sexuality and power. Greenwood argues that if witchcraft is nature religion, it is about 'inner nature' rather than the physical environment. Greenwood discusses differing approaches to gender typologies in Wicca and in feminist witchcraft, and evaluates these by drawing upon anthropological concepts of trance and possession. According to Susan Greenwood, witchcraft is to be understood primarily as 'a form of contemporary shamanic practice whereby . . . witches (re)negotiate their magical and sexual identities for self-empowerment'.

Elizabeth Puttick elaborates on the themes of sexuality and power by reviewing models of female experience in a variety of traditional religions and new religious movements, showing how these can lead to the devaluation of women. Puttick argues that the role of the 'sex goddess' and the associated myth of romantic love have sometimes provided partial escapes from the devaluation of women, but such emancipation is selective and enacted on terms set by men, culminating in domestic slavery. Whereas Tantra offers the prospect of a resacralising of female sexuality, in practice women in western Tantric contexts, as in Asia, may none the less be the objects of male exploitation. Correspondingly, women in new religious movements frequently find themselves the victims of sexual abuse by male cult leaders. Elizabeth Puttick argues that it is necessary for 'women – as well as men – to be in control of their own sexuality and emotional life'.

In the last chapter of this part, Geoffrey Samuel compares Tibetan Buddhism in the west with Paganism. Samuel explores the ways in which Tibetan Buddhism and Paganism represent our relationship to 'nature', recognising that there is no single representation of nature in either of these emergent traditions. Drawing upon ethnography, the author presents ritual parallels which exploit sacred place, symbolic space, possession, dancing and singing, and magical procedures. The role of sexuality in Tantra and modern witchcraft is explored in some detail. This commonality in practice is placed in the wider context of environmental ethics and feminist critiques of contemporary western culture. Samuel suggests that Wicca and other forms of western Paganism, as life-affirming religious practices, develop complementary aspects of religious experience to those stressed by Buddhism in the west.

In the third, concluding part of the book, 'Nature Religion in Practice', aspects of the practical application and appeal of nature religion are presented. Jone Salomonsen presents a detailed and nuanced account of a well-known Californian witchcraft group, the Reclaiming community in San Francisco, founded by Starhawk in 1980. She discusses the importance, as means of female empowerment, of nature and the Goddess to members of the community, and seeks to explain the attraction of the Goddess for a variety of women initiates. Her explanation of the relationship between experience and textuality in contemporary witchcraft draws upon linguistic, historical, existential and semiotic categories. Salomonsen concludes that the 'holy hermeneutics' of feminist witchcraft is diverse and polyvalent, and empowering of women.

As a practising Druid, Philip Shallcrass presents a contrasting male perspective, recalling his personal discovery of the Goddess and her influence on his life as a 'priest of the Goddess'. This account is representative, even typical, of the combination of influences that impel individuals towards dedication to the Goddess, such as childhood experience, a sense of the eminent practicality and eclectic possibilities of Paganism, and literature such as Robert Graves' *The White Goddess* (Graves 1961). Shallcrass is particularly attracted to Welsh and Celtic folklore and to practices in which the role of the woman as initiatrix is central.

Vivianne Crowley outlines the self-image of Wicca understood as a revived religious tradition, focused not least on the veneration of nature, and she examines the ways in which witches practise environmental activism within their religion. Nature is regarded as being ensouled, and most Wiccans would consider themselves to be pantheists, panentheists or even animists. The deities of Wicca are understood as embodiments of a life-force manifest in nature. The Wiccan ritual cycle is based on seasonal myth in which the processes of nature – conception, birth, maturation, harvest and death – are represented through the dynamic interaction of male and female deities, with whom the participants identify. Crowley shows how the Wiccan appreciation of nature has changed as the tradition has become more associated with active environmentalism in the public domain.

Alastair McIntosh, who drew the Ambleside conference to a spirited conclusion, also closes the reflections contained in this book. He presents a passionate exhortation to embed nature religion in the reality of physical nature and the environment, and to acknowledge the specificity of the land on which each of us lives. McIntosh combines the role of environmental scientist with that of an activist who uses techniques and practices drawn from Celtic shamanism and other forms of nature religion as a Bard. His 'Gal–Gael' declamation is a narrative of social, political and environmental struggle in contemporary Scotland. McIntosh provides a detailed commentary upon his epic prose-poem, and this contribution affords indispensable insight into the performance character of present-day ecological activism.

It is our intention that *Nature Religion Today* should confront and engage with a religious development which is often misconstrued by an ill-informed public accustomed to the sensational treatment of phenomena that stand outside the mainstream. Contemporary nature religion is exploratory, as well as traditional, and its growing prominence is clearly a response to social and cultural impulses that are themselves in need of effective explanation. Whereas the socio-scientific study of main-line religion since World War II has been largely the product of sociologists preoccupied with the secularisation paradigm, academic investigators of nature religion and its cognates often combine observation and participation in ways which challenge all claims to reductive objectivity. We therefore hope that this volume will enable the reader not only to gain insight into current religious transformations, but also possibly to reconceive some important aspects of the present-day human condition.

PART ONE

A Chthonic Imperative? Religion and Nature in the Modern World

CHAPTER 1

Globalisation and the Religion of Nature
Peter Beyer

– I Introduction: nature and the technical –

My purpose in this chapter is to discuss the social context in which nature religion has become important; and therefore how nature religion participates in that context, helping to form and being formed by it. The social context to which I refer is a global one, meaning that my primary unit of analysis is a single globally extended society or social system. I will elaborate on how I understand this system below; first, however, it is important to address the question of what the concept of nature religion means.

Nature religion, for my purposes here, is not a particular religion or religious tradition. Rather it is a useful analytic abstraction that refers to any religious belief or practice in which devotees consider nature to be the embodiment of divinity, sacredness, transcendence, spiritual power, or whatever cognate term one wishes to use (cf. Albanese 1990). Having said that, the term is none the less quite ambiguous. Aside from the vexed question of what counts as a religious belief or practice, the word 'nature' includes among its modern meanings notions close enough to the idea of sacredness for the expression to risk being pleonastic. Nature is the way things are aside from human agency, much as the religions are ways of knowing, gaining access to or otherwise communicating with that same extra-human reality, or at least with that which is assumed to serve as the condition for its possibility.

One might object that nature in this label is more restrictive, referring only to the 'natural world' consisting of things like forests, mountains, stars and non-human life-forms. Such a narrowing, however, would still beg the question of what is to be included or excluded as nature, and on what basis. As with the concept of religion, therefore, we can attain better precision if we focus also on what nature is not. Nature would then be one pole in a binary combination, in which the opposing or complementary term would be artifice, the humanly created or the technical. Adding the characteristic of being perceivable, nature would then be the total world available to us through our five senses, but excluding those portions which we deem to be technically, humanly and therefore artificially created. Nature religion, then, concerns itself with an imputed spiritual reality that inheres in this nature.

This way of circumscribing nature religion may seem excessively complicated to some. It is useful in the current context because it allows us to focus directly on how nature religion fits into today's global context. It is that context which gives us the model for what is technical and artificial, and thereby suggests what should be counted as nature. The operative questions then become: why is this distinction important; why do we see the rise of religious activity in terms of it; and what implications does this rise have for understanding what is happening in our world today?

In the remainder of this chapter, I try to answer these questions on the basis of a specific analysis of globalisation and some of its more important consequences. My basic thesis is that the historical development of global society has been spurred by the spread of certain powerful technical rationalities – economy, state, science, medicine, schooling and others – around the globe; that this spread has generated the construction of various cultural and personal identities as ways of appropriating or otherwise responding to those rationalities; and that nature religion is informing a portion of these responses, especially some of those that are critical of the consequences of technical dominance. To aid in the analysis of how nature religion fits into the globalisation picture, I adapt and extrapolate from Victor Turner's (Turner 1969) distinction between structure and anti-structure, rendering the latter term as counter-structure to stress the polar and dialogical relation between the two. Among other advantages, this strategy allows a clear view of how nature functions as a powerful and important symbol that not only embodies a critique of dominant structures, but also helps to define and legitimate them, the latter albeit indirectly.

– II GLOBALISATION: TECHNICAL RATIONALITY AND CULTURE –

A quick look at the growing number of recent publications about globalisation reveals the dominance of a roughly three-pronged conception. First, there is the economic idea that globalisation refers to transformations in the capitalist economic system in such a way as to weaken the independence of national economies in favour of a global market and to strengthen the world-wide operation of business firms (cf. Chorafas 1992; Dunning et al. 1990; Holm and Sensen 1995; Laxer 1993). Second, there is the notion that globalisation refers to the increase and spread of rapid communication technologies, such as satellite television and the Internet, which make all areas of the world more accessible to each other (cf. Bradley et al. 1993; Smith 1991). Third, there is a conception of globalisation as a process of cultural homogenisation as expressed in a wide range of phenomena from food consumption to urban architecture, from entertainment to tourism (cf. Ritzer 1996). The evaluation of this process can be either positive or negative. Some view it as development and progress, others see it as imperialism and the destruction of authentic human life.

This dominant conception, while not inaccurate, is none the less incomplete, and this in at least two important senses. First, it concentrates on very recent developments in a historical process that has been going on for quite some time. Thus, for example, following Immanuel Wallerstein's analysis (Wallerstein 1974, 1979), the world capitalist economy (his name for the global system) has its roots at least as far back as the sixteenth century. The current developments are from this perspective merely the latest chapter in the history of its spread and transformation. Correspondingly, while technologies like the Internet and television are certainly recent, the expansion of the global system has always been connected with technological developments ranging from navigation tools to weapons, from the printing press to industrial machinery (cf. Levenson 1967).

Second, and perhaps more importantly, most talk about globalisation emphasises the extent to which it has been a unidirectional process of western expansion, whether economic, political, technological or cultural. I would certainly not want to deny the central role of European power in this process; on the contrary, I would underline it. Yet a too exclusive focus on this aspect leaves out of consideration the degree to which non-westerners have participated in the formation of global society, increasingly since the end of World War II as powerful players and not just passive subjects. Indeed, one of the reasons for the current popularity of the idea of globalisation is undoubtedly the fact that 'reverse' influences have become far more difficult to dismiss or to interpret simply as non-westerners responding to western dominance. Under this and other pressures, the 'imperialist' west continues to transform as profoundly as the 'colonised' non-west, undermining the whole notion of a unidirectional process under the control of one set of dominant players.

A better understanding of globalisation can begin from Wallerstein's notion of a gradually expanding world capitalist system, but it cannot stop there. To be sure, European imperial expansion was instrumental in leading to the formation of contemporary global society; but it is not the European origins that are important so much as the reasons for European success. What distinguished the European powers in their imperial efforts of the sixteenth to twentieth centuries was that they had begun to shift to a form of social organisation centred largely on the development of technically rational instrumentalities such as economy, polity and science. This shift meant, among other things, a relatively constant expansion of administrative surveillance techniques, wealth in the form of capital, and ever more powerful technologies. Their technical superiority allowed the Europeans to expand their activities around the entire globe. It is this technical expansion that constitutes the basis of globalisation, but it is only one aspect of what globalisation has become (cf. Beyer 1994).

The inadequacy of conceiving globalisation simply as a synonym for western or European-based imperial expansion becomes clear when we look at the modern history of the first non-western country to match the western powers on the level of technical sophistication, namely Japan. After Admiral Perry's momentous visit to Tokyo harbour and the subsequent Meiji restoration of 1868, the Japanese set out to appropriate western technique, but very definitely on a specifically Japanese cultural base (cf. Robertson 1987). By the end of the nineteenth century they had succeeded in this task, becoming a modern imperial power beside the western ones, all the while maintaining and developing their cultural particularity. They had 'modernised' without 'westernising'. To be sure, these historical developments brought about very significant changes in Japanese society, much as European society had undergone epochal changes in previous centuries. Yet they did not lead to anything like cultural homogenisation; quite the contrary. In order to appropriate the originally western technical instrumentalities, the Japanese had to find a way of making only such changes as were necessary. There had to be a large amount of cultural continuity. An intimate part of this task was to (re)construct a modern Japanese cultural and national identity largely on the basis of already long-standing and indeed taken-for-granted Japanese cultural elements (e.g. bushido, Shinto, imperial house). Only with such a reconstructed self-image could they act on the global stage. Anything else would have required such monumental change in Japanese society in such a short period of time that probably only chaos and defeat would have resulted.

The importance of the Japanese example is that it shows how the globalisation that was and is from a certain perspective the spread and development of originally western instrumentalities cannot be conceived simply as cultural diffusion or imperial expansion. Their appropriation is not limited to a small upper ruling caste and their retainers as was the case for traditional empires. The changes required involve increasingly large portions of a region's population and therefore a refashioning of most of their lives. But given that tendency, the changes cannot be too much in discontinuity with what these same people have been, at least not over a short period of time. Indeed, as usual with social change, the new had to be in large measure a reinterpretation and recombination of traditional elements dissolved out of their previous contexts. The result is what Hobsbawm (Hobsbawm and Ranger 1983) has called the 'invention of tradition', Andersen (1991) the creation of 'imagined communities', and Hutton (1996a) 'discovered traditions': cultural constructs that establish the possibility and legitimacy of important cultural differences – that is, world-wide cultural pluralism – in the context of the global and comparatively homogeneous dominance of the systems of technical instrumentality.

The Japanese experience, of course, does not offer 'the model' of appropriation and cultural specification any more than have Western European or North American countries. The idea of some sort of basic 'pattern of modernisation' has been a tempting one; but like the notion of a uniform spread of the capitalist world economy, it is ultimately misleading or at least cannot account for enough of what has actually happened in the world of the last two centuries. Instead, it is more fruitful to look at the rise of pluralistic cultural identities – ethnicities, nations, peoples – as a critical aspect of how the powerful instrumentalities have been and are being particularised in various parts of the world. Again the evaluation of this complex process will vary, as will the specific characteristics from place to place, from incident to incident. In addition and quite obviously, the spread of capitalist economy, the nation-state, scientific technology, medicalised health, academic education and other instrumental systems has not resulted in some sort of equal distribution of power, wealth and life-chances; quite the contrary. What is important to underline, however, is that the modern construction of local or culturally particular identities has become a broadly legitimate and often highly valued strategy for at the same time appropriating the powerful instrumentalities, reacting against them or their perceived carriers, and yet also providing particular socio-cultural vehicles for their development, and even strengthening (cf. Featherstone et al. 1995; Nederven Pieterse 1993; Robertson 1992). And all this not out of some inherent evolutionary necessity, but simply as the contingent outcome of history.

Moreover, what Roland Robertson (1992) calls 'national societies' are not the only manifestation of such particularisation or localising of the globalising universal. The process also happens at the individual level of the self and in terms of non-national or non-ethnic group identities. In the former regard, the rise of the individual, especially but not only in the west, signals the degree to which the globalised instrumental systems do not by themselves determine many aspects of their own particularisation or specification. Rather their rise has led to what Giddens (1990) has called the 'disembedding' of individuals from their traditional cultural and social context with the result that the reconstruction or 're-embedding' must happen as much on the individual as on the group level. As regards the non-national or non-ethnic group identities, we see manifestations ranging from local social networks, to organisations, to social movements based on specific ideologies or world views. Similar to the appropriation/resistance/furtherance of globalisation evident in national or ethnic movements, we find corresponding processes in things such as liberation movements (e.g. socialist, feminist, homosexual) and various religious movements. This idea brings us to the question of the role of religion in the process of globalisation.

– III RELIGION: CULTURE AND INSTRUMENTAL SYSTEM –

Like the instrumental systems, the idea of delimitable religion and especially the idea of a plurality of formally analogous religions is substantially of early modern western origin, much like the idea of the modern nation. All historical cultures and civilisations have of course had what we, as observers, might analyse as religion or religious aspects. But that is different from the notion of religion as a differentiated institutional system that focuses on a special mode of symbolic activity. The latter arose in early modern Europe only in the context of the parallel formation of the other instrumental systems. It therefore represents the attempted instrumentalisation of religion. Moreover, as the instrumental systems expanded with the European imperial projects, so too did western religion in the form of the Christian churches. Here too we witness the attempts by local people to appropriate and adapt the originally western form into local constructions, sometimes through the rise of indigenous Christianities, but at least as often through the formation or attempted formation of parallel religions, formally equal to Christianity, but on the basis of local religious traditions. The changes in the so-called world religions of the last two centuries are instructive in this regard (Beyer 1996).

The most important point to underline in the present context is that religions or religious traditions in the global context are in a critical respect similar to nation-states. They represent both local cultural traditions and a globalising instrumental modality. Much as modern states, the manifestation of a globally extended political system, have relied on the idea of nation as a primal link between local circumstance and global modality, so an increasing number of religions have been selectively (re)constructed on simultaneously universal and particular grounds. Christianity, Islam or Buddhism are examples, and in principle anyone can be a Christian, a

Muslim or a Buddhist; but each of these religions really only gains its concrete specificity in terms of a particular local manifestation, a particular local tradition. The difference between nations and religions, however, is that the latter are not as territorially located as are the former, although they are also that to some degree. This structural similarity and partial overlap with ethnic territory results in attempts, using Prudence Jones' (1996) expression, to 'see traditions' rooted in particular territories and then give them a 'name' through which they can join, not the family of nations, but the 'family of religions'.

There is also a less advantageous side to the foregoing. While, on the interpretative model I am suggesting, the powerful instrumentalities do have to be particularised in a plurality of ways, places and circumstances, they also have their own structures, logics, inherent values and cultural expressions. The universal is not simply subsumed in the particular any more than the particular is simply subsumed in the universal. Evidence of this former aspect is not difficult to find. National or religious particularisation does not, as mentioned before, lead to the equal distribution of the power of the instrumental systems, whether in terms of wealth, political influence, health, or whatever other example one chooses. And indeed, national and ethnic identities are constantly constrained even and perhaps especially where they have been made the necessary expression of states: one can form states on the basis of ethnic or national ties much more easily than one can actually govern them on this basis. Similarly with religions: while religious pluralism is at least as possible as it has been at any other time and place in history, and perhaps more so, that capacity is severely constrained by the tendency towards the privatisation of religion, or what amounts to the same, the difficulty of maintaining religious authority. With religion as with ethnicity, the strong temptation is to resort to state power, with similar limitations and compromises.

With these portions of analysis behind us, we can now consider the place and importance of nature religion in this complex global situation. In the remainder of this chapter, I shall show the degree to which nature religion is a typical reflection of the globalised world in which we live. Both nations, religions and ideological movements, and nature religion, all share in a process of the simultaneous appropriation, critique or resistance, and furtherance of themselves.

– IV NATURE RELIGION AS COUNTER-STRUCTURAL STRATEGY IN A GLOBAL SOCIETY –

As a kind of identifiable religious tradition such as Christianity or Buddhism, nature religion, of course, does not exist. On the other hand, nature religion is not simply an aspect or dimension of all or several religions. Instead, in the context of this book, it refers to a range of religious and quasi-religious movements, groups and social networks whose participants may or may not identify with one of the many constructed religions of global society. What they all have in common that makes them deserving of the label is, on the concrete level, the attribution in various ways of divinity to nature; and, on the societal level, a critical stand with respect to the dominance and negatively judged effects of the globalised instrumental systems. In the light of the degree to which nature is precisely that which is not deemed the result of human artifice or technique, these two aspects go together. Thus, included under the heading of nature religion would be modern witchcraft/Wicca and Neo-Paganism, various revitalised aboriginal spiritual traditions, movements that appropriate aspects of aboriginal spirituality but consist mostly of non-aboriginals, neo-shamanistic groups, various portions of environmental movements, some feminist movements, certain 'New Age' movements, and movements within traditional religions such as Christian creation spirituality. This list could vary somewhat and I certainly do not want to suggest that such classification is an unambiguous matter. Part of the problem in this regard is that few if any of these groups are highly institutionalised and therefore clearly identifiable and circumscribable.

It is neither my purpose nor is it within my competence to detail the specific features of these various groups, movements and networks. Rather, I want to point out certain critical features that one finds quite frequently in nature religion. Prime among these would be the following: a comparative resistance to institutionalisation and legitimisation in terms of identifiable socio-religious authorities and organisations; a concomitant distrust of and even eschewing of politically oriented power; a corresponding faith in charismatic and hence purely individual authority; a strong emphasis on individual paths or at least individually chosen paths to fulfilment and hence on the equal value of individuals and groups; a valorisation of physical place as vital aspects of their spiritualities; a this-worldly emphasis with a corresponding important place for the search for healing, personal vitality, and transformation of self; a strong experiential basis where personal experience is a final arbiter of truth or validity; a valuing of community as non-hierarchical and effectively charged human bond or belonging; a stress on holistic conceptions of reality; and a conditional optimism with regard to human capacity and the future (cf. Champion 1993; Woodhead 1996). While one must be careful not to overgeneralise, I suggest that these features, and combinations of them, occur sufficiently often in contemporary manifestations of nature religion to indicate a pattern.

In order to understand the cultural logic of these features in the context of globalisation, it may be instructive to look at them as symbolic expressions of what Victor Turner (1969) has analysed as the anti-structural style of much religious ritual. Turner argues that religious ritual often symbolises the access it claims to give to transcendent or spiritual power through symbolic action that is constructed in deliberate contrast to the symbols and structures of 'normality'. Turner points to a polar relation between normal structure and religious anti-structure, using such polar opposites as, respectively, transition/status, whole/part, equality/inequality, inferiority/superiority and community/articulated structure. Where normal social/psychological reality is status oriented, complex, clearly structured and hierarchically ordered, the anti-structural and liminal religious reality symbolises its difference as the purported condition for the possibility of normal order through the ritual creation of a counter-order, a kind of reverse image of normality. I wish to adapt Turner's analysis by stressing the dialogical polarity of this religious strategy and thus calling it counter-structural rather than anti-structural, an idea which stresses the oppositional aspect. In addition, we can extend Turner's argument to the realm of personal religious experience. This quite frequently uses non-normal consciousness in dreams, trance, ecstasy, possession and induced visions to accomplish a similar contrast on a psychological level. Following this strategy, religion can act as a constant critique of institutionalised social structures and normal consciousness; but given that its symbolic activity is only possible in terms of that institutionalised and normal world, and indeed refers by contrast to that world, religion also supports it or at least would be impossible without it. Religion is, after all, in the final analysis part of that normative and symbolically mediated order; and it can only claim its difference or distinctiveness through this strategy of counter-symbolisation. Using metaphorical language, religion is like a mirror that makes possible a critical reflection of normal reality by creating a virtual, reverse and thus spiritual image of that reality; but this generation of a spiritual image is only possible in terms of the normal world that is being reflected.

Today's expressions of nature religion can be seen as an analogous counter-structural reflection, critique and confirmation of contemporary social normality, namely global society with its dominant instrumental systems. A large number of its varied features can be understood in this light. To begin, nature is itself a counter-structural symbol: inasmuch as the more dominant global modernities are characterised by a priority of technical, humanly controlled and artificial constructs, so nature is all that which is not technical artifice, but also that which is deemed the condition for the possibility of this globalised world. Indeed, the nature/technique polarity is a defining feature of this arising religiosity.

Other features can be seen in a similar way. There is the stress on holism as opposed to the highly differentiated and specialised world of technical rationality. The instrumentalised world is criticised for having forgotten or ignored not only the holism, but also the ground of its own possibility, nature; so much so that in its hubris it is destroying that nature. The source of more certain spiritual knowledge is not any of the specialised domains of the global systems, including the differentiated and institutionally specialised religious, but the myths, rites and symbols of pre-technical civilisations as these are reconstructed by these groups, individuals and movements: pre-Christian European (e.g. Celtic, Norse, Germanic), aboriginal or eastern inasmuch as these religious traditions are not nearly as identified with the spread of technical dominance. Specific systemic contrasts are also evident. Healing is not to be restricted to the techniques of modern medicine; in fact this is suspect as a source of genuine health and vitality. Science is not just the world of its positivist systemic practitioners, but also the wisdom of the sages, the gurus, the shamans and the spiritually aware. As with medicine, science is deemed to point to its own limitations.

The theme of inferiority versus superiority appears in various ways. Thus nature, while often personified and always divinised, is interpreted as weak and subject to destruction by technical power; it is not a straightforwardly powerful and avenging god, goddess or pantheon. Indeed, nature religion currents represent themselves precisely as the forgotten or suppressed religion of the marginal, of the weak and of the oppressed. Not only does the history of the oppression of aboriginal peoples, of women, of witches, of Third World peoples and traditions not negate the validity of their religious symbols, myths and rituals; rather, as with the proletariat in Marxist thought, such marginalisation from the dominant power structures is interpreted precisely as a warrant of greater authenticity. One senses that any religious culture or symbol system that is or has been the bearer of the dominant, ruling strata, or of imperial power, is for nature religion at least somewhat suspect.

If the analysis remained at this level, however, it would be seriously incomplete. What makes the rise of contemporary nature religion genuinely intriguing is not simply its counter-structural or even counter-cultural symbolic strategy, but the intricate links between the latter and the values and dominant structures of global society. For what we have here (in a way somewhat analogous to, although also quite different from, contemporary so-called 'fundamentalisms') is an oppositional strategy that also furthers some of the basic directions globalisation has taken historically. I refer specifically to the way that nature religion exhibits what Robertson (1992: 173f.) has termed 'glocalisation': what adherents sometimes call 'acting locally and thinking globally', but with more complex meanings than that expression usually has.

On perhaps the most obvious level, nature religion currents frequently stress that genuine human existence should refer primarily to the local place, but with the explicit assumption that others around the world are doing the same with reference to their own places. This belief mirrors a globalised society that encourages and values particularity and exclusivity as legitimate and good: individuals as well as groups should be free to develop themselves, and to develop themselves differently. The stress on holism does not contradict difference since the whole appears differently in different places. In typical counter-structural fashion, however, the link among the differences is not itself differentiated systems, but felt communitas, using Turner's term. The wish to avoid hierarchical ordering through structure dictates this. None the less, we have to observe that structure, in this case globalised instrumental structure, is in fact a condition for the possibility of this counter-structural felt community, even though the logic of nature religion symbolisation may wish to ignore this.

Corresponding to the unstructured nature of the global community and also growing out of the counter-structural character of nature religion is the frequent wish to avoid institutionalisation: structure with its concomitant statuses and stratifications is to be avoided or at least downplayed, but this precisely to allow the stress on local place, on individual and group difference. The polytheism of much nature religion is another symptom of this aspect. In this way, nature religion often becomes highly individualistic in its expressions, varying according to the individual, and to the small group, but always on the assumption that what one is doing is formally similar in terms of goal and function to what everyone else is doing. The atomisation, as with the stress on equality, springs from the counter-structural strategy. Yet here again, what in one sense goes against what the dominant globalised structures are deemed to be is also a reflection and thus reinforcement of them. The instrumental systems that dominate global society after all encourage this sort of individualism.

The situation, however, also tends towards the privatisation of such local, individual and group difference: another way of saying that it has little systemic authority or power.

– V CONCLUSION –

The issue of institutionalisation and power within global society raises a number of important questions with regard to how the movements based in nature religion relate to one another and to the global systems. I shall discuss two of these here. The first concerns the sharing and 'ownership' of symbolic resources. Inasmuch as nature religion is globally oriented, individuals and groups construct their local differences in principle on the basis of universal traditions, or at least traditions that are, like those of the world religions, supposedly open for adoption by anyone and everyone. In addition, the combination of the elements of these traditions is also open for uncontrolled variation: as the Wiccans put it, if you harm no one, do as you will. But this is not always as straightforward as it sounds. A good example is the mostly implicit conflict between aboriginal peoples seeking to reconstruct their own nature-religion-based particularity on the basis of what they see as their own traditions, and those non-aboriginals attracted to the expressive power of those same symbolic resources (cf. Porterfield 1990). To some degree, the construction of aboriginal particularity, as elsewhere, depends on being able to control those elements that count as aboriginal traditions; outsiders who use these in 'un-authorised' ways will tend to weaken the particularising power of these elements for the aboriginal people themselves. The issue in this case is made more complicated by the fact that many aboriginal peoples are engaged not only in a symbolic project of recovering and reconstructing their traditions, but also in a political project of self-determination along standard political systemic lines (in Canada, the issue of self-government and the independence of native peoples), in which the religious/cultural traditions play an important part. The matter of religious authority becomes important here, but the anti-institutional tendency of much nature religion works against this. Thus, in the terms I have been using in this chapter, counter-structural strategy clashes with the desire to legitimate structure, in this case, aboriginal political structure.

In a related way, the anti-institutional and counter-structural character of much nature religion today affects the relation between this current and the dominant instrumental and globalised systems. Unlike in most societies of the past, these instrumental systems do not depend for their legitimisation on the counter-structural resources of religion. This differentiation, as has frequently been observed, is a prime condition for the possibility of technical specialisation. As I have pointed out elsewhere (Beyer 1994), however, this does not imply the necessary secularisation of global society, or even the necessary privatisation of religion, although neither of these is excluded. What it does mean is that making religious resources effective beyond the restricted and private sphere of the individual and voluntary group will depend on mobilisation strategies that go beyond the straightforward production and reproduction of religious ritual and action. A frequently successful tactic in this regard has been to politicise religious resources in the form of religio-political movements which can, on occasion, even succeed in taking over the levers of a sovereign state.

Beyond this, however, there is the not insignificant influence of religiously based social movements. In the orbit of contemporary nature religion, ecological and feminist movements spring to mind as the most important categories of the latter. Both movements have been notably effective in translating their goals into the structures of the dominant instrumental systems; but in both cases, this has occurred largely because the movements have become partially institutionalised in such organisations as Greenpeace, green political parties, and national and international women's organisations, in all cases downplaying the overt nature-religion component, at least in public. In other words, their relative success has depended to some degree on their becoming structured, abandoning to some extent the counter-structural form. Far from indicating the futility of nature religion as a potential force in global society, however, what this points to is how the social movement has become a vital factor in the context of global society. This is probably the prime form through which counter-structural currents like nature religion can influence some of the directions in which the dominant systems pull us without becoming thoroughly institutionalised and especially politicised. Indeed, as the fate of Marxist-Leninist socialism has shown, although eschewing institutionalisation in the form of the dominant systems does mean giving up some very powerful tools, it may none the less be the only way of maintaining the advantages of counter-structure in a society where technical forms of social organisation are as powerful as they now are.

CHAPTER 2

Reflections on New Age and the Secularisation of Nature
WOUTER J. HANEGRAAFF

– I INTRODUCTION –

In her instructive *Nature Religion in America*, Catherine L. Albanese discusses New Age religiosity in general, and Neo-Paganism in particular, as representative of a certain type of 'nature religion'.[1] She discusses the Native American Sun Bear as an example, and emphasises the continuity between his New Age message and transcendentalist traditions in American culture. Of particular interest is her comparison with the very different type of 'nature religion' represented by the American writer Annie Dillard. In the following pages I intend to follow up on Albanese's discussion by further investigating what is at stake in the contrast between these two perspectives.

My own research confirms that Sun Bear's perspective, as summarised by Albanese, is highly representative of basic presuppositions of the New Age movement.[2] New Age religion affirms an essentially harmonious and benevolent universe, matched by an equally optimistic view of the human self. The human soul is basically good and pure, but human beings lose contact with their inner perfection as a result of social conditioning. Alienated from and ignorant of their true self they tend to harm everything around them, including the natural environment. Spiritual development as advocated by New Age religion will restore inner psychological harmony and conscious contact with the higher self; and this will restore harmony between human beings and nature. Healing the mind leads to the healing of Mother Earth. When harmony is fully restored, all will be well. Catherine Albanese points out convincingly that this perspective is fundamentally incompatible with a view of nature such as that presented by Annie Dillard.[3] Dillard's nature is not sweet and harmonious, but decidedly 'red in tooth and claw'. An experience of the sacred – a mixture of fear and fascination in the face of an inscrutable mystery – is fundamental to Dillard's world view but conspicuously absent in New Age religion.

– II THE BASIC RIFT IN MODERNITY AS ANALYSED BY THOMAS MANN –

I suggest that the contrast between Sun Bear and Dillard is not merely based on the contingency of personal preferences but reflects a basic opposition which is fundamental to modern western culture. More convincingly than in any scholarly study I know of, this opposition has been analysed in a literary work: Thomas Mann's great novel *The Magic Mountain* (1927).[4] I will therefore take Mann as my guide in what follows. *The Magic Mountain* is situated in the health resort of Davos, high up in the Swiss mountains. The resort is peopled by a colourful mix of patients from various European countries, which enables Mann to use it as a microcosm of European culture. Seven years before World War II, a young man of independent means – his name is Hans Castorp – comes up to visit his sick nephew in Davos, intending to stay for only three weeks. However, he quickly falls under the spell of this strange place and its inhabitants. Instead of returning home he stays on the mountain for a period of seven years, and in the *Reinkultur* (pure culture) of this peculiar environment he undergoes an extraordinary inner development which may legitimately be described in alchemical terms as a *transmutatio*.[5] Among other things, Hans Castorp partici-pates in long and intricate discussions between two other patients, who stand for two fundamental strands in modern western culture. The first one is the Italian Settembrini, the champion of the Enlightenment. He holds optimistic views about the possibilities for human progress by means of education; and he is motivated by a humanistic ideal of harmony among all people, in the context of a secular, naturalistic world view. His opponent is Naphta, who scorns naive beliefs in human progress and considers pain and violence to be basic to existence: they point to the numinous mystery at the heart of being, a supernatural dimension which is not bound to human norms (i.e. is in-human). Settembrini's ideals are rejected by Naphta as sentimental. In short: according to Settembrini we live in an essentially benevolent universe. Evil and suffering are created by society, and can be corrected by humanistic education. According to Naphta we live in a dangerous and uncertain universe, a fallen world. Evil and suffering are not human inventions but point to an inscrutable, supernatural mystery at the very heart of being.

Anyone who has read *The Magic Mountain* and is somewhat familiar with the New Age movement will, I think, agree that New Age religion is much closer to Settembrini's than to Naphta's world view. New Age beliefs mirror the Enlight-enment ideal of a harmonious society based on benevolent humanistic principles. It shares with the Enlightenment a firm belief that humanity can and will achieve happiness by learning to live in accordance with universal laws. Naphta's perspective, on the other hand (which is closer to Annie Dillard's), is completely alien to New Age thinking.

What has this to do with 'nature religion'? Let us look at a fragment from *The Magic Mountain*, where Hans Castorp is in discussion with Settembrini:

> 'What have you against the body?' – interrupted Hans Castorp suddenly and looked at him with wide blue eyes, the whites of which were veined with blood . . . 'You are a humanist, are you not? What can you have to say against the body?'
>
> Settembrini's smile this time was unforced and confident . . . 'You will always find me ready to answer you, Engineer', he said with a bow and a sweeping downward motion of the hand, 'particularly when your opposition is spirited; and you parry not without elegance. Humanist – yes, certainly, I am a humanist. You could never convict me of ascetic inclinations. I affirm, honour, and love the body, as I affirm, honour, and love form, beauty, freedom, gaiety, the enjoyment of life. I represent "the world", the interests of this

life, against a sentimental withdrawal and negation, classicism against romanticism. I think my position is unequivocal. But there is one power, one principle, which commands my deepest assent, my highest and fullest allegiance and love; and this power, this principle, is the spirit. However much I abhor hearing that dubious conception of moonshine and cobwebs people call "the soul" played off against the body, yet, within the antithesis of body *and* spirit, the body is the evil, the devilish principle, for the body is nature, and nature – within the sphere, I repeat, of her antagonism to spirit, to reason – is evil: mystical and evil. "You are a humanist?" By all means I am a humanist, for I am a friend of mankind, like Prometheus, a lover of humanity and human nobility. But that nobility reposes in the spirit, in reason, and therefore you will level against me in vain the reproach of Christian obscurantism'.[6]

Remarkably, the humanist Settembrini appears to be as deeply suspicious of nature as he is suspicious of religion. He distrusts 'nature' because he feels it stands for the body; and the body, for him, is the locus of disease and ultimately of death (a theme which recurs again and again in this novel about a community of people whose only bond is the fact that they are all ill, often moribund). As such, according to Settembrini, nature is inherently hostile to the spirit of humanitarianism, which affirms life. This argument may seem similar to a proclamation of metaphysical dualism and asceticism, as Hans Castorp suspects, but it is not. Settembrini defends a monistic ideal of *mens sana in corpore sano* - a healthy mind in a healthy body – rather than preaching the denial of the body. The solution to this paradox has to do with a presupposition which may not be immediately apparent. Nature is good, according to Settembrini, as long as it is subservient to spirit. But behind an interest in nature for its own sake, he suspects an unhealthy fascination with the realm of disease and death. And one thing discovered by Hans Castorp during the course of his development is that this fascination is ultimately based on the irrational attraction of the sacred. Thus we come to what lies at the heart of Settembrini's aversion to nature. To him, the sacred is the realm of the irrational and the inhuman, that is, the complete opposite of his own rationalistic humanitarian ideals. Throughout *The Magic Mountain* Settembrini tries to warn his pupil Hans Castorp not to submit to this most dangerous of all temptations, which is ultimately the temptation of death.

The nature of the opposition which Thomas Mann has in mind is subtle, and may easily be misunderstood. This may happen especially when Settembrini's opposition to the sacred is interpreted as an opposition to the supernatural. What he really objects to is what he regards as unhealthy fascination with the numinous and the invocation of irrational mystery. But whether or not the sacred is explained with reference to the supernatural in any traditional sense is clearly a matter of secondary importance (Settembrini simply does not believe in the supernatural; the sacred, however, is a power which he recognises but rejects). Thus, in spite of his rejection of 'nature', Settembrini's own Enlightenment alternative is nevertheless inspired by an ideal state in which human beings live in a natural world, harmonious in body and spirit. The real opposition, in other words, is not between nature and anti-nature (or supernature), but between two different views of nature: a sacral one, and a secular naturalism. Settembrini rejects the fascination with 'nature' in the name of secular naturalism; his rejection of the body in the name of the spirit is a reflection of this.

I have already referred to the remarkable fact that, although New Age religion purportedly attempts to 'resacralise' Nature, its worldview is actually much closer to the type of secular naturalism defended by Settembrini. That New Age religion allows for invisible entities and higher worlds creates no greater problem than does the presence of the Homeric gods for Settembrini's admiration of classical, Apollonian Greece. In spite of its belief in higher realities, New Age religion has no room for the supernatural: rather, like the proponents of the Enlightenment, it believes in universal natural laws which operate on all levels of the universe, both visible and invisible.[7] The idea of a reality which is radically outside the realm of nature and does not answer to its laws conflicts too evidently with the great – although paradoxical – respect of New Agers for the authority of 'science'. New Age approaches to the problem of suffering and apparent evil follow logically from this naturalistic framework. Evil can be regarded neither as a metaphysical reality nor as an inscrutable mystery, without disrupting the monistic presupposition. It therefore has to be illusory, and it must be affirmed that, from a cosmic perspective, 'whatever is, is right'. Suffering must have a rational explanation, and the explanation proposed by New Age religion is essentially the one of Settembrini's humanistic pedagogy: suffering results from ignorance, and can be healed by right education. Of course, New Age religion goes beyond the likes of Settembrini in applying this principle on a radical cosmic scale: the evolutionary process is presented as one grand educational play, in which conscious souls learn from painful experience over many lives. Elsewhere I have demonstrated that this similarity is not just phenomenological but based on actual historical influences. New Age beliefs of spiritual evolution through many lives in this world and in other worlds (popularly but incorrectly summarised by the term 'reincarnation') were derived not from oriental religions but from popular eighteenth-century theories of 'ascendant metempsychosis', interpreted in terms of nineteenth-century naturalism.[8]

– III DEATH AND THE SACRED –

Critics have often associated the New Age movement with the 'irrational' Counter-Enlightenment, presenting it as opposed to Enlightenment values. This assumption is simplistic and incompatible with the evidence.[9] But most adherents of New Age religion, as well, do not see themselves as heirs of the Enlightenment; rather, they like to think of themselves as contemporary representatives of a universal wisdom which has never been without its representatives during all periods of history and in all cultures, east and west. Actually, however, a closer analysis demonstrates that their worldview is unambiguously western and did not exist before the nineteenth century. It is true that fundamental New Age ideas are ultimately rooted in western esoteric currents; but there yawns a gulf between traditional pre-Enlightenment esotericism, on the one hand, and its secularised reinterpretations in the New Age movement, on the other. One way to explain this gulf, especially in connection with 'nature religion', is to make use of the celebrated concept of 'the sacred', understood in Rudolf Otto's terms as a *'mysterium tremendum ac fascinans'*.[10]

From Settembrini's perspective, both the fascination and the fear inspired by the sacred have the same root: death. At bottom, fascination with the sacred is fascination with death; and to choose nature over humanity is to prefer death over life, darkness over light. His opponents, however, suspect that death and life, darkness and light, are so intimately interwoven that they cannot be separated without taking the essence out of life itself.[11] Nature itself is a mixture of light and darkness. Hans Castorp's development during his seven years on the Magic Mountain can be interpreted as a process in which he learns to integrate death into life without submitting to it (unlike Settembrini's 'Counter-Enlightenment' opponent Leo Naphta, who finally commits suicide). In the key chapter 'Snow', Castorp comes very close to the edge, however. On a reckless solitary ski trip in the winter, he ventures deep into the silent and inhuman recesses of nature, in a half-conscious flirtation with death. Overtaken by a snow-storm he finds a tenuous shelter behind a snow-hut, where he falls asleep and has a dream. The dream is evidently modelled on Friedrich Nietzsche's celebrated opposition of the Apollonian versus the Dionysian. Hans Castorp beholds a landscape of classical poise and serenity, where beautiful men and women are engaged in happy and carefree activities. Then, following the earnest gaze of one of these people, he realises that he himself is sitting on the steps of a large temple. Entering the temple, among rows of giant pillars, a feeling of dread and fear slowly grows on him while he finds himself drawn towards the inner sanctum. There, he beholds the horror: two terrible, half-naked old women, standing at a fire, are tearing up with their bare hands the body of a small child, devouring the pieces. Then, spotting Hans Castorp, they come after him.

Hans Castorp wakes up in terror, and suddenly finds himself able to define his own position between the perspectives of Settembrini and Naphta.

> I will let death have no mastery over my thoughts! For therein, and in nothing else, lies goodness and love of humankind. Death is a great power. One takes off one's hat before him, and goes weavingly on tiptoe. He wears the stately ruff of the departed and we do him honour in solemn black. Reason stands simple before him, for reason is only virtue, while death is freedom, desertion,[12] un-form and lust. Lust, says my dream, not love. Death and love – no, they make a bad poem, in bad taste, false! Love stands opposed to death. It is love, not reason, that is stronger than death. Only love, not reason, gives kind thoughts. Form, too, can come from love and kindness only: form and civilisation of the sensible-friendly community and the beautiful state of humanity – always in silent recognition of the blood-sacrifice. Ah, yes, it has been dreamed clearly and well contemplated! I will think of it. I will keep faith with death in my heart, yet will remember that faith with death and the dead is only wickedness and dark voluptuousness and enmity against humankind, if it is given power over our thought and contemplation. *For the sake of kindness and love, man shall let death have no sovereignty over his thoughts.* And with that, I wake up.[13]

Hans Castorp's dream of the temple's inner sanctum, and his attitude towards the body, illness and death throughout the book, are classic examples of the experience of the sacred as *mysterium tremendum ac fascinans*. While describing his hero's development, Thomas Mann again and again uses motifs which refer to western esoteric traditions. Hans Castorp's development is characterised as 'hermetic pedagogy'; alchemical analogies are evoked in crucial places; and it can be proved that Mann has loosely modelled his story upon the grail legend. These references, I suggest, are not of merely anecdotal value. Mann evidently recognised that the logical alternatives to Settembrini's secular naturalism have a close affinity with traditions of an esoteric philosophy of nature, especially as represented by German Romantic *Naturphilosophie*. Hans Castorp's *Todessehnsucht* (nostalgia for death) is a major theme in this literature.[14] His mature position, as formulated after his dream, is the outcome of a long interior struggle (which was also Thomas Mann's struggle) with this perspective. He finally comes to integrate death as a vital (sic) part of life, the power of which must be recognised but – in contrast to Naphta's position – should not be allowed to have dominion over the supreme values of love and human kindness.

One can have different opinions about whether this 'solution' is really convincing; I only mention it here as one particular attempt to come to terms with a basic opposition in modernity. Ultimately, as I suggested, the opposition is between a sacral nature and a secular naturalism. The issue which most strongly divides these two is the question of how to deal with the dark sides of existence: suffering, illness, violence, cruelty, death. The former perspective experiences them as mysteries, somehow connected with an inscrutable and irrational dimension at the heart of nature. This is what unites such otherwise different personalities as Leo Naphta, Hans Castorp and Annie Dillard; the differences between them – and these are considerable – concern their different reactions, as human beings, to the experienced power of the sacred. From the second perspective, that of secular naturalism, these dark sides of existence are not mysterious at all and carry no sacred connotations: they are neither *tremendum* nor *fascinans*. They are simply the unfortunate result of human ignorance and an as yet imperfect condition of society, and they can be corrected or overcome by an 'education of the human race'.

– IV THE SECULARISATION OF NATURE IN ESOTERICISM –

The 'secularisation of nature' as exemplified by New Age religion involves a shift in which the former perspective is rejected in favour of the latter. In this particular case, the process corresponds to the shift from traditional forms of esotericism to forms of secularised esotericism (or 'occultism').[15] Elsewhere I have discussed this process in detail. Here I will merely illustrate it by a brief comparison of New Age naturalism with the *Naturphilosophie* of the Christian theosopher Jacob Boehme, whose influence permeates the esoteric traditions of the seventeenth and eighteenth centuries.[16]

Boehme's central cosmogonic vision describes the birth of God out of a primal abyss beyond all concepts and all human understanding, named the *Ungrund*. The birth of God is the birth of what Boehme calls 'eternal nature': it is the body of God in a real sense of the word. Our natural world, in contrast, is a fallen nature which has lost the integrity of eternal nature. This concept of a fallen nature already demonstrates the huge difference between Boehme's philosophy of nature and the cosmologies found in New Age religion. For Boehme, New Age aspirations to restore harmony between humanity and nature would be bound to fail, as long as nature herself (including human nature) was not reintegrated and redeemed.

Boehme's eternal nature, prior to the fall, is born in a sevenfold process. It is not appropriate to describe this process as taking place in historical time, much less to describe it as 'evolution', as has been done almost without exception since the Romantic era.[17] Boehme would have said that history and evolution are concepts appropriate to the fallen world, not to the original divine world (which is not called 'eternal' for nothing). One might say that to describe the birth of God in eternal nature as 'evolution' amounts to a reversal of the well-known hermetic dictum 'As above, so below', which was fundamental to Boehme as well as to others in his tradition. It means, in effect, to say 'as below (where we have history), so above': that is, the higher is modelled upon the lower.[18] Boehme's perspective would be, rather, that history and evolution are imperfect reflections of eternal archetypes. This in itself already makes New Age evolutionism incompatible with Boehme's traditional esoteric perspective.

The sevenfold 'process' by which God is (eternally) born, has a dark and light part. One may picture it approximately as follows.

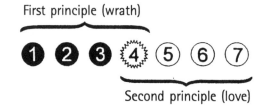

The first three phases are dominated by God's wrath, and are described by Boehme in no uncertain terms as a hellish prison, an insane circling wheel of pain. In the fourth phase, the dark fire of God's wrath is revealed as a flash of lightning, which is the beginning of a change: the dark fire which burns now becomes a benevolent fire which gives warmth and light. Thus, the last three phases of the process are ruled not by God's wrath but by his love: darkness is overcome by light. The dark half of the process is referred to by Boehme as the 'Father' or the 'first principle'; the light half of the process is called the 'Son', or 'second principle'. Father and son together – which means wrath and love, darkness and light – constitute eternal nature: the body of God. It would be a fatal misunderstanding of Boehme to conclude that the Son replaces the Father, that love replaces wrath, and light replaces darkness. Boehme means to say that, in eternal nature, the wrath of the Father remains present, but is eternally redeemed by the love of the Son.

Our world, also called the 'third principle', is a broken world, resulting from Lucifer's fall. God himself was born in darkness and reborn in light; but Lucifer, as a child of eternal nature, was born in light. He had a perfect light body, but wanted to be reborn as well. Driven on by this urge, there was nowhere for him to go except by returning: back, that is, to the dark origin of all being. This fatal plunge back into darkness meant his fall, because it was an 'unnatural' regression: a precise reversal of the supreme spiritual law that light is born from darkness, and redeems darkness. Lucifer's fall disrupted the integrity of eternal nature, and thus resulted in a fallen world: the very world in which we live. In this world, nature is divided against itself: love and wrath, light and darkness, good and evil, now fight each other. Darkness is no longer redeemed by light, but stands opposed to light. In this tragic situation we daily find ourselves. Boehme's goal is to point his readers to the way of spiritual reintegration, by which the body of eternal nature may be restored.

Nothing could be further from this Boehmian perspective than New Age concepts of nature, where 'nature' stands for harmony, and disharmony is created by human ignorance. In the context of Catherine Albanese's opposition, with which I began this chapter, Boehme's nature is much closer to the 'nature religion' of Annie Dillard. I will not repeat Albanese's analysis of Dillard and her comparison with Sun Bear's 'nature religion'. A single example will have to suffice. In a famous passage from *Pilgrim at Tinker Creek*, Dillard describes how she used to watch small frogs around the creek. If you came too close, these frogs would splash into the water, 'emitting a froggy "Yike".' Then, however, Dillard noticed something strange:

> At the end of the island I noticed a small green frog. He was exactly half in and half out of the water, looking like a schematic diagram of an amphibian, and he didn't jump.
>
> He didn't jump; I crept closer. At last I knelt on the island's winterkilled grass, lost, dumbstruck, staring at the frog in the creek just four feet away. He was a very small frog with wide, dull eyes. And just as I looked at him, he slowly crumpled and began to sag. The spirit vanished from his eyes as if snuffed. His skin emptied and drooped; his very skull seemed to collapse and settle like a kicked tent. He was shrinking before my eyes like a deflating football. I watched the taut, glistening skin on his shoulders ruck, and rumple, and fall. Soon, part of his skin, formless as a pricked balloon, lay in floating folds like bright scum on top of the water: it was a monstrous and terrifying thing. I gaped bewildered, appalled. An oval shadow hung in the water behind the drained frog; then the shadow glided away. The frog skin bag started to sink.
>
> I had read about the giant water bug, but never seen one. 'Giant water bug' is really the name of the creature, which is an enormous, heavy-bodied brown bug. It eats insects, tadpoles, fish and frogs. Its grasping forelegs are mighty and hooked inward. It seizes its victim with these legs, hugs it tight, and paralyses it with enzymes injected during a vicious bite. That one bite is the only bite it ever takes. Through the puncture shoot the poisons that dissolve the victim's muscles and bones and organs – all but the skin – and through it the giant water bug sucks out the victim's body, reduced to a juice. (Dillard 1974: 5–6)

To all intents and purposes, the event observed by Dillard is an example – in Boehme's terminology – of God's wrath unleashed in nature. Like Boehme, Dillard does not draw the common but shallow conclusion that if there is such cruelty there can be no God, unless God himself is evil. She comments:

> Cruelty is a mystery, and the waste of pain. But if we describe a world to compass these things, a world that is a long, brute game, then we bump against another mystery: the inrush

of power and light, the canary that sings on the skull. Unless all ages and races of men have been deluded by the same mass hypnotist (who?), there seems to be such a thing as beauty, a grace wholly gratuitous. (Dillard 1974: 7)

Nature contains both realities, and there is no easy way to reconcile them.[19] Boehme was sensitive to the same thing[20], and would have referred to beauty and grace as manifestations of God's love. He would have recognised the defenceless frog and the giant water bug as expressions of God's love and God's wrath; and the fact that the latter may so often be victorious over the former indicated to him that, somehow, there was something wrong with the universe. Boehme devoted most of his life to developing a theosophy which would help him understand what had gone wrong, which would analyse the dynamics of wrath and love, and point to the means of their reintegration.

There is clearly a world of difference between Boehme's Christian theosophy, on the one hand, and the basic perspective of New Age religion, on the other. This begins with the fact that Boehme takes cruelty and suffering – but also beauty and grace – seriously, as realities. There could be no stronger contrast with the dominant tendency in New Age religion to describe evil as illusion created by human ignorance. Boehme sees cruelty and suffering as basic and irreducible mysteries, not as a puzzle waiting to be solved by human understanding. New Age religion, in contrast, has developed a closed and essentially rational system of morality. This system is capable of explaining all 'negativity' out of spiritual ignorance, which can and will be corrected by experience (i.e. suffering) through many lifetimes. Finally, Boehme would not have sympathised with the idea that human souls will eventually, at the end of this spiritual evolution, come to understand with perfect clarity the very depths of divinity and the cosmos. This depth, for him, remained ultimately an abyss of darkness beyond all human concepts – the *Ungrund*; and the very attempt to penetrate that abyss had been the cause of Lucifer's fall and the disruption of eternal nature.

– V CONCLUSION –

I have argued that New Age religion is rooted in western esoteric traditions, but that the increasing secularisation of these traditions under the impact of and following the Enlightenment caused its adherents to become deeply alienated from traditional esotericism. At the heart of the latter, we find an experience of the sacred as a *mysterium tremendum ac fascinans*. New Agers, in contrast, tend to make each private individual (not the sacred) into the centre of his or her symbolic world; and they tend to seek salvation in universal explanatory systems which seem devised to replace mystery ultimately by the certainty of perfect knowledge. Their theoretical frameworks are heavily dependent on those of a secular naturalism in the Enlightenment tradition.[21]

There may be different opinions about the question of whether the process of the secularisation of esotericism is to be valued positively or negatively. Some will see it as an advance, arguing that it makes ancient traditions suitable for the contemporary world. Others will see it as a decline, arguing that it produces merely shallow caricatures of profound teachings. The point I have tried to make is merely this: adherents of New Age like to believe that they represent the (frequently hidden or rejected) wisdom of the ages, while critics say that New Agers merely repeat the superstitions of the past. Both views are equally simplistic, and in need of being corrected by serious historical research. In studying traditional esotericism, historians should beware of projecting their own biases back into the past, and be prepared to make the effort of trying to understand a strange world on its own terms. In the course of such exploration they may encounter an equally strange nature, which contains even more things between heaven and earth than are dreamt of in New Age philosophy.

– Notes –

The research on which this chapter is based was supported by the Foundation for Research in the Field of Philosophy and Theology in the Netherlands (SFT), which is subsidised by the Netherlands Organisation for the Advancement of Research (NWO).
 1 Albanese (1990: ch. 5)
 2 Hanegraaff (1996). Whether Sun Bear is also representative of Neo-Paganism seems somewhat questionable.
 3 See especially Dillard (1974, 1982).
 4 The following discussion refers to *Der Zauberberg* ([1924] 1967).
 5 This is suggested by Mann himself. See for example Hans Castorp in a conversation with Clawdia Chauchat: 'By chance – call it chance – I have been driven highly upward to this genial environment . . . In one word: you probably do not know that there is such a thing as alchemical-hermetic pedagogy, transubstantiation to a higher state, *Steigerung*, if you understand what I mean' (Mann 1967: 630). Note that the crucial word *Steigerung* is untranslatable in this context. Literally it means 'rising up', but it is also used for a state of fever (high temperature), a condition common to all the patients in Davos. This allows Mann to play a subtle game with the concept of sickness (fever) as related to a 'higher state of being', including the implication that death is related to the attainment of such a state.
 6 Mann (1967: 264). Here and elsewhere my translation is modelled on that of H. T. Lowe-Porter (Mann 1972), but I have not followed him in all respects. Note in particular that, in the present quotation, I translate the crucial word *Geist* as 'spirit', whereas Lowe-Porter sometimes uses 'intellect', sometimes 'mind'.
 7 For this point see Isaiah Berlin (1955 and later editions); and see my discussion (Hanegraaff 1996: ch. 15, section 1).
 8 Hanegraaff (1996: ch. 15, section 3B).
 9 Hanegraaff (1996: ch. 15, esp. section 1). Cf. also Godwin (1994).
 10 Rudolf Otto (1919). In my opinion, it is possible to make critical use of Otto's concepts without necessarily accepting his theological and religionist presuppositions.
 11 Similar arguments may be found quite frequently in Neo-Paganism. In this chapter I restrict myself to the general trend of New Age religion, without taking into account the complicating factor of Neo-Paganism.
 12 A reference to Hans Castorp's 'desertion' from normal social life, entranced by the

community of the sick and dying on the Magic Mountain. I do not see how Lowe-Porter can translate 'Freiheit, Durchgängerei, Unform und Lust' as 'release, immensity, abandon, desire'.

13 Mann (1967: 523). Emphasis in the original.

14 See for example the novel Die Heimatlosen (The Homeless) by the Romantic poet and investigator of the occult Justinus Kerner, behind which stands the philosophy of Gotthild Heinrich Schubert's enormously influential Ansichten von der Nachtseite der Naturwissenschaft (Views on the Night-side of Natural Science). For these connections, see my article on Justinus Kerner and the "Seeress of Prevorst" (Hanegraaff forthcoming).

15 I use the term 'occultism' in a precise sense, distinguished from 'occult sciences' or 'the occult' (see Hanegraaff 1996: ch. 15, section 1B).

16 For splendid analyses of Boehme's thought, see Deghage (1985, 1992). See also Weeks (1991). For a more extensive discussion of Boehme's concept of 'wrath', see Hanegraaff (1993).

17 Boehme has been a major influence on German Idealism, and on Schelling in particular. Paradigmatic for the Idealist interpretation of Boehme is the great book by Ferdinand Christian Baur, Die christliche Gnosis (1835). For a contemporary example of an evolutionist Boehme-interpretation, see Nicolescu (1991).

18 Cf. Needleman (1992: xxviii).

19 Cf. the impressive reflections in Dillard (1974: 240–2).

20 Boehme has described how he fell into a deep depression, 'when I beheld the great profundity of this world, as well as the sun and the stars, and the clouds, as well as rain and snow, and contemplated in my mind the whole creation of this world. In which I then found evil and good in all things, love and wrath; in the unreasoning creatures as in wood, stones, earth and elements as well as in the human beings and the animals' (Aurora 19.5–6; my transl.; cf. De Tribus Principiis, Vorrede 13).

21 My interpretation of the New Age movement in terms of a 'secularisation of nature' is not incompatible with a process which has been referred to as the 'sacralisation of nature' by Paul Heelas (1996). What seems like a contradiction actually results merely from two different definitions of 'sacred': the sacrality of traditional esotericism is replaced in New Age religion by a 'sacrality' of a very different, post-Enlightenment type.

Chapter 3

Between Apocalypse and Self-realisation: 'Nature' as an Index of New Age Religiosity

Steven Sutcliffe

To find nature . . . is frequently to find something internal and mystical.

(Coward 1989: 33)

– I Introduction –

I argue in this chapter that the informing hermeneutic of New Age religiosity has developed under the influence of the polarities of the title – 'apocalypse' and 'self-realisation' – ever since New Age's adoption by networks of individuals in the post-war years. New Age subsequently grew through a limited public face in the 1960s into full flower as a phenomenon of heterodox religiosity in the 1970s. In the 1980s the term became a diffuse populist emblem attracting widespread comment; by the 1990s it had become an adjectival noun permeating popular, middlebrow and academic cultures, qualifying rather than defining specific products or activities.[1]

In the course of this development, the category 'nature' has emerged as one of several convenient indices of the phenomenon's underlying metaphysic; it is convenient here to draw upon Raymond Williams's essay on the word (Williams 1976: 184–9). Of three broad historical differentiations of meaning he identifies, it is the most recent referential tendency, from around the seventeenth century onwards, that will concern us, namely 'nature' as 'the material world itself . . . including or not including human beings' (ibid.: 184). This field of reference incorporates both what Williams terms a 'very early and surprisingly persistent personification of singular Nature' – by which he means 'Nature the goddess, "nature herself"' – as well as the later Romantic connotations of nature as 'the "countryside", the "unspoiled places", plants and creatures other than man' (ibid.: 186, 188).

'Nature' in New Age is sharply distinguished from the sociological and historical dimensions of 'culture'. In contrast to the latter, nature is all that is absolutely primary – culture's raw material, so to speak – that original world of vital organicity from which western values have only subsequently, and ultimately artificially, been wrought, and from which in the process they have largely become severed and alienated. As Paul Heelas puts it, according to New Age 'it is essential to shift from our contaminated mode of being – what we are by virtue of socialization – to that realm which constitutes our authentic nature' (Heelas 1996: 2).

Following a primary differentiation between 'nature' and 'culture' we can distinguish a secondary typological polarity wherein nature is cast in terms either of an obscuration of ultimate reality, or as its revelation. Writing of the American religiosity she terms 'nature religion', Catherine Albanese describes a similar polarisation between 'a view of matter as "really real", the embodiment of Spirit and the garment of God, and – on the other hand – a view of matter as illusion and unreality, ultimately a trap from which one needed to escape' (Albanese 1990: 82). More succinctly yet, Michael York writes of New Age as an 'unresolved dialectic' between 'a numinous materialism and a world-denying idealism' (York 1994: 16).

In this chapter I want to examine in the light of this 'unresolved dialectic' certain themes and episodes exemplifying New Age 'nature', understood both in the general sense of Williams' 'material world itself' and with the more particular connotations of extra-cultural, 'natural' reality. I take my examples largely from contemporary phenomena in Britain, particularly the Findhorn Community[2] and the alternative health milieu[3] but I also touch upon the important historical contribution to New Age of former theosophist Alice Bailey, and certain developments in the ideology of human potential in North America.

– II THE APOCALYPSE –

A particularly dramatic historical manifestation of what York terms 'world-denying idealism' is the genre known, in Jewish and Christian traditions, as 'apocalyptic'[4] widely and popularly associated with 'doomsday' prophecies of the impending destruction of the status quo. Common motifs include angels and demons, notions of divine or cosmic judgement, descriptions of battles, and extraordinary natural phenomena (Hinnells 1995: 43). According to one celebrated historical account, apocalyptic traditions typically promote a 'revolutionary eschatology' along these lines:

> The world is dominated by an evil, tyrannous power of boundless destructiveness . . . imagined not as simply human but as demonic. The tyranny of that power will become more and more outrageous, the sufferings of its victims more and more intolerable – until suddenly the hour will strike when the Saints of God are able to rise up and overthrow it [and] shall in their turn inherit dominion over the whole earth. (Cohn 1978: 21)

Now, we find a somewhat similar picture in early New Age, although participants were more likely to be middle-class and middle-aged 'metaphysical seekers'[5] in contrast to Cohn's 'rootless poor' (ibid.: 14). In any case, in this worldview nature – the totality of the existing, taken-for-granted order, 'the material world itself' (Williams 1976: 184) – drastically impedes revelation. In fact, empirical reality and materialist science are part of the problem. According to activist Anthony Brooke in 1967:

> We are on the threshold of a New Age – a New Dispensation – and the world will evidently not long continue in the way in which day to day living everywhere is now going on . . . We are without question in the time of the winding up of human history as we have hitherto known it. (Brooke 1976: 62)

An early 'channelled'[6] entity in Britain, 'Gildas', consolidates this perspective: 'To bring about changes . . . to a world which is materialistic, dark and grasping will inevitably cause pain and destruction because of the sudden contrast . . . as vibrations are raised to the heights to which they *will* be raised' (Brooke 1976: 79).

The American activist David Spangler, whose New Age career to date has spanned four decades, expands upon the apocalyptic presuppositions of early New Age:

> The earth was entering a new cycle of evolution, which would be marked by the appearance of a new consciousness within humanity that would give birth to a new civilization. Unfortunately, the present cultures of the world were so corrupt and locked into materialism that they would resist this change. Consequently, the transition . . . would be accomplished by the destruction of the old civilization, either by natural causes such as earthquakes or floods, or by a great world war, or by social collapse of an economic or political nature, or by combinations of these. However, those individuals whose consciousness could become attuned to and one with the qualities of the new culture would be protected in various ways . . . They would then enter a new age of abundance and spiritual enlightenment – the Age of Aquarius. (Spangler 1984: 17)

There are clearly a number of common features to the forecasts of Brooke, Gildas and Spangler. First, we should note the overtly millennialistic implications of this 'New Dispensation': a 'sudden contrast' – triggered by 'natural causes', perhaps, or the cultural stimuli of warfare and economic slump – will precede a 'new age of abundance and spiritual enlightenment'. In other words, the New Age will be a literal, and not a metaphorical, event. Second, the prevalent metaphysic is highly dualistic, recalling certain gnostic cosmologies (for example, Manicheanism) wherein the world is construed as being in the grip of, or constituting a battleground for, two irreconcilable principles: light and dark, spirit and matter, good and evil. Third, the millennium would appear to privilege a special cadre, or avant-garde, of individuals promoting theocracy or oligarchy as the appropriate organisational forms for this 'new order'. Spangler, for example, alludes pregnantly to 'those individuals'; and Peter Caddy (1996: 226) writes: 'Our purpose at Findhorn was to establish a place that demonstrated a God-centred lifestyle . . . to aid the reconstruction of civilization in the event of catastrophe.'

However, the anticipated apocalypse never transpired: at least, not in any public sense. Consider Findhorn again. Co-founder Eileen Caddy describes a dramatic episode involving a small group from Findhorn on a local hill on Christmas Eve, 1967, an auspicious period in that extravagant decade's calendar:[7]

> As we stood together holding hands, I felt my body fill with light. I began to tremble violently and then collapsed, unconscious . . . Finally, as I came to, I experienced an absolute oneness with Peter [husband], with Joanie [friend] and with the entire universe. I felt I was plugged into the cosmic power source and that we three had provided some sort of anchor or earthing point . . . Something truly momentous had occurred – for us and the whole world. (Caddy 1988: 121–2)

'Guidance'[8] received by Eileen subsequently provided a satisfactory interpretation:

> The day many have been waiting for is over. The cosmic power released at that appointed moment, felt by you and many others, has begun to reverberate around the universe . . . Some may be disappointed because there was no outer manifestation. Nothing has gone wrong. It is simply that man has misinterpreted what has been prophesied. (ibid.: 122)

In other words, in place of 'the winding up of human history' forecast by Brooke or the 'destruction of the old civilisation' alluded to by Spangler, Caddy offers a subjective hermeneutic, the object of which lacks 'outer manifestation', as she puts it. That is, there are no exterior signs of this release of 'cosmic power'. Human response has been internalised: agency has gone (or returned) underground, so to speak, into the realms of thought and affectivity.

– III THE INWARD TURN –

Lest such a hermeneutic turn – from catastrophic destruction to subtle 'reverberation' – be thought a minority position, plenty of corroboration is available to attest to its significance. David Spangler, for example, spent much of his catalytic residency at Findhorn in the early 1970s expounding a similar esotericism:[9] 'Since we believed that the new age was not so much an event as a state of mind, it was something we could create and express now, not wait until after some eventual catastrophe' (Spangler 1984: 34). Thus the classic problem facing an apocalyptic movement – namely, how to rationalise invalidated prophecy – is neatly resolved by reconfiguring the ground on which interpretation takes place. Exterior – and hence public – apocalypse becomes interior – and hence private – gnosis, and the New Age is thus safeguarded against disconfirmation.

One consequence of this hermeneutic revision – a prime example of what Needleman (1970: 13) has termed 'the inward turn' taken by western religiosity in the late 1960s – is that nature is released from its role of obscuring the real to become a source of revelation in its own right. In contrast to its former negative state – Gildas' 'materialistic, dark and grasping' world, thwarting abundance and spiritual enlightenment – nature begins to acquire the properties of a distinctive realm, a subtle world of 'numinous materialism' accessible only to emic – and specifically esoteric – exegesis. As Faivre and Voss (1995: 60) summarise this perspective: 'Multi-leveled, rich in potential revelations and meanings of every kind, Nature can be read like a book.'

One such engagement with nature was offered in early New Age circles by R. Ogilvie Crombie, a venerable Edinburgh theosophist who became an early supporter of the Findhorn Community. Crombie recorded several encounters with beings such as Kurmos the faun and the god Pan in places like Edinburgh's Botanical Gardens and the island of Iona. The following account comes from a visit Crombie made in the mid-1960s to the Shropshire Adult College at Attingham Park, Shrewsbury, an important early venue for New Age interests in Britain.[10] Attingham Park had been bequeathed to the National Trust in 1947 and became one of a number of venues promoting adult education in the post-war period: it is an imposing eighteenth-century mansion in the classical style – a 'stately home' – with extensive grounds. Here Crombie visited the Rhododendron Walk, 'considered by some to be a place of great spiritual power':

> I felt a great build-up of power and a vast increase in awareness . . . I became aware of Pan walking by my side and of a strong bond between us. He stepped behind me and then walked into me so that we became one, and I saw the surroundings through his eyes . . . The moment he stepped into me the woods became alive with myriad beings – elementals, nymphs, dryads, fauns, elves, gnomes, fairies . . . I now had pan pipes in my hands and was aware of shaggy legs and cloven hooves. I began to dance down the path, playing on the pipes. (Walker 1994: 94–5)

That an esoterically vitalistic, magical nature – a multidimensional realm of subtle inference and experience – was not a marginal theme in New Age can be seen from the Findhorn garden. Here the gardeners followed from the earliest days (and continue so to do) the guidance of 'nature spirits'.[11] A 'Nature Sanctuary', a small, circular, semi-underground chamber for meditation and singing, has in recent years been constructed in the settlement from stone, wood and turf, and 'being in nature' is a popular expression in the community for spending reflective, even mystical, time out of doors. 'Nature' thus becomes the repository of ideals of beauty, mystery and authenticity: a paradisal, revitalising realm beyond the pale of modern urbanity.

Crombie's nature is clearly in sharp contrast to the 'dark and grasping' realm of Gildas. And yet nature thus re-enchanted is ambiguously related to the interiorising trajectory of Eileen Caddy and David Spangler, as Crombie himself inadvertently demonstrates in subsequent speculations:

> We turn away from the outside world, the material world which so many believe to be the only reality, to seek that true reality which is within and yet everywhere.
> In that sense, Pan is within me, the whole universe is within me, the elemental kingdom, the angelic hierarchy, God himself is within me. (Walker 1994: 97).

Through sleight of hand the ontology of nature has significantly changed. The previous picture of an enchanted reality – in which, writes Crombie, 'I was aware of every single leaf on the bushes and trees, of every blade of grass on the path standing out with startling clarity . . . as if physical reality had become much more real than it normally is' (ibid.: 94) – has given way to an abstracted, introverted, quasi-solipsistic understanding. Nature is no longer represented as a vividly autonomous reality set over against Crombie, and with which he dynamically engages, but – to recall the words cited as an epigraph to this chapter – 'something internal and mystical', a trigger for 'attending to the inner being' (Coward 1989: 33).

This points to an exegetical ambiguity that has come to typify New Age, in which the empiricist's conventional boundaries regarding what belongs 'within' (the individual) and what belongs 'without' (in the world) are relentlessly undermined. The softening of boundaries has encouraged a wide range of populist exegeses sympathetic to the mixing and compounding of properties, 'planes' and realms of reality and imagination. The apocalyptic genius may in the process become a function of the private sphere rather than, as traditionally, an inexorably public prophecy of the end of the world. Apocalyptic traces may now manifest as psychological and affective states – fear, anxiety, excitement – as psychology and cosmology merge. Indeed, one emic commentator explicitly considers the 'psychological thrust' of 'modern esoteric spiritualities' to be 'intensely relevant to the modern crisis': 'More and more, the modern man or woman has been driven to the individual self as the locus of healing and meaning' (Needleman 1993: xxiii).

– IV SELF-REALISATION –

Thus far, nature in New Age circles has appeared as something of a 'stumbling block' to the idealistic – not to say apocalyptic – urge: it is 'dark and grasping' (Gildas), it hinders the 'New Dispensation' (Brooke). However, we have also begun to uncover an esoteric position according to which 'Nature can be read like a book' (Faivre and Voss 1995: 60) and wherein boundaries blur between 'inner' and 'outer' events. On the one hand this seems a step towards York's 'numinous materialism'; but on the other we have seen how a doubting idealism may – under the cloak of esotericism – re-enter the picture to keep the material realm in its proper – thoroughly contingent – place: that is, as a weak ('lower' or 'outer') reflection of other ('higher' or 'inner') realms. If not quite a 'stumbling block', then, this position is not quite a 'stepping stone' either in the manner of the methodology of the early human potential movement, for example, where human nature – the embodied, biological self – was typically promoted as an inescapable site of, and means towards, the work of self-realisation.[12] We can now begin to grasp the background to the ambiguity attendant upon the nature of New Age in contemporary culture, since the exegetical norms of different settings in the highly fluid and syncretic milieux within which this equivocal emblem has been articulated may be not only not obviously apparent, but even fundamentally polarising.

Let us now look at these hermeneutic options in some contemporary circles associated with New Age. Take, for example, the general movement for alternative or holistic health, variously described as 'part of the bedrock of the New Age experience' (York 1995: 38) and a 'key catalyst in recruiting for the Aquarian movement' (English-Lueck 1990: 1). Let us take a specific proselytising activity: the public fair or exhibition. In Britain the foremost example of this is the annual 'Mind Body Spirit' exhibition in London, which celebrated its twentieth anniversary in 1996. This is an annual gathering of experimental therapies, healing systems and associated goods which harbours an eclectic range of underlying metaphysics and cosmologies. Its founder, Graham Wilson, emphasises qualities of 'self-improvement', 'healing and self-empowerment' and 'personal growth' in the event's programme (Mind Body Spirit 1996: 5). Yet his summary of what amounts to an implicitly realised or 'achieved' New Age (he writes 'we have moved beyond the threshold of the Age of Aquarius') conflates self-realisation with a reassuringly mild millennialism:

> This is a time when we are discovering the inter-relatedness of mind, body, spirit and nature. We are learning to listen to our own inner needs, developing closer attachments and opening up channels of love that take us beyond the boundaries of human potential towards the mastery of our own destinies. (ibid.: 5)

The phrases chosen here – 'opening up', 'beyond the boundaries of human potential', 'the mastery of our own destinies' – convey just enough of the new, the dramatic and the revelatory without being committed to a particular interpretation. Meanwhile, a gentle tension can be traced in the events of the opening day of the event. Four lectures are offered: 'Angels! Angels! Angels!' ('Meet your personal Angel in a beautiful guided meditation'); 'How to Heal and Regenerate' ('an introduction to energy healing and ways of regenerating the life force within you'); 'The Quest for Enlightenment' ('Enlightenment isn't what you think it is . . . Simplify your quest'); and 'The Earth Dance' ('acknowledge the earth, open to universal energies and entities'; facilitated by a Canadian medicine man, an African shaman and a German druid). We can see a movement in the content of these presentations from the idealism of angelology through the more pluralistic ramifications of vitalism ('the life force within you') to the primal or chthonian materialism of the 'Earth Dance'.

A similiar tension permeates many of the workshops on offer. 'The Art of Channelling' ('the development of one's subtle energies and receptivity to other dimensions') and 'The Game of Life' ('you can create anything you want simply by aligning your thoughts and words with the perfect good that resides divinely within you') are both oriented towards idealism, the realm of thought typically revealing the good and also providing the technology for transformation. On the other hand, 'Qigong for Healing' ('special exercises for inner organs, heart, kidneys, lung and liver and how to achieve a balance of energies') and 'Creating Sacred Space with Feng Shui' ('how to clear stuck energies in the places where you live and work') would appear to privilege a more obviously biological – and hence material – level, setting store by physical organs (qigong) and 'natural' environment (feng shui).

Smaller versions of 'Mind Body Spirit' now regularly take place in most larger British cities. Edinburgh, for example, features an annual 'Alternative Health Exhibition' weekend in a large city-centre venue. The complete list of workshops offered by practitioners on the Saturday of the 1996 event features a broadly familiar curriculum: Tai Ch'i, channelling, spiritual healing, aromatherapy, reflexology, circle method, Alexander Technique, crystal therapy, Takion, Shiatsu, homeopathy, meditation, craniosacral therapy, vega testing, internal alchemy and psychic art.[13] Again, these practices are usefully illuminated by the present typology. Thus, whereas the techniques of aromatherapy, reflexology and the Alexander Technique, for example, would seem – like qigong – to privilege the senses and internal structures of the human body (including ever finer degrees of organismic sensitivity and control), the very *modus operandi* of practices such as channelling, spiritual healing and crystal therapy would seem to lie in miraculous or supernatural intervention.

On the one hand, of course, one might well expect a thriving healing movement valorising sensitive, non-invasive treatment to affirm physical well-being, if only implicitly, rather than promoting non-empirical or posthumous rewards. Albanese (1990: 117–52) expresses some implications of this position in her compound term 'Physical Religion', a category which indicates the synthesis of religiosity and health that she deems characteristic of nineteenth-century 'nature religion'. In fact, what Albanese says of the aetiology of Thomsonian herbalism might equally stand for the general worldview of contemporary alternative healing: 'Nature was everywhere the norm, and disease was rebellion against it' (ibid.: 130).

On the other hand, an undertow of Manichean apocalypticism persists at the margins of alternative health. For example, the Aetherius Society has maintained a presence in these milieux, offering workshops and demonstrations in healing, 'pendulum dowsing' and 'psychic powers' at recent Mind Body Spirit fairs. This group is intimately bound up with the craze for unidentified flying objects (UFOs) which reached a peak in the 1950s and early 1960s.[14] The metaphysical implications of UFOs – according to the Aetherius Society the harbingers of the New Age – retain a central stake in the Society's diversified ideology of the 1990s. A leaflet advertised a recent workshop in Glasgow entitled 'UFOs: Their Mission to Earth' with the claim that 'the coming New Age will encompass concepts literally out of this world'. Presenters made reference to a planetary 'cleansing' said to be in progress in preparation for the millennium, which was to be catalysed by the imminent appearance of the 'Space Intelligences'.[15]

Indeed, it may be that New Age's apocalyptic or Manichean undertow is currently resurfacing. Best-selling paperbacks like Brian Weiss's *Many Lives, Many Masters* (Weiss 1988) – an account of 'past-life therapy' that includes material channelled from 'Master Spirits' – and James Redfield's *The Celestine Prophecy* (Redfield 1994) – effectively a New Age 'Pilgrim's Progress' which advocates the goal of a 'lighter, more purely spiritual' humanity (ibid.: 276) – mine rich, persuasive and persistent seams of gnostic psychologism and millennialism. As I write, the fiftieth anniversary of the first UFO sighting is being celebrated in popular culture, where *The X-Files* – an American television series fictionalising paranormal investigations and extra-terrestrial contact – garners popular and critical acclaim.

Conversely yet in complementarity, other strands of New Age bear witness to exploration of the depths and intricacies of human nature: that numinous biology of one's own self. I have already touched upon this briefly in the context of human potential ideology, but a little more needs to be said to complete this chapter. This dimension of New Age-associated activity has been appositely characterised by Heelas (1996: 28) as a 'highly optimistic, celebratory, utopian and spiritual form of humanism'. The satisfaction, exploration and experimentation of the individual – what Heelas (ibid.: 18) terms 'Self-spirituality' – is paramount here. Under this aspect, supernatural signals are demythologised: emphasis is upon the immanence, even the 'naturalness', of the divine. 'Natural' food (whole, organic, vegetarian or vegan),[16] clothing (unbleached cotton, craft-spun wool, non-western garments and accessories) and behaviour (casual, affective, individualistic) is the norm. As Coward (1989: 15) remarks: 'To claim that a therapy, medicine or food is "natural" is to validate it instantly'. Examples of this orientation include much of the Findhorn Foundation's curriculum in recent years; the Skyros Centre for holistic holidays in the Greek islands; and Neal's Yard, a small pedestrianised enclave on the fringes of London's Covent Garden supporting commercial ventures in alternative health, therapy and goods.[17]

Indeed, in historical terms it can be argued that it was the collision of the largely American human potential movement with the eschatological apocalypticism of the 1960s networks that prepared the ground for the emergence, in the 1970s, of a genuinely populistic and cross-generational mix of eclectic religiosity under the broad heading of 'New Age'. In other words, humanistic psychology brought New Age millennialism literally down to earth, reminding participants of the microcosmic dimension intrinsic to the esoteric cosmologies most espoused, and helping to reroute the outer, upward gaze within. In this cross-fertilisation of ideologies and generations, a familiar position was recouped and strengthened, for 'inner' dimensions and their means of access have always been a specialism of the esoterically inclined.[18] As Alice Bailey wrote in the early 1920s: 'Only in the thorough comprehension of the axiom "Know Thyself" will come that understanding that enables man to wield the law and know the inner working of the system from the centre to the periphery' (Bailey 1983: 2).

But if, as I am suggesting, it was the prerogative of the 'growth' movement to compound the quest for 'consciousness' and 'raised vibrations' on the part of early New Age activists with a distinctively biological focus, nevertheless a hermeneutical ambiguity concerning the final nature of the human organism persists even here. The doctrine of self-realisation advocated by American humanistic psychology carried the seeds of an idealistic transcendence of naturalism from the beginning, as the list of examples of those 'human capacities and potentialities' deemed appropriate for investigation by the field, included in the introduction to the inaugural issue of the *American Journal of Humanistic Psychology* in 1961, implies: 'Creativity, love, self, growth, organism, basic need-gratification, self-actualization, higher values, ego-transcendence, objectivity, autonomy, identity, responsibility, psychological health, etc. (Alexander 1992: 41).

Now, most of these categories denote fairly concrete concerns, but several – most obviously 'love', 'growth', 'self-actualization', 'higher values' and 'ego-transcendence' – point to a complex of values less easily accessible to empirical – that is, naturalistic – verification. It is perhaps then little surprise that before the decade was out – in 1969 – a sister publication, the *Journal of Transpersonal Psychology*, had appeared, launched by the same editors (Abraham Maslow and Anthony Sutich). This publication, however, left no question as to its interests:

'Meta-needs, ultimate values, unitive consciousness, peak experiences, ecstasy, mystical experience, B values, essence, bliss, awe, wonder, self actualization, ultimate meaning, transcendence of the self. The list goes on. The primary emphasis . . . was on inward and transcendent experience and on self-realization. (Gordon-Brown and Somers 1988: 226)

Significantly, the sole term shared by the lists of these two journals – humanistic and transpersonal – is 'self-actualization'. But what is the ultimate nature of the actualised or realised self?

The transpersonal view can be exemplified by the ideas of the Italian Roberto Assagioli, whose method, psychosynthesis, has been variously described as amongst 'the most "transpersonal psychologies" of the modern era' (ibid.: 225) and 'a major school of psychotherapy for New Agers' (Melton *et al.* 1990: 247).[19] Assagioli posited the existence of two selves: the conscious ego and the 'higher self', or 'personality' and 'soul' (Gordon-Brown and Somers 1988: 229). The transpersonal task lies in pursuing ever more consciously and intentionally the 'journey to the self' (ibid.: p.231). This is, of course, the 'self actualization' also promoted by humanistic psychology, but the actualised self of transpersonalists is something more, something other, than mere organismic or existential creaturehood, for 'the experience of the self, the transpersonal centre, the soul *includes* the personal but goes beyond it' (ibid.: 229). Indeed, ultimately it is the ego or personality, and not the 'transpersonal centre' or 'soul', that is said to be derivative: 'It is generally said that each of us "has a soul". The transpersonal perspective turns this statement on its head: "The soul has us – the personality is a reflection and a fragment of the soul" (ibid.: 230). The ontological implications of this can only sit obliquely to the hedonistic spirituality of a Skyros holiday, the goods on offer at Neal's Yard, or the serenity of Findhorn's nature sanctuary, whatever the degree of numinosity attached to such naturalism. In contrast the transpersonal position proposes the primacy, indeed the agency, of pure idea.

Certainly the search for and realisation of the self have become a formative ingredient of post-1970s New Age, and find a sympathetic parallel in much modern heterodox religiosity. The proliferation of esoteric terminology relating to these concerns is itself one index of supply and demand. Alice Bailey, for example, lists a bewildering variety of cognate terms for the ultimate object of this kind of religiosity:

The Soul; the Ego; the Self; the One Self; the Higher Self; the Spiritual Self: the One; the Inner Ruler; the God Within; the Inner Reality; the Divine Inner Ruler; the Inner Spiritual Sun; the Divine Indweller; the Master Within the Heart; the Indwelling Flame; the Inner God; the Christ Within; the Christ Principle; the Individuality; the Divine Reality; the Real Man; the Thinker; the Spiritual Thinker; the Solar Angel. (Bailey 1983: 23)

This is hardly an empirical, naturalistic or humanistic construction of self. Rather, it is romantic and symbolical. Self here retains little trace of biological or organismic objectivity: it is purely idealistic, a wholly other, sealed and perennial capsule, immune to time and acculturation. Its realisation represents the re-emergence of the supernatural, this time from within, rather than from above, 'nature'.

– V CONCLUSION –

In summary, then, I have argued that the category 'nature' constitutes a useful index to New Age religiosity. I employed a polar typology derived from Albanese and York to indicate the hermeneutical oscillations of the 'natural' in various New Age-related settings. As I have tried to indicate by reference to both historical developments and emic thought, each type – the natural as 'real', the natural as 'illusory' – contains the seed of its opposite. That is, there is no self-realisation without apocalypse (however diluted or psychologised) and vice versa. The theological and cosmological implications of particular emic articulations of 'nature' or 'the natural' can thus be illuminated by recourse to this typology.

– NOTES –

1 Whether New Age can be categorised as a 'movement' in anything more than an extremely loose sense of the term remains a moot point. For detailed accounts, see Storm (1991), Steyn (1994), York (1995) and Heelas (1996). In what follows I intend a weak distinction to be made between a tradition of more-or-less self-conscious, highly motivated activists (for example, Alice Bailey, Peter and Eileen Caddy, Sir George Trevelyan) and specific projects (the Findhorn Community, the Wrekin Trust, 'Alternatives' in London, certain enterprises in Glastonbury); and a diffuse, populistic 'New Age', a term that in the 1990s may denote anything from a total lifestyle (of 'travellers' or, quite differently, 'yuppies') to a category of book, music or religiosity, with many shades of equivocation in between.

2 A settlement on the Moray coast, north-east Scotland, consisting in two large sites hosting caravans, houses, substantial community buildings, and several hundred people. The community dates back to late 1962, when three unemployed adults (with three children) occupied a caravan on scrubland near the sea. The story is told in Maclean (1980), Caddy (1988) and Caddy (1996).

3 For an illuminating ethnography (conducted in California, but highly relevant to Britain now), see English-Lueck (1990); for a provocative critique, see Coward (1989).

4 Literally 'to uncover', from Greek *apo*, from, *kalyptein*, to cover. My reference to this genre fits the wider Jewish-Christian cultural context from which New Age emerged and with which participants are typically familiar and often in tension, for many see themselves as innovators within, or 'apostates' from, the religious mainstream. David Spangler's seminal text, for example, is significantly entitled *Revelation: The Birth of a New Age* (Spangler 1977).

5 A term used by Balch and Taylor (1977: 840).

6 'Information . . . accessed and expressed by someone who is convinced that the source is not their ordinary consciousness' (Riordan 1992: 105).

7 Caddy (1988: 121) records that 1967 attracted 'a great many predictions from all sorts of sources that the world was going to end . . . that Judgment Day was at hand'.

8 Caddy's preferred term, broadly analogous to 'channeling' (see n 3) but with an interioristic – that is, gnostic/psychologistic – focus. Obtaining 'guidance' was a pervasive activity in Frank Buchman's Moral Rearmament movement (MRA) of the 1930s and 1940s, in which Eileen Caddy was involved for a time.

9 For a detailed discussion of the epistemology of esotericism, see Faivre (1994: 3–110). He considers esotericism to be a 'form of thought' concerned principally with acquiring 'knowledge – in the sense of "gnosis" ' (ibid.: 4, 11). Faivre's remark on the central dynamic of the term in the modern period is relevant here: 'Whoever said "esotericism" said "go to what is more *interior*" ' (ibid.: 7).

10 Its principal between 1948 and 1971 was Sir George Trevelyan, described by Peter Caddy as 'the father of the new age in Britain' (foreword in Trevelyan 1986: 8).

11 See Findhorn Community (1978) and Maclean (1980).

12 See Reichian, Encounter and Gestalt approaches in particular. On the history of humanistic psychology and the ideology of human potential, see Rowan (1976), Stone (1976), and Alexander (1992). St John (1977: 9–97) gives a participant's account of the vivid physicality and affectivity – touching, hugging, hitting cushions, expressing feelings – of a typical encounter group.

13 Programme: Scottish Alternative Health Exhibition 23 and 24 March 1996, Assembly Rooms, George Street, Edinburgh.

14 It was formed in 1955 by George King as an organization to promote messages he claimed to receive from a Venusian being. See Wallis (1974); also Clark (1990). UFOs and 'space brothers' quickly became important foci of speculation in early New Age networks: for example, in 1954 Findhorn co-founder Peter Caddy distributed his paper on the topic amongst British government ministers (Caddy 1996: 115–18).

15 Aetherius Society workshop, Glasgow: 26 November 1995 (fieldnotes). The most recent publication of the Society is 'Contacts with the Gods from Space' (1996), of which a promotional leaflet promises 'You will be able to take advantage of Spiritual opportunities you never dreamed possible and understand as never before the real meaning of the New Age' (fieldwork collection).

16 See Twigg (1979) and Hamilton *et al.* (1995) on the intimate relationship between religious and dietary alternativism.

17 Programme brochures are obtainable from: Findhorn Foundation, The Park, Findhorn, Forres IV36 OTZ; Skyros, 92 Prince of Wales Road, London NW5 3NE; Neal's Yard Agency for Personal Development, 14 Neal's Yard, Covent Garden, London WC2H 9DP.

18 See the six characteristics of esotericism and the brief history of western groups and currents offered by Faivre (1994: 10–15, 51–110).

19 It should also be noted that Assagioli was closely associated with Alice Bailey in the 1930s. He published early work in her magazine The *Beacon* and was for a time a trustee of the Lucis Trust, Bailey's umbrella organisation, after World War II.

CHAPTER 4

Assumed Affinities: Wicca and the New Age
JOANNE PEARSON

– I INTRODUCTION –

Academic study[1] is sometimes inclined to assume that Wicca is part of the New Age, although many Wiccans disagree. The response, 'we are not New Age' comes a close second to the assertion 'we are not Satanists'.[2] In the course of firsthand communication with Wiccans in Britain, and on the basis of their responses to a widely distributed questionnaire, it became apparent that the majority of Wiccans surveyed (86 per cent) did not regard Wicca as part of the 'New Age movement'. Reactions ranged from horror at the prospect of such an association to an acceptance that, although there may be some similarities, there was no evidence to support an overall categorisation of Wicca as New Age. Some respondents even crossed out the option in the questionnaire and added exclamation marks, as if to show their surprise that the researcher had even considered the possibility that Wiccans could regard their religion as 'New Age'. A parody of Hamlet's famous soliloquy, written by a Wiccan priestess, provides a striking summary of the way in which the New Age is viewed by many Wiccans:

New Age or not New Age? That is the question
Whether tis nobler in the mind to join
With fluffy bunnies, crystals and the like
Or to take arms against that sea of fads
And by opposing end them?
To die, perchance to have a near-death experience
And write a book about it
To sleep, perchance to dream and through regression
Find that fantastical past life in which
The ego can rejoice
For who would bear the whips and scorns of Pagan Gods in whom
Both dark and light are met
And so make moves to be more whole?
The Witch, the Druid, the Magus are but mad enough to walk
The realms of night where light New Agers
Fear to tread![3]

On the one hand, the apparent antagonism of Wiccans to the term 'New Age' does not invalidate the description of Wicca as New Age by academic researchers. An examination of this research into New Age, however, indicates that Wicca has been assessed with reference to its North American contexts,[4] and is regarded as having marginal importance.[5] On the other hand, the self-identification of Wiccans as separate and distinct from New Age is an area of investigation which has not been sufficiently explored.[6] Thus, the present chapter does not begin with the assumption that Wicca has an affinity with the New Age; rather, it will focus on an examination of the evidence for British Wicca's rejection of identification with the New Age, and concentrate on their self-identification. The following argument is based on on-going fieldwork in Britain, and the conclusions reached do not claim to encompass any other forms of Wicca than that of Gardnerian/Alexandrian, initiatory, coven Wicca as practised in Britain.

In order to pursue this investigation, I shall first analyse the three central principles of New Age teaching as formulated by Paul Heelas in his study of the New Age movement, which, as the most recently published volume on the New Age, will be used for the sake of convenience. Each principle will be applied to Wicca and, given the apparent inapplicability of these three characteristics, I then argue that there are two more relevant characteristics which make clear that there are fundamental differences between Wicca and the New Age. Whilst the self-identification of Wiccans may exclude interpretations which assimilate it to the New Age, it may nevertheless be likely that researchers of the New Age will continue to use such inappropriate interpretative categories. It is therefore important that such assumed affinities are subjected to serious critical interrogation.

– II THE CHARACTERISATION OF THE NEW AGE MOVEMENT –

Any formal assessment of the so-called 'New Age movement' must confront the extraordinarily eclectic, variable, flexible and diverse phenomena which have, over the last thirty years, been gradually drawn together under this heading. The undisputed diversity of New Age practices can be understood in terms of a vast array of characteristics, none of which applies universally except for, perhaps, the one unifying principle proposed by Paul Heelas: the 'authority of the individual'. However, Heelas has formulated three principles which, he claims, lie 'at the heart' of New Age teaching. The first and second of these are statements, 'Your lives are not working' and 'You are gods and goddesses in exile'; the third is an instruction, 'Let go/drop it' (Heelas: 1996: 18–20). These three principles of the New Age constitute, according to Heelas, the 'essential *lingua franca*' of the New Age, which can be expressed alternatively as 'Self-spirituality' (ibid.: 18). We can therefore surmise that, in order to characterise Wicca as 'New Age', it should fit Heelas' three main principles. Let us therefore examine each principle in turn and apply it to Wicca.

The first statement is 'Your lives are not working.' The premise from which New Age teaching launches its practices is the assumption that we are all indoctrinated by mainstream society and culture and are therefore no longer aware of who we essentially are. We thus live mechanically, enslaved by an unnatural established order imposed upon us by parents, schools, modern institutions. In consequence, we are limited, victims, unable to express our real selves. The vast variety of New Age practices may help us become aware of this, and, through expensive workshops,[7] can show us how to break free from mechanistic existence.

It is apparent that Wicca is neither based on this assumption, nor does it refer to the statement made above. In the questionnaire mentioned at the start of this chapter, none of the hundred Wiccans who responded indicated that they had become involved in Wicca because 'their lives were not working', and supplementary fieldwork does not indicate that these Wiccans assume their lives or the lives of other Wiccans are, or were, dysfunctional. Rather, the fieldwork suggests that Wiccans operate within a different polarity. Whereas the New Age operates along a 'dysfunctional-self/fulfilled-self' polarity, Wiccans work within a tension between a pragmatic response to the demands of everyday life and pursuit of a holism which involves the interaction and fusion between 'two worlds'. Observation indicates that Wicca has a recognition of and regard for the problems which are experienced in everyday life, whether bereavement, rape, divorce, exam nerves, moving house or learning to drive, to name a few examples. At the same time, Wiccans understand themselves to be actively engaging with an equally real magical world through ritual, meditation and other practices.[8]

The Wiccan attitude towards such 'problems' does not suggest the assumption that 'your life is not working', but it does not suggest either that Wiccans pretend that life is always easy. This realistic view of living in the modern world can be seen reflected in Wicca's refusal to claim that the gods, a high priest or high priestess, or even someone's 'higher self' has all the answers to life's problems. The response of one high priestess upon receiving a letter from someone interested in Wicca is typical. She reported that the person seemed to have a 'funny idea that Wicca could somehow solve all his problems', and that this was, in her opinion, the wrong reason for getting involved in Wicca.

Does the evidence suggest that Wicca fits the first tenet of New Age teaching? Wicca does not regard humankind as malfunctioning, yet it does not present a romantic notion that human life is problem-free. Observation indicates that Wicca chooses to operate within the boundaries of a pragmatic realism; that is, the modern world in which we now live may not be 'ideal' and certainly has its problem areas, but this is the case with any period of history we may wish to consider. We live in a world which has its 'good' parts and its 'bad' parts; it is sometimes easy, sometimes hard. The Wiccans, it would appear, elect to live in the world rather than attempt to overcome or escape from it:

> the outer daily world [is] transformed and yet remains the same, with the same demands, same problems as before. Spirituality is not an escape from, but an enhancement of life . . . the priestess [of Wicca] learns as much from coping with two children, doing a job, and running a home, as from erudite books, and other witches and priestesses . . . this is the world of the ordinary and extraordinary in which I live, slipping back and forth, blending and combining them to create an experience called Priestess of the Goddess. (Wadsworth 1997)

The evidence suggests, therefore, that 'your lives are not working' is neither a central theme of Wicca nor a starting point for entry into the religion. Whilst Wicca appears to celebrate both the 'ordinary and extraordinary' and 'walk the realms of night' as well as light, the New Age seems to emphasise a dysfunctional life in the 'dark' before entering the 'light' of New Age practices. Rose (1996: 347) has argued that the New Age can be seen as monistic, or at least non-dualistic, yet on a fundamental level the New Age emphasis on a lack of interconnectedness of dark and light does appear to be dualistic. The attitude of the New Age that reality lies on a spiritual level set apart from the physical, and the Wiccan acceptance of the reality of death, pain and suffering along with celebration of the joy of living, is summed up by York (1995: 147): 'In general, in place of the New Age's stress on the "White Light", Neo- Paganism – especially Wicca – incorporates the interplay between light and dark.'[9]

The theme of separation is developed further in the second statement presented by Heelas in characterising the New Age, 'You are gods and goddesses in exile'. By this he means that, 'Perfection can be found only by moving beyond the socialised self – widely known as the "ego" but also as the "lower self", "intellect", or the "mind" – thereby encountering a new realm of being' with the consequence that 'the most pervasive and significant aspect of the New Age is that the person is, in essence, spiritual' (Heelas 1996: 19). This second principle therefore suggests that the New Age upholds something akin to a Manichean dualism of matter/body versus spirit. In the context of popular culture, Heelas uses the song *Spirit* by the Waterboys to show the virtues of the shift from dogmas, beliefs and codified moralities to spiritual disciplines and practices.

The message of the song is one of exhortation to become 'Spirit', for spirit is better than 'Man' and indeed, there seems to be nothing good to say about 'Man'. The song seems to suggest that we are divine, or at least spirit, trapped in a body, exiled in the modern world and on earth. Correspondingly, New Age practices facilitate a movement from one state of being to another, from body/matter/imperfection to spirit/godhead/perfection. To attain the goal of living as 'Spirit', the body must, at least mentally (though, in extreme examples such as the Heaven's Gate deaths in March 1997, literally), be left behind. In sum, Heelas argues that:

> Ultimacy – God, the Goddess, the Higher Self – lies within, serving as the source of vitality, creativity, love, tranquillity, wisdom, responsibility, power and all those other qualities which are held to comprise the perfect inner life and which, when applied in daily practice, (supposedly) ensure that all is utopian. (Heelas 1996: 28)

In response to the assertion that 'Spirit' is superior to 'Man' and that the divine lies within, there is evidence to support the view that for Wiccans self-development is a natural by-product of Wicca. As a result of this, some feel comfortable using terminology borrowed from Jungian psychology, as in Vivianne Crowley's ([1989] 1996) popular account, *Wicca: The Old Religion in the New Millennium*. This is a text imbued with Jungian psychology and yet acclaimed by many Wiccans as a classic portrayal of British Wicca. Yet these Wiccans do not claim to be seeking perfection; rather, they say that they are developing towards 'wholeness' or 'completeness'. Such 'wholeness' contains, by its very nature, all of an individual's traits, not just those listed by Heelas above which comprise the perfect New Age inner life. Thus, as well as 'vitality, creativity, love, tranquillity, wisdom, responsibility, power', Wiccans also accept that there may be anger, stupidity, irresponsibility, ruthlessness, weaknesses and pain. According to these Wiccans, being 'whole' means being aware of and gradually confronting these traits. As a contemporary Wiccan puts it, 'She [the Wiccan] is not perfect, nor does she aspire to be, even if she could define such a concept' (Wadsworth 1997).

Whilst there is no single view of the nature of deity in Wicca (and indeed there is no formal dogma or creed to which Wiccans subscribe), Heelas' idea that we are 'gods and goddesses in exile' implies that exclusive importance should be accorded to the inner realm. By contrast, there is evidence that although a small number of Wiccans do not believe in the gods as external reality (using concepts of deity as archetypes existing only within the psyche), the majority of the Wiccans surveyed indicate that they worship their gods and goddesses in a form of invocation that involves both an external reality and an inner, psychological component. For many of this group, the gods are regarded not as perfect but as evolving just as humans are. Thus, to seek perfection through becoming a god or goddess would be, to them, a futile fantasy and a waste of time.

There is one symbol used throughout Wicca, the pentagram, which is often employed to explain the nature of 'Man' inclusive of 'Spirit'. In Wicca, each point of the pentagram is said to represent one of the five elements – earth, air, fire, water and aethyr/spirit. Since the pentagram is drawn in one continuous succession of lines, all of the elements are regarded as equal, and the aim of Wicca is to integrate them into one whole as much as possible. The New Age conception of a 'Spirit/Man' divide therefore differs from the basic teachings of Wicca symbolised in the pentagram, where the body is celebrated as well as the spirit.[10] In esoteric lore, the pentagram is generally regarded as a symbol of the human being, for it forms the shape of a human figure with arms and legs outstretched. In this sense, Wiccans regard the pentagram as a symbol of all that humans are, of which spirit is merely one component. As a contemporary Wiccan has written:

> Many religions praise spirit over the other elements, as though it is superior, but in fact as witches and priestesses we say all five are essential, and no one element, whether in Nature or in a personality, is more important than another. Hence the reason the pentagram is our best known symbol, being the five point star, with all arms interwoven equally . . . since most other spiritual paths ignore the mundane world, it comes as a surprise to meet one [i.e. Wicca] which embraces it fully. (Wadsworth 1997)

The symbol of the pentagram expresses the basic teaching of Wicca and in principle it encompasses all the constitutive elements of humanity. As such, this symbol affords a view of reality in conflict with the New Age understanding of the development of 'spirit' at the expense of everything else that comprises the human. Again, the evidence thus suggests that the second New Age principle, like the first, should not be applied to Wicca.

The third key principle is the instruction 'Let go/drop it', which, according to Heelas, 'provides the means for obtaining salvation'. Although Heelas speaks of the 'utopian vision' of the New Age, he appears to represent salvation as the 'exorcism' of the 'tyrannical' hold of the ego Heelas (1996: 20). Wicca is neither utopian nor a salvation religion in this sense. Wiccans do not seek to construct a utopian reality, or to escape from an irredeemably flawed world. Although some Wiccans draw upon psychological theory and make use of the concepts of 'ego' and 'self', they place a different emphasis upon 'ego'. Unlike New Age perceptions of ego, Wicca does not regard it as 'tyrannical' or as in some way 'bad'. Interviews with Wiccans in a number of different covens indicate that the ego is often perceived as being a necessary defence mechanism, a barrier between the self and the world. The ego acts as a filter, essential to the health of the psyche, and it does not need 'exorcising' or destroying. An awareness of the relationship between the ego and other aspects of the psyche is regarded as an interpretative tool employed to help understand development in the spiritual, personal and day-to-day dimensions of life. According to Wicca, deliverance from the ego *per se* is neither necessary nor desirable.

To a certain extent, then, this third principle of the New Age can be applied to Wicca. In terms of working with the ego and the self, Wicca does overlap with the New Age. The negotiation of the relationship between the ego and the self is undertaken in the context of a religious practice characterised by extremely strong and established commitment on the part of all participants. However, the applicablility of this third principle is limited, for the Wiccan attitude towards the ego appears to differ quite markedly from the New Age emphasis on seeking to separate from the dysfunctional socialised self that is manifest as ego.

On the basis of the foregoing considerations, entry into the religion of Wicca is not undertaken on the basis of the statement that 'your life is not working', and does not demand either the attainment of perfection or that the ego can and must be destroyed. Rather, the pragmatic realism which was seen in the earlier examination of the first principle underlies Wicca's attitude towards life and thus towards the idealism of the New Age. In realistic terms, Wiccans see life as composed of good and bad times. Realistically, there is no perfection grounded in the recovery of the uncorrupted self, for the ego is a necessary component of the psyche which may be understood in various ways. Instead Wicca focuses on its perceived reality of worshipping the gods and developing a more integrated approach to being human.

In the first section of this chapter, I have argued that Wicca is distinctive in ways which make it difficult, if not impossible, to assimilate it into 'New Age' as defined in a recent leading presentation. In the second stage of the present argument, I proceed to outline and examine two factors which allow me to clarify a comparison between Wicca and the New Age. The two connected concepts of 'authority' and 'commitment' as used in Wicca are indicative of a form of cultural practice distinct from that of the New Age.

– III AUTHORITY AND COMMITMENT –

An important characteristic of the New Age as presented by Heelas is the location of authority within the individual and the associated rejection of anything perceived by the New Ager as an external form of authority. Heelas states that, in the New Age, the limits of religion lie within the self alone, for 'if there is too much external authority – theistic, traditionalised, polytheistic – one can conclude that one is no longer with the New Age' (Heelas 1996: 35). There is much evidence, in terms of both established studies and current research, that authority in Wicca is not rejected, but has a recognised role.

The concept of authority is of central importance for the identity formation of both New Agers and Wiccans. The way in which authority functions is, however, very different. Whereas in the New Age authority resides in the self, in Wicca there is a complex process that involves the interaction of individual and group, which mediates the authoritative call of the gods and the corresponding committed response. Fieldwork observation provides examples which can clarify the distinctive Wiccan understanding of authority in practice. On this basis it will become apparent that authority in Wicca anticipates sustained commitment on the part of initiates markedly different from the 'consumption' of spiritual self-realisation characteristic of New Age.

The definitions of authority provided by the *Oxford English Dictionary* (1996) are a good starting point for an initial conceptual exploration which can enhance under-standing of the different applications of authority in the New Age and Wicca. First of all, authority is defined as 'the power or right to enforce obedience', and this appears to be the negative meaning of authority against which the New Ager reacts. Authority is defined in two further ways, as 'delegated power', and as 'an influence exerted because of recognised knowledge or expertise'. Both these latter definitions appear more accurately to reflect the meaning of authority in Wicca. The two latter types of authority, and in particular the third type, are a function of experience, that is, the 'actual observation of or practical acquaintance with facts or events; knowledge or skill resulting from this'.

Authority in Wicca is not embodied within a priesthood in the same way that it is in institutionalised religions such as Christianity. This is because Wicca specifically initiates each practitioner both as witch and priest or priestess, but this should not be taken to imply that authority is vested in a static, unchanging way in any particular individual. Thus the function of the individual initiate within the context of the coven is processual: as the Wiccan becomes more fully incorporated into the priestly role so she or he grows in authority. High priestesses and high priests often speak of being 'put on a pedestal' by new initiates who, as they grow in experience, then 'kick away' that same pedestal. This is a process which is sometimes quite subtle, sometimes blatant. Wiccans explain this process with reference to authority: the new initiate, seeing in his or her initiator the God or Goddess practically made manifest, invests the high priestess or priest with great power and authority.

Wiccans work to prove themselves worthy of the power and authority which the new initiate has automatically given them. During that same period of time, or longer, however, the initiates also learn their own capabilities and limitations, that they too can also participate fully in ritual, and to trust their own experience, built from mistakes and successes. Once the initiates have stopped worrying about getting everything right, they begin to realise that their ideas and opinions are being sought after and listened to, not just those of the high priestess and priest, and that they too have become a source of authority. This is especially true once an initiate starts exhibiting particular skills. For example, in a coven one might typically observe one Wiccan particularly interested in Qabala, another in Tarot, another in astrology, another in incense making; the priestess or priest becomes the 'coven authority' within her or his area of expertise. The high priestess and high priest, on the other hand, would usually be the ones with a developed expertise in running rituals, practising magic and training others, and so they wouldl typically be observed as the authority on these matters.

The distinctive Wiccan perception and application of authority becomes clear if we analyse the organisation of autonomous covens. Authority is tacitly expressed in the taking of vows at the time of initiation, something a self-respecting New Ager would be unlikely to do. New initiates are priests and priestesses from the start, for in Wicca there is no passive, non-participatory role, no 'congregation' as such. In Wicca, all are priests and priestesses, and all are progressing towards the role of high priest or high priestess, though some may leave before they reach this stage. In terms of the New Age, though some individuals may attend workshops or training groups and then decide that they also want to train others (Heelas mentions est graduate Robert D'Aubigny, who went on to found Exegesis in Britain), they appear to be the exception rather than the rule. Fieldwork has shown that the structure of Wicca provides many opportunities for all members of a coven to try their hand at writing and running rituals, and to have an input into the training of new initiates. In these ways they gain experience and authority.

With regard to the question of 'external' authority rejected by the New Age, Wiccans recognise the authority of the gods. In principle, Wiccans may identify themselves as polytheistic, pantheistic or panentheistic religionists. Wiccans believe in and worship a multitude of gods and goddesses. The gods do not impose authority; rather authority is accorded to them in a similar way to that by which authority is given to the high priestess and high priest. As the deities of Wicca are not assumed to be perfect, they can be argued with, and thus, as with the high priestess or high priest in the coven, their authority is not seen as absolute. A high priestess reported that she had vented her anger at the gods because she did not want to go to the part of the country she thought he was telling her to move to (she got her way in the end!). This high priestess pointed out that the gods of Wicca are powerful beings, and they ought to be able to cope with the expression of human anger. This example is indicative of the relationship Wiccans have with their gods; the deities may give instructions and may even know what is best for the priestess or priest, but they do not impose their will and they can be argued with.

The evidence suggests that authority within Wicca is diffuse; there is no absolute authority located either in the divine or in the high priestess and high priest. Through observation or reading of a ritual, it becomes apparent that during ceremonies authority in Wicca is not static, for the flexible nature of both the Wiccan working space and the Wiccans who operate within it allows for constant shifts of focus from one person, direction or object to another. Authority is, however, focused on two interrelated processes: the interaction between initiate and initiator, and that between both of the latter and the gods. Fieldwork indicates that, among Wiccans, the experience, knowledge, thoughts and ideas of all participants may be regarded as authoritative, and are seen as resources available to be drawn upon. Authority is not simply located within the individual, the individual's 'higher self', or the individual's experience and intuition. It is to be found in other Wiccans and in the gods as well as in oneself. There are always external perspectives available, and Wiccans actively engage with each other as they draw upon these. Clearly this attitude towards authority is different from the New Age view that external authority – whether from other people or from external gods – is invalid.

In terms of commitment, Heelas notes that only 5–10 per cent of New Agers belong to and are faithful members of particular New Age organisations (Heelas: 1996: 38). Bruce follows Heelas in suggesting that New Age practices do not require sustained commitment on the part of the 'consumer', but only from leading figures. Thus, those having an intimate long-term involvement in the New Age are few (Bruce 1995: 95). From this, the impression is given that the New Age is characterised by short-term, serial involvement in a variety of practices, and indeed, Heelas cites sixty hours of seminars for est and five days of intensive training for 'i am'. The New Ager would thus appear to expect quick results and to be result-centred, taking specific courses for specific ends.

Wicca, by contrast, demands sustained commitment and every Wiccan is intimately involved. The nature of the commitment is long term, for it is process-centred rather than result-centred. It is not unusual to find Wiccans who have spent five or more years with the coven into which they were initiated, participating in circles every two weeks throughout that whole period. Those who go on to form their own covens tend to expect the same level of commitment from their own initiates, which they match with their own continued level of commitment. Dedication to the gods, to Wicca and to the coven is taken very seriously, and it is noticeable that those who lack dedication often leave whilst they are still first degree initiates. This may be due to the fact that the second degree initiation is considered to be a far greater commitment, as Vivianne Crowley points out:

> It is the initiation that makes him or her a High Priest or High Priestess of Wicca. The second degree initiation confers the authority to transmit the tradition and the power to initiate first degree Witches. In most traditions, the second degree is considered a much more important and binding initiation than the first. The commitment of the second degree is considered to have an effect beyond this particular life and must not be undertaken lightly. The initiation is seen as a permanent commitment to the priesthood and to the service of the Gods. (Crowley 1996: 193)

The length of time taken by first degree initiates before they are ready for second degree is typically two to five years. Some may choose to remain at first degree, but most will leave the coven during this period if they cannot make the second degree commitment. It could therefore be argued that Wiccans initiated to second and third degree make up the equivalent of Bruce's New Age 'committed core'. Nevertheless, field observation of the level of commitment expected of, and exhibited by, first degree Wiccans reveals it to be considerably greater than that suggested by Heelas and Bruce with regard to New Agers. Wicca involves rituals of initiation, and even at first degree level, the ritual includes an oath of commitment 'to protect our brothers and sisters even unto death and never to reveal the *secrets of the Art* except in an appropriate fashion' (Crowley 1996: 116). Commitment to the coven and to Wicca is emphasised through the binding of the initiate and the taking of the initiate's measure, which act as reminders of the commitment which has been made by both the initiate and the initiator.

Analysis of the application of 'authority' and 'commitment' in Wicca and the New Age exposes significant differences, which can, however, be interpreted using recognised definitions of the key terms. Commitment as 'an engagement or obligation that restricts freedom of action' is linked to authority as 'the power or right to enforce obedience'. The New Age makes negative use of these two definitions in a mutually reinforcing way by which the New Ager views external authority as something which is imposed and which restricts freedom. In Wicca, the alternative definition is utilised, whereby commitment is taken to mean 'dedication' or 'application'. By making positive use of this definition, Wicca reinforces the definition of authority as influence gained through knowledge or expertise. In Wicca, authority and commitment thus facilitate each other. This reinforces the impression that Wicca can be described as a long-term initiatory practice, whereas the New Age can essentially be understood as an amorphous amalgam of short-term, therapeutic practices.

– IV CONCLUSION –

This chapter forms an integral part of a larger, on going study. It does not claim to have covered all characteristics of the New Age or of Wicca, but has instead focused upon a selection of concepts central to the identification of both groups. The perception of Wicca by academics researching the New Age and the self-perception of Wiccans may well frequently diverge. In this chapter it has been shown that Paul Heelas' three central principles of the New Age are not easily applicable to British Wicca. Moreover, the two characteristics of authority and commitment have been shown to be applied positively in Wicca, but to be unsuited to the characterisation of the New Age. On these two counts, it is difficult to sustain the customarily assumed affinity between Wicca and the New Age. Popular and media perceptions of Wicca have often been misleading, but there is no reason why similar distortions should continue to affect the academic representation of this religion. Wicca is distinctive in ways that allow it to claim a position as an integral religious tradition and to resist reduction to misleading representation.

– NOTES –

1 Heelas (1996); Lewis and Melton (1992).

2 See Harvey (1997: 217–21) where he asserts that Paganism is most often misunderstood as either Satanism or New Age, and discusses why Paganism is neither of these.

3 Talking Stick, London-based producer of 'the world's first Pagan comic' *Wizard and Whips* (1995), provides more 'tongue-in-cheek' examples of the Pagan/Wiccan attitudes towards the New Age through a series of spoof adverts, for example: 'Start your own business – Make a fortune as a New Age counsellor – No experience, common sense or wisdom needed – Talk bollocks and con vulnerable people today' (ibid.: 4); 'The *Real* Talisman – Individually Charged for *You* – "Cosmic Vibes Mega-Talisman" – only £18.00 (plus £34.50 p&p)' (ibid.: 9); and lastly, 'Powernetics – Yes! You too can have lots of money! You too can have lots of sex! You too can drive a fast car! To find out how, send a non-refundable donation of $295.95 to The Plaza Suite, The Regency Hotel, California' (ibid.: 19). To spot a New Ager, Talking Stick tells us to 'Look out for sycophantic cheesy grin and "off my face on planet bong" glazed expression' (back cover). See also York (1995: 174, n. 14), in which he quotes from Talking Stick a 'checklist of indicators by which "pagan and magick groups" might identify and eliminate their increasing "infiltration" by New Agers', as an example of (Neo-)Pagan distancing from the New Age.

4 I am grateful to the North American Wiccans present at the 'Re-Enchantment' conference held at King Alfred's College, Winchester 1997, who pointed out that they also disliked being labelled 'New Age'.

5 Heelas' account of the New Age appears to include Wicca on the basis of a single line (taken out of context) from the two page 'Charge of the Goddess' as published by Crowley (1989/1996); Barker (1989) includes Wicca in her list of new religious movements, but only mentions it once in the main text of her book. Research on Paganism (Harvey 1997, Adler 1986), however, tends to mention the New Age briefly in order to point out that Paganism is not part of the New Age. Michael York's detailed study (1995), though encompassing both (Neo–) Paganism and the New Age in one volume, does provide examples of the differences and similarities between the two. Steven Sutcliffe, who has conducted a historical study of the New Age, does not mention Wicca at all and, significantly, Sutcliffe disagrees with many recent characterisations of the New Age (pers. com. August 1997). In his chapter in the present volume, Hanegraaff (n. 11) leaves Paganism out of his examination of the New Age because it is a 'complicating factor'.

6 Some Wiccans, however, have indicated to me that such an investigation is not really necessary, that to explore Wicca in terms of the New Age is as much a waste of time and energy as exploring Wicca in contrast to Satanism or Christianity, for example. Since neither the New Age, Satanism nor Christianity is regarded as having any bearing on Wicca, these Wiccans do not think Wicca needs to be justified in contrast to any of them.

7 See Adler's comment that the difference between Paganism and New Age is the decimal point (Adler 1986: 420, also cited by Harvey 1997: 219). Workshops run by Wiccans which I have attended as part of my fieldwork have typically cost c.£2.00 if held in someone's house (to cover cost of tea/coffee/milk and handouts, with everyone bringing food to share) and £20 and £38 (for a London-based one-day workshop and a non-residential weekend workshop respectively) to cover room hire. The Wiccan ethic tends to be that a charge is made to cover costs but not to make a profit. Reduced-fee places are always available for those unable to afford the full cost. Stuart Rose (1996: 330), arguing that some

New Age workshops are cheap, cites the cost of a non-residential weekend workshop, again in London, as '£110 average waged, £80 low waged, £45 unwaged'. Note that the New Age unwaged fee cited here is still more expensive than the highest fee for a comparable Wiccan workshop. The 'average waged' fee of £110 would have almost covered the £115 fee for a week-long, self-catering, residential Wiccan gathering including rituals and workshops held in 1997.

8 See Jone Salomonsen in this volume.
9 See also Samuel in this volume for a brief discussion of Buddhist and Wiccan 'responses to the darker sides of the human condition', and Hanegraaff's note (this volume) that Neo-Paganism similarly argues that 'death and life, darkness and light, are . . . intimately interwoven'.
10 Cf. Samuel in this volume.

CHAPTER 5

The Chthonic Imperative:
Gender, Religion and the Battle for the Earth

RICHARD ROBERTS

– I INTRODUCTION –

The rediscovery of the spiritual significance of the earth and a reawakening of consciousness of the Goddess are central features of Paganism.[1] As such, they are aspects of the identity of a widely diffused and increasingly differentiated new social movement. The latter is also an 'imagined community', composed of many networks, groups and individuals impelled by a revisionary account of human, in particular western, history and prehistory. It is this comprehensive vision that concerns me, for, in its more developed forms, it proposes a radical account of the human condition that affords inspiration to an increasing number, even as it challenges both those who study religion within the paradigm of agnostic neutrality and others who are committed reflexive practitioners within traditional main-line religions.

The basic concern of this chapter is with this earth-centred vision of human existence, apostrophised here as the 'chthonic imperative',[2] which is presented and enacted in the experiential ritual and mythology of the Goddess (Christ 1987). This cluster of beliefs and cultural practices embodies in its most reflexive forms a wide-ranging interpretation of the human condition. The core of this consists in a kind of megalithic idealism, a conviction that there was once an integrated human reality, a matriarchal connectedness[3] that pre-existed the 'Fall' that took place with the discovery of metal, the emergence of an aggressive patriarchal division of labour, the consequent enslavement of women, and a pervasive loss of an integral relationship with nature. The full range of reversals implied by the chthonic imperative as informed by the reassertion of matriarchy does not simply consist in the demand that humankind recognise the requirements of the earth, Mother Earth, Gaia, Erda, as the condition of ecological survival (see Adams 1993; Cooper 1992; Daly 1991; Lovelock 1979; Nasr 1968; Odum 1953; Ponting 1988; Sachs 1993; Seed et al. 1988; White 1967). The chthonic imperative also requires that the focus of human identity and ultimacy be shifted away from the received and dominant mediations and identifications associated with the long-unfolding, male-specific compact of western thought as a whole. In its latest stage of development and dissemination as globalised capitalism, the latter is seen as a threat to the integrity of the whole world.

Whilst the literature promoting this vision is now considerable (see Gimbutas 1989;

Goldenberg 1979; Starhawk [1979] 1989; Thompson 1981), the essential features are displayed with great clarity and rhetorical power in one of the foundation texts of the re-emergent cult of the Goddess, Monica Sjöö and Barbara Mor's *The Great Cosmic Mother* ([1987] 1991). As highly effective communicators, Sjöö and Mor focus upon a series of basic theses which serve as the starting point of a corresponding reflective response. The issues that arise are in number and scale beyond what can be handled here in more than the briefest terms. My intention is, nonetheless, to open up lines of communication between the passionate commitment of those who embody and enact the chthonic imperative, and those (like the present writer) who continue to struggle with the inner crisis of the western Christian religious and intellectual tradition as theologians, scholars in the humanities, and social scientists.

For men, this inner crisis now extends to all aspects of identities built upon ancestral male hegemony, the full discovery and uncovering of which may well precipitate the pain and violence (both psychic and physical) of resistance. To speak out of a manhood erected upon the successive interconnected mediations of the western identity through God, Christ, church, capitalism, denatured nature, the punitive super-ego, 'being-unto-death', and now the virtual aura of a globalised world system is to utter *de profundis*. To encounter the 'death of God' thus understood as a 'moment' in this train of mediation is indeed to confront the 'death of man' in a gender-specific sense. In a typically suggestive but convoluted manner, Michel Foucault writes of the 'new gods' that are 'swelling on the future Ocean' after the 'absolute dispersion of man' (see Foucault 1990: 384–5).[4] For those in the western Christian tradition this is seemingly the end of a long road; and where to go and what to do are questions that have far from obvious answers. Words can scarcely express the conflictual distress of the dissolution of tradition for those who believe, or who have believed; it is therefore worth recalling that there is no gendered monopoly of pain when humankind tries to confront what we have made of the human condition and its earthbound setting.

– II Utopian megalithic matriarchy –

The redoubtable Pagan and radical feminist activist Monica Sjöö originated, and with Barbara Mor developed, one of the first truly comprehensive accounts of resurgent matriarchy in their jointly authored text, *The Great Cosmic Mother*. This book is a *tour-de-force*, a whirling synthesis mercifully informed by a lively humanity and compassion. Their renewal of matriarchal vision is concerned not simply with the reconstruction of its historic and (more questionably) its prehistoric origins, but also with the visionary dimension, nothing less than the provision of a new *mythos* for the human condition. Despite her intense feminism, Monica Sjöö issues the (for a male reader) very welcome declaration that, 'I do not believe that it is biologically given in men to be violent and destructive' (Sjöö and Mor [1987] 1991: xix). Moreover, Sjöö and Mor do not rule out the possibility that men too may have powerful intuitive and supra-rational sensitivities to particular places, the earth, and ancient (or reinvented) traditions.

In presenting itself as a visionary account of the human condition, *The Great Cosmic Mother* is reminiscent in tone and strategy of the panoramic textual method employed to great effect by the German Jewish Marxist revisionist Ernst Bloch: a vast cornucopia of cultural artefacts is poured out before the reader, and out of this a pattern emerges (Roberts 1990: ch. 1). Moreover, the affinity is in fact more than that of genre, for looked at in the broader scheme, Sjöö and Mor (like Bloch) are at least in part Marxist revisionists. They know their Marx, and they share a Marxian urge to research and promote a total renovation of the human condition grounded upon a revolutionary transformation of material relations, in their instance those of gender, rather than class. Given the location of the fulcrum of history in the patriarchal hegemony that perverted an original matriarchal order, then the inversion of this relation and all that goes with it will in effect restore and promote the truest goals of socialism, which were lost in crude dialectical materialism. Whereas Bloch was overwhelmed by the complicities of a decadent past and thought in terms of anticipatory consciousness and the undetermined future, Sjöö and Mor project their vision of an ideal prehistorical past, and a new scheme of creation, fall and redemption in which the earthly-spiritual, the chthonic imperative, is central. This imperative acts through the equivalent of the Marxian proletariat, that is through the concrete universal of womanhood comprised under matriarchy and empowered by the Goddess. Both visions are in the final analysis utopian; both involve mythopoesis on a grand scale; both invoke the divine as critical horizon; each programme attempts to discern and direct the *Zeitgeist*.

'In the beginning,' so Sjöö and Mor inform us, 'was a very female sea' (Sjöö and Mor [1987] 1991: 2). The planetary ocean is 'womb-like', full of parthenogenic life-forms moved by lunar-tidal rhythms which swim in an amniotic ambience that eventually transfers itself to land with the microcosmic egg. By contrast, the penis, 'a mechanical device for land reproduction', emerged a mere 200 million years ago into a world in which the male was essentially secondary and drone-like in comparison with female capacities. Maleness itself is therefore understood as an effort-laden deviation from female primacy. This is a first reversal: the biological primacy of phallocentrism repeatedly enshrined in the metaphysics and science of the west (from the primal Semitic Adam to Aristotle, Aquinas and Francis Bacon), and enacted in its myriad social and cultural artefacts, is thereby overturned.[5]

The biological primordiality of the female is, however, confronted by histories of human culture that are narratives based on the suppression of any consciousness of its true origin, a strategy supported by 'something called "God" ' (Sjöö and Mor [1987] 1991: 5). For them, as for Feuerbach, Marx and Engels (besides Nietzsche and Freud), this 'God' is a false mediation to be stripped out and suppressed; but unlike these male slayers of 'God', Sjöö and Mor and other Goddess feminists do not, however, advocate the elimination of the projective tendency of human beings through a policy of total atheism. The chthonic imperative in broadest form sanctions the rebirth of the gods, an active polytheism; in its specifically matriarchal expression the chthonic imperative promotes the rule of the Goddess. To understand more fully precisely how this marked pluralism is to be managed within the obvious ideological differentiation of contemporary nature religion would require further research.[6]

From the standpoint of Sjöö and Mor, the suppression of womankind can be regarded as the world's most successful ideological conspiracy based upon the exercise of raw male power. Whereas few of us may be scientifically qualified to judge whether, as Sjöö and Mor suggest, the male sexual organ is the under-developed female or the reverse, the assertion of female primacy on the basis of biology does have points of contact with other strands of contemporary feminism and some scientific findings. The representation of evolutionary priorities in metaphysical terms is risk-fraught, not least because science itself is not free from a degree of social construction.[7] The role of non-reproductive sex and the powerful inscription of 'nature' are all highly complex matters which can be made to serve very different ideological agendas, both within and beyond the wide range of positions, constitute the full spectrum of resurgent female consciousness. The invocation of science in support of a comprehensive quasi-metaphysical scheme runs into more obvious dangers. Marx, and in particular Engels drew upon then contemporary science and thus legitimated a tendency to allow ideology to override empirical research science, with disastrous consequences for later Soviet science. There is no reason why matriarchal Goddess feminism should not experience the same difficulties if it fuses a gendered concrete universal with a selective appro-priation of legitimatory ideas drawn from changing science (see Ronald Hutton's contribution to this volume).

The social and cultural derivation of original matriarchy is largely constructed by apologists such as Sjöö and Mor from sympathetic interpretations of the image of the human female who lived in the Upper Palaeolithic to the Middle Neolithic periods. It is therefore the Stone Age that comes to represent an idealised cultural norm; subsequent developments are in many significant senses a 'fall' away from the 'primal visions, images and gestalts of human experience . . . [that] still resonate in our psyches' (Sjöö and Mor [1987] 1991: 7). Again, as with the biological dimension of their argument, the assertion of pre-historic female primacy on the basis of the reconstruction of prehistoric societies (to which there is of necessity strictly limited access) draws upon specialised areas of research that are also subject to constant change and development.[8] It is therefore important to bear in mind that both the biological and prehistoric societal dimensions as exploited by Sjöö and Mor are functioning as aspects of a creative vision that has a reciprocal relationship with the cultural practices and thus the plausibility structures of a new social movement. Yet it is important to acknowledge that the feminist primordialism represented by Sjöö and Mor is highly reflexive, and whilst it operationalises a set of presuppositions concerning the cultural significance of an inherited biological and prehistoric past, it is not to be regarded simply as a chthonic fundamentalism.[9]

Sjöö and Mor's account of the origins of female identity in the biological primacy of female sexual organs over those of the male, and the prehistoric embodiment of this priority in a lost universal primordial matriarchy, requires a realist theory of the efficacy of myth in order to prevent their reduction to mere 'archetypes of the unconscious'. In order to 'approach our human past – and the female God – we need a wagon with at least two wheels: one is the mythical-historical-archaeological; the other is the biological-anthropological' (Sjöö and Mor [1987] 1991: 9). What they therefore recognise is that 'many feminists today are unsure whether studies of evolutionary biology, or of religious mythology, can have political relevance for contemporary women' (ibid.: 11). Sjöö and Mor have no such doubts.

For Sjöö and Mor such a mixed approach is indispensable; but it is arguable that what amounts in their case to the merging of myth, history and archaeology with material extracted from biology and physical anthropology involves many ambiguities. Whereas the scientific study of religion in its post-Enlightenment forms has striven for 'objectivity' and the reductive explanation of religion, the simultaneous scientific and personal commitments of those involved in the study of nature religion is a remarkable reversal worthy of comment. Yet, in assessing the mythopoetic potency of the chthonic imperative and primal matriarchy, it is essential to discriminate between those parts of the project which are more obviously sustainable from others which are little more than sophisticated wish-fulfilment, that is, thinking that has to be understood in the context of the plausibility structures of a nascent religious movement. Whether it is possible for those who draw upon such movements for self-empowerment to make these discriminatory judgements at the same time as they study them is a relevant question.

– III THE DILEMMAS OF PRIMAL WOMANHOOD –

As has been suggested above, Sjöö and Mor's vision runs considerable risks when it includes the study of 'nature' and biological origins in the context of contemporary feminism (Butler 1990, 1993). There are many possible consequences when 'nature' is drawn upon to support the drama of female existence as a programme of self-empowerment. Thus, for example, whilst Sjöö and Mor lay claim on behalf of women to the origins of human culture in the ante-and post-natal care of offspring, they do not pretend that this is a cost-free process:

> Among humans, males help with protection and food acquisition; but it is the communal group of females that surrounds the child, in its first four to six years of life, with strong physical, emotional, traditional, and linguistic presence. And this is the foundation of social life and human culture. (Sjöö and Mor [1987] 1991: 11)

In other words, the extraordinary stress that Sjöö and Mor lay upon the natural origins of womankind might initially seem to imply a form of biological essentialism with regard to gender and sexual identity.[10] The psychological realism of their emphasis upon the specifically female role in the primary care of offspring is counterbalanced (albeit paradoxically) by the assertion of primordial parthenogenesis and bisexuality, which might free women from other potentially burdensome gender-defined roles. Correspondingly, whilst sexuality might seem to pertain to biological primordiality, it is of primary importance because of its cultural role:

The Human race has been definitively shaped by the evolution/revolution of the female body into a capacity for non-reproductive sex. This is not just a physical fact. It is a cultural, religious, and political fact of primary significance. (Sjöö and Mor [1987] 1991: 11)

There is a malleable core to *The Great Cosmic Mother* in which biological predetermination and the social and cultural emancipation of women are dynamically fused. Indeed for Sjöö and Mor, all culture, all science, all technology originate at the matriarchal hearth and in the prehistoric integrity of the community of women:

The fact is that from this first inner circle of women – the campsite, the fire-site, the cave, the first hearth, the first circle of birth – that human society evolved. As hominids evolved into Palaeolithic *Homo sapiens*, and then into settled and complex Neolithic village people on the time-edge of 'civilisation,' these tens of thousands of years of human culture were shaped and sustained by communities of creative, sexually and psychically active women – women who were inventors, producers, scientists, physicians, lawgivers, visionary shamans, artists. Women who were also the Mothers – receivers and transmitters of terrestrial and cosmic energy. (Sjöö and Mor [1987] 1991: 12)

Such passionate holism is reminiscent of the more rhapsodic passages in the so-called young, Romantic Marx and Engels' depiction of a condition freed from scarcity and oppression in which all human beings enjoy their spontaneous creativity. Unlike Marx and Engels, who had little sympathy with primitive life-conditions (or what Marx disparagingly referred to as the idiocy of rural life), Sjöö and Mor present a highly idealised vision of primaeval womankind. As with the postulation of a Soviet New Man endowed with Stakhanovite potency, so with Sjöö and Mor, social and cultural contradictions of the female human condition are putatively resolved in the prototypical figure of a magically-empowered, quintessentially politically correct 'black Athena', the primal superwoman:

The original witch [who] was undoubtedly black, bisexual, a warrior, a wise and strong woman, also a midwife, also a leader of her tribe . . . The nature of the Goddess was in no way the pale, meek, and solely maternal one that has been associated with 'femininity' in patriarchal culture. (Sjöö and Mor [1987] 1991: 216)

Sjöö and Mor have to confront the eclipse of this rhapsodic female life-order. Somehow this primal reality underwent an almost Atlantean disappearance, a sudden and total submersion attributed to the intervention of men. In short, a 'Fall' took place when men invented and then used metal, supremely iron, as the means of aggressive domination that displaced and destroyed megalithic matriarchy. This account of the origin of evil in the context of original female goodness is reinforced by male perversity paralleled and mirrored in the Hebraic and Christian elements that inform western culture. As in the Christian scheme, where the old Adam is recapitulated in the new Adam, Jesus Christ, so what we are invited to think of as the much-wronged black, lesbian, parthenogenic first Eve becomes the paradigm for the re-enactment of the cycle of existence of the Great Mother in the practice of nature religion. Yet, the reader might be forgiven for asking, should this witch/ Goddess paradigm be spared all critique of the kind which called the male self-projection of an omnipotent, omniscient, misogynistic God the Father into question? Should utopian matriarchy and the chthonic imperative be insulated from the insights of Feuerbach, Marx, Freud or their successors? On a more obvious and banal plane, the reader of this exciting and imaginative text might well be reminded of those nineteenth-century writers of lives of Jesus who were said to have gazed down a deep well only to see their own distant reflection.

Sjöö and Mor's critique of patriarchy shares much with received traditions of successive waves of feminist theory. Where they diverge from the mainstream of the latter in a distinctive way is in the very high status they accord to the 'politics of mythology' (Sjöö and Mor [1987] 1991: 256) and the conscious assimilation of female and male identities into oppositional mythic space, rather than the monopolar ontological exclusions and negativity characteristic of, say, Mary Daly's *Pure Lust* (Daly 1984). As with Ernst Bloch (but unlike Marx, Engels and their dialectical materialist successors), Sjöö and Mor at least reckon with an on going dialectics of gender. With regard to their mythological representation, the contrast of the solar and the earthy becomes a systematic categorisation into which male and female principles and their respective attributes are respectively allocated. This is at the very least an arena in which dialogue (albeit contestatory) might possibly take place, such as is expressed in many forms of Pagan ritual performed through the cycles of the year (Crowley 1996).

For Sjöö and Mor, the primacy of prehistoric female identity as grounded in what we might venture to describe as the primordial passion of the Great Mother has special, but limited historical impact. Such has been the success of aggressive patriarchy that anything more than a closely confined emphasis upon the actual historic achievements of women would appear pointless. It is far more important to re-energise contemporary women with a vision of their prehistoric 'imagined identity' in the Fore-Mother and Goddess with a view to inspiring present and future action instead of engaging in the archaeology of female reverses under patriarchy. Thus Sjöö and Mor seek to promote the ritual release of a repressed consciousness rather than engineer the rehabilitation of neglected achievement.

The celebration of 'success' during the era of repressive patriarchy and its attendant technology would be difficult, if to be a woman involves evocation of the chthonic imperative, the rediscovery of earth-relatedness, rather than competition in terms of outcomes within a scheme of a male-specific, falsely conceived history. Yet might it not be, contrary to Sjöö and Mor, that effective empowerment implies participation in mediation and thus the partial recovery of 'alienation' as objectification, a divorce from, rather than identification with, nature? Here the problem of the status of western cultural artefacts pointedly highlighted by T. W. Adorno from a revisionist Marxist standpoint arises once more. Adorno could refer to Beethoven's *Missa Solemnis* as an 'alienated masterpiece' (Adorno 1976); an enduring work of genius was also the product of a perverted bourgeois consciousness and supposedly opposed to the interests of a deprived working class. Likewise, the chthonic imperative juxtaposes symbolic, mythical and magical identification, even spiritual symbiosis with 'nature', with a patriarchal culture which has in certain respects been astonishingly successful in its refraction of universal human concerns.

Apologists for western 'democratic capitalism' like the Catholic theologian Michael Novak argue that adolescent alienation in the 'empty shrine' of capitalism is the rite of passage all must undergo if they are to attain maturity (Roberts 1993). In this setting, 'nature' is but the gift upon which humankind may exercise its ingenuity within the framework of property, patent and copyright law. In short, from this standpoint it could be said that the chthonic imperative and Goddess matriarchalism of the kind advocated by Sjöö and Mor, like some varieties of deep ecology, celebrates nature in a way open only to a tiny minority; that is to those who, through the privilege of wealth or the assumption of exemplary self-imposed marginality, may enjoy forms of self-realisation closed to the urban masses who depend for their economic and psychic survival upon complex forms of mediation unassimilable to the chthonic imperative. It is the displacement of a patriarchal by a matriarchal theological horizon to which we now turn in order to examine in more depth and detail the problem, and yet the necessity, of mediation.

– IV CHRISTIANITY AND NATURE: THE NECESSITY OF MEDIATION –

Central to Sjöö and Mor's mythological critique of the west is the loss of matriarchal universality attributable to the God of the Hebrews:

> The Hebrew patriarchs tried to destroy the world's original, most widespread, and enduring religion by branding it as 'evil,' and by portraying the Mother Goddess and her magic snake-lover as the source, not of all life, but of 'all wickedness' – hated and condemned by their new tribal God Jahweh. To the degree that they were historically successful in this attempt, Western biblicised peoples have lost their original concept, and memory, of what the Goddess and her Serpent really meant – to all people, and all time. (Sjöö and Mor [1987] 1991: 58)

Thus in its turn, Christianity perpetuates and universalises patriarchy, and, furthermore, it organised the extirpation of the residuum of Paganism; moreover, as Sjöö and Mor maintain, 'Everything alive in Christianity (especially its heresies) is taken from the Old Religion' (ibid.: 116). When considering the advent of early western industrialised modernity, Sjöö and Mor identify at least in part with Marx and Engels' critiques of Judaism and Christianity. In particular, Engels, following Bachofen (Bachofen 1967), early argued for the primacy of matriarchy and the historical relativity of the patriarchal bourgeois family. Marx, Engels and Marxism failed, unfortunately, to distinguish between formal religion and the life of the spirit and the heart. Glossing Sjöö and Mor, it could be said that in reproducing a dichotomy between material and spiritual existence, Marx and Engels merely repeat and reinforce in a different way the perverse alienations analysed in the *Paris Manuscripts*. The co-founders of so-called scientific socialism reacted against the alienation characteristic of the capitalist system of production. Yet at the heart of their paradoxical admiration of the achievements of the bourgeois class, expressed *par excellence* in the *Communist Manifesto* of 1848, they laud the conquest and mastery of nature as the prelude to the final abolition of human need. Seemingly as oblivious as the most ruthless competitive capitalists to any questions relating to the intrinsic value of nature, Marx and Engels thus eliminated further common ground, with catastrophic ecological consequences now apparent across the former Soviet bloc. In the place of matriarchy, and following the careers of Christianity and Marxism, for Sjöö and Mor there continues to subsist a culture unworthy, apparently, of the name:

> Western history does not show us any evolution toward greater spirit, greater meaning, greater culture. The Western Roman-Christian contribution to the world, when we look at it, has been almost entirely in the area of technology, and of analytical intellect; combined with a notorious spiritual and cultural alienation, and perhaps the loneliest individuals the world has ever seen (Sjöö and Mor [1987] 1991: 85)

The foregoing general condemnation of the western project understood as the triumph of alienation and the apotheosis of instrumental reason is not new. Not least, it echoes the response of the Romantics to the early stages of the Industrial Revolution, and the critique of the Frankfurt School. Thus, from rather different but not wholly unrelated positions, Wordsworth, Ruskin, and Thoreau might well have echoed Sjöö and Mor's contention that 'Human survival does indeed depend on a sacramental relation to nature' (ibid.: 80).[11] In order to grasp more fully what this might mean, it is first necessary to outline in brief but with some care the history of those mediations which Sjöö and Mor reject in the name of ritual and of affective immediacy with nature, a relationship legitimated and empowered by the mythology of the Goddess.

The debate concerning the interconnection on the religious level between western Christian culture and the transformation and degradation of nature has been dominated by contrasting interpretations of the Genesis narratives. Since Lynn White's renowned article (White 1967) exegetes have mined this vein to the point of exhaustion (see Northcott 1996: ch. 5). The centrality of the man Adam and the derived status of the woman Eve have been used to further the denigration of women. It is, however, God's injunction in Genesis 1. 28 to 'Be fruitful and multiply, and fill the earth and subdue it; and have dominion over the fish of the sea and over the birds of the air and over every living thing that moves upon the earth' (RSV) that has (however misguidedly) been used to legitimate the destructive exploitation of nature. The assumption that biblically legitimated God-given rights have had this damaging role compounds the increasingly problematic character of European and North American religious identity, not only for feminists and environmental activists interested in the role of religion within the western tradition, but also for whole populations threatened by ecological degradation which look to their traditions for positive resources.

In reality, the western Christian rehabilitation of attitudes to nature is an intellectual possibility, but it is burdened not simply by the need to counter and reinterpret major elements in the tradition as such, but also because it has to come to terms with an extravagantly ambitious scheme of mediation. This scheme, regardless of the range of critical interpretations placed upon it, has a definite shape, continuity, and stages, the last state of which is complex disintegration.[12] Moreover, far from being the monopolistic assertion of patriarchal divine priority, Christian theology is itself built upon resolutions imposed upon its own set of inherently unstable reversals. The received orthodoxies founded upon these resolutions were conserved through the creation of social institutions capable of exerting power of enforcement in the name of ecclesiastical authority. Thus as regards the person of Christ (and the doctrine of the two natures, human and divine), power, the role of women, the original prohibitions upon military service, the displacement of immediate eschatological expectation by the appearance of the Church, the adoption of Roman law, and so on, the western Latin tradition has exhibited an astonishing flexibility. All these transformations, traced, amongst others by Weber (1979), Troeltsch (1931) and Michael Mann (1986) in their respective studies concerning the role of economic ethics, the social teachings of Christianity, and the sources of social power, arguably involve reversals of original intent. Herein lies both a source of the theological vitality of Christianity and a potential basis for a hermeneutics of self-transformation. Any such latent possibilities do not, of course, exonerate a tradition from the consequences of actions attributable to it.

Fundamental to the evolution of the Christian scheme of mediation is the very remarkable transformation of the original Palestinian Jesus from a remote figure in an obscure Jewish group to the *Christus Cosmocrator*, the Christ Ruler of the Cosmos exemplified in Byzantine mosaic iconography. This process, along with the development of the doctrine of the Trinity, has been studied exhaustively in the theology of the Church Fathers, both Greek and Latin. The attainment of what the Scottish theologian Thomas F. Torrance calls 'classical Christology' was ultimately crystallised in the *unio hypostatica*, a wholly unique and unrepeatable union of the 'two natures', divine and the human, in the person of Jesus, whose equally unique status as Incarnate Word and Son of the Father provided an uncompromising 'inner logic' of revelation (Torrance 1965: ch. 8). The achievement of the traditions which peaked at such great Councils as Nicea (325) and Chalcedon (451) (see Andresen 1985: vol. 1; Kelly 1968: pt III) was the creation of an immensely powerful theological ideology, which exercised an imaginative grip upon western consciousness for over fifteen hundred years.

Those who resort to prehistoric legitimation for their identity might well maintain that from their point of view the time span of Christianity is limited, even unrepresentative of the human condition. Knowledge of the latter extends with each new paleontological find; but equally the interpretation of such discoveries offers as little solid comfort to those who seek to postulate a potentially recoverable Golden Age of matriarchal holism as to those others who struggle to impose selflessness and altruism upon evolutionary drives. The significance of the Christian legacy lies not so much in the validity of cultural practices, or even its truth-claims, in the extraordinary self-confidence of a culture which came to be convinced of its incarnation of the Absolute made flesh. By virtue of his status as *logos* (i.e. word/grammar/ explanation – even, as it were, the science of) the Incarnate Christ was also understood to be the immanent embodiment of the integrative principle of the universe, the divine rationality that underlies and infuses creation and the whole of nature. The progressive divinisation of the Christ figure from the early *logos* Christology through to the triumphant apotheosis of the *Christus Cosmocrator* tended to problematise both the humanity of Christ and the relationship of that humanity to humankind at large. Whereas compensatory responses become obvious, not least as seen in the growth of Marian devotion in its many forms (which include the Christian assimilations of the equivalent of the Great Mother, the *Magna Mater*), these do not detract from the paradigmatic male-specific hegemony of Father and Son communicating in and through the Spirit. Given this masculinist emphasis in the Western conception of the Trinity, it is remarkable how this can have retained the religious loyalty of women for such a long time.

The treatment of 'nature' (*phusis/natura*) in Christian antiquity involves a complex ingestion of Greek and Latin terms with their own etymological and philosophical histories and a relation with Stoic origins. The meaning of the concept of nature within theology was influenced by the struggle with Gnosticism (which tended to emphasise the ephemerality of matter) and the Christian obligation to recognise that the world and human bodies were created (and thus at least originally good) and the objects of redemption (and thus potentially restorable through salvation and resurrection) (Brown 1990; Kuhn 1963). The derivation of the ultimate meaning of the natural from the act of creation meant, however, that the status of nature remained somewhat ambiguous: did goodness reside in the natural as such, or was it derived and dependent upon divine grace? The late Scholastic dispute between nominalists (followers of Duns Scotus) and realists (followers of St Thomas Aquinas) was on the surface a passionately driven philosophical argument about whether individual contingent objects had 'universals' to which they corresponded and from which they derived their meaning. At a deeper level this dispute touched upon the value that might be attributed to the created world and the Incarnate Son. The eventual triumph of nominalism, which underwent revolutionary expression in the thought of the young Martin Luther, made the 'value' of the material world dependent upon divine *fiat*; that is, the will of God to impute goodness to creation which in and of itself was mere animate and inanimate matter (Blumenberg 1961). Thus the mediatory principle of the divine and human natures uniquely embodied in the Incarnate Christ, and extended through history in the church understood as the *Christus prolongatus*, was fatally undermined.

In the theology of the Reformation, nature was thus 'fallen' and denuded of intrinsic virtue with the first man Adam; but in Luther's reworking of the basic principles of Christian theology, the price of freedom from ecclesiastical power and corruption was severance from the ecclesiologically conditioned, divine-human nature embodied in the person of Christ. The restoration of the relationship between God and nature had to rely upon atonement, the redemptive death of Christ and realised eschatological judgement, rather than upon a divine-human nature which mediated a quasi-physical reality through incarnate and sacramental presence. The consequence was that the created world, nature, subsisted as the object of the divine redemptive will (and as the theatre of election or predestination in Reformed theology) rather than as the object of an affirmative love which might allow for the celebration of the intrinsic goodness of created and grace-infused nature. Moreover, given St Augustine's association of original sin and its transmission with the sexual act, the practical efforts of the Reformers to promote the ideal of marriage (as against obligatory celibacy for the priesthood) did not confront in an effective way the negative and problematic meaning of sexuality within western Christianity. The eschatological devaluation of nature and obsessive attitudes towards sexual sin, seen (for example) in modern North American Protestant fundamentalism, are the understandable outcome of unbalanced expressions of this tradition.

It is no accident that the masculinist capitalism attacked by Sjöö and Mor grew most readily (according to Weber's enduring account of the Protestant ethic and the spirit of capitalism) on Reformed soil. Main-line Protestant Christianity further recast the theologies of St Paul and St Augustine rediscovered by Luther in a way which exacerbated the problematic nature of the relation between nature and transcendence and prepared the way for deism. Of course, Catholic Christianity was resistant to collusion with the modernisation processes later to be associated with Liberal Protestantism and the Enlightenment. The price of the continued identity of the Catholic Church was an intellectual isolationism, sustained by concepts of 'nature' drawn from the theology of St Thomas Aquinas as revitalised through Neo-Thomism, which were used in a reworking of the relationship of 'nature and grace'. It is only in the very recent past that the Catholic Church has ceded ground to the extent of recognising the validity of evolutionary theory in relation to biological nature and the development of *Homo sapiens*. As a rider to this brief sketch of western theological tendencies, it is worth remarking that Eastern Orthodoxy, which according to some of its apologists has not experienced (or needed) Renaissance, Reformation or Enlightenment, is regarded by some as intrinsically more friendly towards nature than either Catholicism or Protestantism. This is not least because of its highly symbolic trinitarian liturgy, which recapitulates the whole cosmic order; furthermore, it can lay claim to no history of active collusion with modernisation, as is the case with regard to Protestantism.

The later freeing of reality from theological constraint and the concentration of the religious and spiritual dimensions in the 'turn to the subject' went a long way towards creating the situation in which, when once the residual reality of God was challenged, then the world could sink into instrumentality in early industrialism, use value in political economy, and pervasive commodification under the conditions of late capitalism. The received western mutuality-in-identity of 'God' and 'man' was such that the 'death' of the former could, as Nietzsche and Foucault argue, entail the demise of the latter. Christian theology (above all in its Protestant forms) is identified with its collusive relationship with the dramatic career of capitalism and thus with the damaging tendencies of globalised modernisation on the one hand; yet methodologically, it has resisted effective engagement with social science and is thus largely unable to relate positively to the contemporary, differentiated religious resurgence. These tendencies compound self-preoccupation and a failure to engage in critical, comprehensive and convincing innovation.

The history of modern theology is largely that of a progressive accommodation with modernity and thus with changing conceptions of nature. There are, however, such figures as that of the leading Swiss-German theologian Karl Barth (1886–1968), who uncompromisingly restored central doctrines and synthesised on a grandiose scale.[13] Yet in the twentieth century such efforts have succeeded only in consolidating the isolation of theological reflection from contemporary religious change, of which emergent nature religion is a powerful recent example. In essence, the last great syntheses between the categories of nature and the core doctrines of Christian theology are to be found within Protestantism in the philosopher Hegel, and on the Catholic side in the work of Pierre Teilhard de Chardin, respectively. The chthonic imperative challenges the residual Christian west. With regard to matriarchy and gender relations, its positive attitudes to sexuality, immediacy in our relation with nature, the democratisation of ritual, and experience of the sacred in terms of the Goddess run largely beyond the resources and categories at present available to the Christian tradition (Nelson 1992; Weber 1979: 602–10).[14] The very power, exclusivity and patriarchally centred universalism of the Christian vision are now an ironic handicap: the lordship of Christ can know no compromise within pluralistic or polytheistic schemes. Theological bricolage which recasts Christianity in terms of sexuality[15] or creation-spirituality[16] subverts what is in the final analysis the essentially ascetic character of the Christian Gospel.

– V CONCLUSION: 'NATURE', COMMON GOODS AND THE FUTURE OF THE HUMAN –

Given the rapid disappearance of nature as 'wilderness', and thus the shrinking of the potential context of earth-centred self-realisation for all but a tiny minority in western culture, advocacy of the chthonic imperative and the practice of the Goddess will soon face, if it is not doing so already, the demand that it routinise its charisma if it is to initiate and help sustain a mass transformation of attitudes.[17] Alienation from nature is now the normative human experience for those experiencing global urbanisation. Yet such is the pressure upon residual nature through direct physical appropriation (not least through industrialised mass tourism) that additional use for large-scale ritual purposes may well, without very sensitive management, further destroy the object of dedication. The development of effective ritual, symbolic and mythological means of developing this spiritual sensitivity in urban and ecologically damaged contexts would seem a priority.

In more technical terms, as Klaus Eder has argued, the idea of 'nature' is a social construction swayed by many influences (Eder 1996). Monica Sjöö and Barbara Mor's project appears to amount to a demand for a return from 'second' (industrial) nature to a 'first' (unreconstructed) nature that for many in effect no longer exists. In reality, however, information technology, as now energised by globalised capitalism, has functionalised and commodified a 'third', virtual 'nature' that operates through the circulation of 'signs' removed from a now distant and problematic 'signified'. In other words, is it not possible that the 'nature' available to an over populated, environmentally degraded world will amount to a virtual memory of the once-real? The concept of 'nature' therefore requires very careful elaboration within the wider one of global change if 'nature religion' is both to preserve its critical and distinctive edge and effect significant social change.[18]

The idea of the chthonic imperative serves as a useful organisational and rhetorical device that allows us to show how one remarkable and representative book may be interpreted on a range of different levels. In my judgement, the most positive aspect of the matriarchal assertion made in *The Great Cosmic Mother* is the universalism that stems from the passionate recognition of the dependence of all humankind upon the earth and its well-being. Monica Sjöö and Barbara Mor in this way avoid the rarefied intellectualism of partisan attempts to theorise the reification and self-empowerment of any sectional interest in an era of political, philosophical and religious exhaustion. Furthermore, they succeed in relating a supreme 'common good' to the future of the human through postulating a concrete universal, the highly mythologised witch/ Goddess, whose mediatory role requires the reversal of all previous western mediations. The question as to how far each aspect of the project requires the other is, of course, a different matter.

As a man, I cannot help being moved, and indeed intellectually influenced, by Sjöö and Mor's rediscovery and reconfiguration of matriarchy. Indeed, I have much sympathy with the impatience of such male writers as Henry Adams, D. H. Lawrence and Robert Graves with the masculinist culture of catastrophe characteristic of the last two centuries. Yet the experience of the twentieth century indicates that the abandonment of critical reason and communal commitment to thoroughgoing mythopoesis is a high-risk strategy. Moreover, were I, as a man, simply to hand over my autonomy to womankind this would imply an imprudent and unrealistic trust in the existence of a gender-based, uncorrupted natural virtue. Human life involves a necessary objectification:[19] we stand over against our selves in a reflexive relationship attained through labour and struggle. Ritual, symbolic and mythological retreat into the psychic womb of the *Magna Mater* exerts an undoubted attraction; but the allure of the Eternal Feminine is fraught with ambiguity and risk, and trespasses upon the most sensitive territory of primal identity-formation.[20] Immediate encounters through access to the unconscious with the cosmos, the earth, particular landscapes, gods or goddesses – or individual bodies – can be devastating when they imply an absolute identification and thus a total recapitulation of personal identity.[21]

In conclusion, critical advocacy of the chthonic imperative is of importance because it sanctions and enhances the recovery of the intrinsic, rather than the merely instrumental, secondary or utilitarian (exchange) value of nature. Taken in isolation, however, immediate and integral identifications with the earth, nature and the Goddess require appraisal in the context of an informed reflexivity. Without critical discussion, the displacement of class struggle by a gender-driven 'battle for the earth,' may well involve a range of attempts by both women and men to place their respective opposites in unwelcome areas of mythological, psychological and affective space. This is a powerful but dangerously partisan strategy, which has wide-ranging social and political implications.

As a cultural practice, earth-centred, matriarchal Paganism embodies a relatively cohesive belief-system enacted through a core of common practices, of which the central and decisive feature is the ritual celebration of the annual life-cycle of birth, childhood, sexual maturity, fertility, old age and decay, death, and so on. In, its matriarchal manifestation, however, the chthonic imperative shares with Christianity a drive towards the integral and the total. Unlike diversified New Age, in which any unifying ideological drives are undercut by pragmatic eclecticism enacted in a marketplace of spiritual hybridities, Paganism and Christianity are effectively incompatible. The former celebrates earthbound existence, not least through sexuality; the latter involves constant vigilance with regard to the flesh (*sarx*) that wars against the spirit (*pneuma*) (Fox 1986a: ch. 7).[22] The former promotes psychological and ritual integration of *anima* and *animus* – and even happiness; the latter raises creative alienation to exquisite levels, in a reality tolerable only to an elite for whom the attainment of strength through pain comes, as it were, naturally. Such a mutual estrangement is doubly unfortunate.

– NOTES –

1 The term 'Pagan' and its cognates (as opposed to 'Neo-Pagan') are used in this chapter for reasons elucidated in the Introduction.
2 The English word 'chthonic' is relatively recent. The term 'chthonic imperative' as here used is based on the conflation and partial reorientation of two usages drawn from Jane Harrison's *Themis* (Harrison 1912). She refers to the 'Chthonioi', the 'earth-people' (ibid.: 292) (who are of course the dead), and to a 'social imperative' in her discussion of Durkheim's concept of the collective conscience (ibid.: 485). The *Oxford English Dictionary* indicates that there is evidence of earlier usage of 'chthonian', meaning 'dwelling in or beneath the earth', as, for example, by Andrew Lang (1887), and of 'chthonic' in the *Nineteenth Century* (1885). The term 'chthonic imperative' thus encapsulates a perceived obligation to relate to the earth characteristic of the groups examined in this book.
3 The term 'matriarchy' and its cognates are used in a way that respects the sense given to them by Sjöö and Mor (see Sjöö and Mor [1987] 1991: 433–4).
4 It is not possible to do full justice here to the richness and complexity of this passage in Foucault's *The Order of Things*.
5 There is of course a very sophisticated discussion of this in contemporary French theory.
6 At the conference 'Nature Religion Today' it was apparent that there were some powerful latent tensions, which would sometimes emerge in an unpredictable way given a general commitment to spontaneous as well as ritual access to the unconscious. Thus the ecstatic cry 'Banzai!' from a southern English Nordic Pagan in appreciation of a Celtic bard's epic declamation of Scottish cultural nationalism was not untypical.
7 The publication of recent evidence supporting the view that early groups of humankind engaged in widespread cannibalism (a view running counter to earlier palaeo-anthropology, which stressed the relatively gentle character of prehistoric primitives) is a trend perhaps not unconnected to the recent shift in cultural primacy from a benign, co-

operative Keynesianism in the 1960s and 1970s to the socio-biology of enterprise culture and neo-Malthusian Thatcherism.

8 Primordial claims in relation to assertions of identity are not uniquely confined to gender. National and cultural identities may also incorporate equivalent assertions that apply to the land. A remarkable Scottish example (of much contemporary relevance) is the geological imagery used in the cultural nationalist poetry of Hugh MacDiarmid. (See also Alastair McIntosh's contribution below and Roberts 1995.)

9 It would be instructive to apply Martin Riesebrodt's suggestive analysis of the cultural strategies employed by North American and Iranian fundamentalists in the management of the past as paradigm of social reconstruction with Sjöö and Mor's approach (Riesebrodt 1993).

10 As a man, it is highly instructive to explore the quite remarkable divergence in feminist opinion on the matter of biological and social construction, which can be placed on a scale running from writers like Sjöö, who endorse (albeit in a qualified way) the acceptance of a given biological constitution as important to women's self-identity, to cyborg anthropologists such as, for example, Adele Clarke and Linda F. Hogle, who investigate 'technomoms' and 'living cadavers' in a setting informed by Donna Harraway's agenda in 'The Cyborg Manifesto' (in Harraway 1991). In the Cyborg Handbook, Harraway states that 'The global and the universal are not pre-existing empirical qualities; they are deeply fraught, dangerous, and inescapable inventions' (Hables Gray 1995: xix). Women may exploit cyborgic enhancement as a means of transcending biological destiny, whilst men use virtual reality as a means of escape from the unwelcome consequences of women's emancipation: this scenario presents a striking technological parallel with the mythological location of the chthonic female and the solar male. (See also Harraway 1991.)

11 It is, perhaps, difficult to imagine either Wordsworth or Ruskin uttering Thoreau's call to nature as wilderness: 'Give me the wildness whose glance no civilisation can endure – as if we lived on the marrow of koodoos devoured raw' (Gottlieb 1996: 18). Nature is a tricky ally.

12 More accurately, it is a potentially terrifying juxtaposition of power and nihilism, a 'glocalised' (to borrow Roland Robertson's much-used term) juxtaposition of globalising capitalism confronted by ever more powerful local atavisms.

13 As far as Barth was concerned, all 'nature' is consequent upon the revealed 'two natures' uniquely given in the hypostatic union of Christ's own person. For a contemporary critique of Karl Barth's theology, see R. H. Roberts (1992).

14 Weber's remark is typical: 'Despite the widespread belief that hostility towards sexuality is an idiosyncrasy of Christianity, it must emphasized that no authentic religion of salvation had in principle any other point of view' (Weber 1978: 606).

15 James Nelson's peno-phallic Christology in The Intimate Connection is an extreme example of this desire to develop sexuality-friendly forms of contemporary Christianity (Nelson 1992).

16 Matthew Fox's 'creation spirituality' occupies a borderland between Catholic theology and New Age. Fox's efforts have recently been censured by the magisterium.

17 Weber's account of the 'routinisation of charisma', the process that takes place when religious innovation adapts to institutional self-propagation, is a challenge to all traditions, Paganism not excepted. See Weber (1978: 241–54), 'Charismatic Authority'.

18 Others, for example William Huntington (Huntington 1992) and Edward Tiryakian (Tiryakian 1996), have recently argued that contemporary modernity can be represented

as involving the clash of 'metacultures' or 'civilisations', respectively. Huntington has written of the 'clash of civilizations' in which an ancestral (and largely male) culture of Christian provenance is confronted by a hostile rainbow coalition of ethnic, feminist, religious and environmental forces. Tiryakian outlines a useful categorisation of Christian, gnostic and chthonic strands in late modernity.

19 Istvan Meszaros' classic study would provide a useful starting point for such a comparison (Meszaros [1972] 1975).

20 On the theological representation of male identity in the Christian tradition see R. H. Roberts' 'Masculinity' (Roberts forthcoming).

21 I make this observation on the basis of fieldwork experience. The borderline between empathetic understanding and the psychological vortex of identity-transformation is often hard to discern and even more difficult to control.

22 Recent developments in North American and British Protestant evangelicalism are indicative of a recovery of the ancient Christian tradition of virginity and total sexual abstinence, with (for example) the Christian male-bonding Promise Keepers and similar pledge-keeping commitments groups associated with the Jesus Army. Robin Lane Fox provides an informed and sensitive account of early Christian practice, in which, it was hoped, 'Through virginity, a Christian equalled the angels' (Fox 1986a: 366).

PART TWO

The Pagan Alternative: the Goddess and Nature

CHAPTER 6

The European Native Tradition
PRUDENCE JONES

– I INTRODUCTION –

Catherine Albanese's account of modern nature religion, the starting point for my discussion, describes the American experience, that of fiercely Protestant settlers coming to terms with alien indigenous culture. This culture was Pagan in that it was nature-venerating, animistic or polytheistic, and recognised divine beings both male and female (see below). Professor Albanese's account of two main strains in the modern American movement, the 'traditionalists' or Native Americans, who politicise the past, and the 'New Agers', presumably the descendants of the white settlers, who transcendentalise it (Albanese 1990: 155), implies that Native Americans have a nature tradition and are thus able to be 'traditionalists', but immigrant (white) Americans do not or, perhaps better, that theirs is only derivative from, reactive against, a non-nature tradition which conceptually predates it.

Such an analysis, however illuminating for the American situation, has little relevance to the situation in Europe and could appear idiosyncratic as a starting point for a chapter concerning traditions on this side of the Atlantic. Here the native, nature-based tradition forms the background to everyday life, embedded in place-names, in civic and rural ceremonies, in historical tradition, and even in Christian ritual. Modern Paganism or nature religion in Europe cannot be seen simply as an imaginative reaction against Puritan reality, but must include a reconnection with, a bringing to consciousness of, an outlook which is already contained in the existing cultural framework. Paganism in Europe is simply, as it is for Native Americans, a case of bringing widespread principles and practices to awareness and recasting the ancient ones into an appropriate form for the present day. Native Americans, of course, have the advantage of being closer to their oral tradition than most Europeans. Europeans, on the other hand, have the advantage of possessing a detailed written tradition, which is lacking on the other side of the Atlantic and which fills in many of the gaps which archaeology and folklore alone would leave in our knowledge of Europe's Pagan heritage.

– II PAGANISM –

Following the analysis in Jones and Pennick (1995: 2), by 'Paganism' I understand a religious outlook which venerates nature and which recognises many divine beings, both goddesses and gods. Venerating nature does not simply include a diffuse awareness of a greater power but regularly extends to a strong sense of the spirit of the place, of the sanctity of particular locations. Recognising many divinities is not simply formal polytheism or henotheism, but may involve reverence for the more diffuse spirits of animism, and for the spirits of the ancestors, both in the family shrine and in local and national hero-cults. This description encompasses the ancient religions of Europe, both tribal and civilised, the ancient and modern indigenous religions of India (Hinduism) and Japan (Shinto), the modern forms of nature religion in Europe and the European-settled countries abroad, and probably most tribal religions elsewhere, with which I am less familiar. Native American traditional religion certainly falls under this description; but generally in what follows I will use the word 'Paganism' as shorthand for the indigenous religions of Europe, both ancient and modern.

– III EUROPEAN NATURE DIVINITIES –

The deities of the ancient world were seen as invisible inhabitants of everyday life, to be related to according to traditional customs whose effectiveness were verified by experience. In the case of the Greek divinities and their Roman equivalents, modern commentators are sometimes so mesmerised by the poets' tales of the immortals' activities in their own world, the famous Greek myths, that they overlook the human record of how these divinities were related to by humans in ordinary life. Hence they minimise the involvement of these divinities in the world of nature and of natural human functions.

Sky gods are widespread. The 'di' syllable of the word 'divinity' itself is embodied in the names of many such throughout Europe: Zeus for the Greeks, Tiwaz for the Germans, Jupiter (*Dies Piter*) for the Romans, Dievs for the Lithuanians, and so on. In many instances the god simply is the rain: at the end of the Eleusinian Mysteries the priestess would look up at the sky and say 'Rain!', then down at the earth, saying 'Be fruitful!' Greek children in the ancient world had a rhyme, 'Rain, Rain, O Zeus', and adults even a hundred years ago would colloquially say, 'The god (Zeus) is raining' (Rodd 1892: 132). The Roman Jupiter Pluvius, the rain, and Jupiter Fulgur, the lightning, are too well known to need introducing here. Zeus was also the lightning, and wherever this struck, the Greeks would set up a shrine to Zeus Descending: *Zeus Katabaites*. As all-seeing sky god, Jupiter/Zeus was also the guardian of oaths, and strangely enough in this capacity the Romans identified him with a stone. *Iuppiter Lapis* (Stone Jupiter) was kept in the oldest temple of Jupiter on the Capitoline Hill and used by Roman ambassadors for the swearing of international treaties (Cicero *Epistles*. VII, 12, 2; Polybius, *History* III, 25, 7ff.).

The Romans also used a stone, the *lapis manalis* or Stone of the Ancestors, in a rainmaking ceremony (Paulus Diaconus, section 128, on Festus section 93). Unlike *Iuppiter Lapis*, this stone was not specifically known as a divinity, but its use recalls other ceremonies involving divine stones which are part of Pagan tradition elsewhere. For example, in modern Rajasthan, some of the tribal peoples have a god called 'Grass

Bhairon', an aspect of the chief god, Bhairon. It is a large unhewn stone, which during a drought is placed on a triangular cart with small wheels and pulled around the boundary of the village. If the cart can be pulled easily, then there will be a good monsoon; if not, the drought will continue (Kothari in Elliott and Elliott 1982: 24). Meteorites and other stones as divinities are widespread: for example, Pausanias (IX, 27, 1) tells us that at Thespiae the most ancient image of Eros was an unwrought stone. In modern Britain sacred stones are venerated by custom as well, for example the Coronation Stone in Westminster Abbey, above which the British monarch has to sit (nowadays, on a throne), in order to be crowned legitimately, and which as the Stone of Scone was said to emit a shriek when touched by the rightful monarch of Scotland. Folklore credits some megalithic standing stones with healing properties, and others are personified, not usually as nature spirits but with a historical gloss, as for example the Whispering Knights, said to have been turned to stone by a witch at Rollright in Oxfordshire.

The Roman god Janus, whose name means 'door', personified the revolving Roman door with one central hinge, looking now this way, now that. In public ceremonies he was the first deity to be invoked, and Vesta, goddess of the hearth fire, was the last, symbolically encompassing the known world from boundary to centre (Ovid, *Fasti* I, section 171f.). In Roman state religion a double gate represented Janus in the Forum, left open in times of war, and a ceremonial hearth represented Vesta, tended by the Vestal Virgins. Janus, to whom the Kalends (first day) of each month was sacred, became the god of the boundary of the year, depicted in images as a two-headed or two-faced man, looking back to the old and forward to the new, and he gave his name to the month January. He thus developed in complexity from a simple personification to a more elaborate image, but his mythology was simply that he was 'the origin of the gods' (Juven, 6, 393). His counterpart Vesta, whose circular temple, the oldest in Rome, contained the sacred hearth of the goddess but no image, later received a new temple on the Palatine, built in 12 BCE by Augustus, which did contain an image of the goddess, seated and holding in her outstretched hand the Palladium, the sacred talisman of Troy (Wissowa 1912: 144). But the Vestal cult in the old temple remained simply that of tending the sacred fire, baking and offering the ritual cakes, and when in 381 the Christian emperor Gratian ordered that the temple was to be closed and its fire put out, there was a general outcry.

The Greek goddess Demeter was identified with the corn and to some extent with the earth from which it grew, the first by speculative etymology ('de-meter' = Corn-Mother) and the second through the ritual of burial rites, where the dead were called *demetrioi* (Demeter's people), and through the myth and ritual of the Eleusinian Mysteries, the story of Demeter and her daughter Persephone (Victorious-in-Death), the queen of the underworld (Harrison 1903: 271–2). In the Roman world, where Demeter had been assimilated to Ceres, a distinction was made between the corn and the earth. Ovid tells us, in the *Fasti* I, 673–4:

Ceres and Tellus [the earth] share a single function:
The one gives the grain its origin, the other its home

Ceres was originally an Italic goddess of growth and vegetation, whose festival on 19 April involved formal sacrifice, but her first Roman temple was built after the Greek model of Demeter in 493 BCE, probably for Greek merchants visiting Rome. Tellus, on the other hand, remained in her primitive Italic mode, having a temple built to her in 268 BCE (following an earthquake – she was associated with the underworld spirits of the dead), but never being assimilated to a Greek equivalent. She shared a festival, the Seed Festival, in January, with Ceres, at which a pregnant sow was sacrificed, and her own festival, the *Fordicidia* on 15 (Ides) April, included the sacrifice of a pregnant cow on the Capitol by the chief priests. In imperial times, however, she dwindled to something of an abstraction.

In Greece, the goddess Earth (Ge, Latinised as Gaia) was honoured in speech and offered libation in practice, but she had no temple and no priesthood, being linked by poets and artists with Themis (natural law) and Pandora (all-giver) or Aneisidora (giver-from-below). She appears on vase paintings as a figure half-emerging from the ground, sometimes next to an omphalos (navel) stone, and tradition (Aeschylus, *Eumenides* I) tells how she gave the omphalos at Delphi to her daughter Themis (law, propriety), who gave it to Phoebe (the Shining One), who then freely gave it to her brother Phoebus (the Shining One = Apollo). *Delphys* is an ancient word for the womb, and so Delphi may originally have been a shrine to the Earth's fertility, with a sacred stone to mark its entry point. But Ge (Earth) as we know her from literature is a personification of numinosity only, around whom some local traditions and poetic legends cluster, but who was never assimilated into organised religion with a priesthood and temple (or even, like the Roman Tellus, a feast day) of her own.

Deities of nature in the sense of that which is outside civilisation existed in the ancient world and had differing functions according to the needs of the society which recognised them. After the birth of a Roman child, three men would ceremonially beat the threshold (the god or personification Limen), with a broom, an axe and a pestle, to drive away such outdoor deities as Silvanus, god of the woods, and Faunus, god of wild animals. The Greek god Dionysos, named in inscriptions as early as Mycenean Crete, later claimed as divine ancestor by the sixth-century BCE Bacchiadai, rulers of Corinth (Burkert 1985: 294), and worshipped by the Satrae, a tribal people in ancient Thrace (Herodotus, VII, 110), appears in later worship as a god of dismemberment: ruling the wine, drugs and mania which tear our normal ego-adaptation apart, tearing his enemies to pieces, and himself being dismembered according to myth. Euripides in *The Bacchae* argues that he has a place in even the most well-ordered state, like the carnivals, masking and guising (later forbidden by the church as heathenish practices but continuing to this day throughout Europe) which allow people to let off steam under ritual conditions. Dionysos remained, however, an equivocal influence in Classical Greek society, and, as Bacchus, in Rome, until his worship was assimilated into the Orphic Mysteries, where the dismemberment it involved became symbolic rather than literal. In imperial Rome every drinker of wine honoured Bacchus, and in nineteenth-century Naxos, St Dionysius was venerated as the discoverer of wine (Rodd 1892: 142). In modern London the name of the pub Bacchus's Bin is recognised by Christian, atheist and Pagan alike.

International syncretism in the ancient world also assimilated Dionysos to the Egyptian dying and resurrecting god of vegetation, Osiris, where once more he functioned as a saviour god of the mystically twice-born, as well as being seen, through Osiris' rulership of the green shoots in the spring, as a god of vegetation. Mosaics from British villas in the late fourth century CE show Dionysos/Bacchus as a god of fecundity, a sort of Green Man (Henig in Gilley and Shiels 1994: 17–18). From being a breaker of boundaries he became a symbol of the unbounded creative power of Nature; from presiding over an unsophisticated shamanic cult he developed into an initiator into the mysteries of spiritual life.

Deities of natural forces in the ancient world could thus be conceptualised as undifferentiated numinous presences alone, or could gather forms of organised worship such as an image, a priesthood, a feast day, a mystery cult and so on, or could even develop beyond their original practical function into a more abstract signification. A prime example of the latter is Hermes. The word *herma* means a pile of stones, and such cairns, or herms, were the original boundary markers in Attica. If we look at a modern tribal society, villagers in Rajasthan use piles of stones in a similar way. A visitor to the village not only understands that he is crossing into the territory of its human inhabitants, but routinely stops and makes an acknowledgement or an offering to the god of the boundaries (Kothari in Elliott and Elliott 1982: 7–8). In Attica in the late sixth century BCE, one Hipparchus instituted a series of pillars instead of cairns halfway between Athens and each of its outlying villages. This innovation resulted in the minimalist design of a square-edged stone pillar bearing an erect phallus halfway up and the head of a mature bearded man at the top. Walter Burkert suggests that this ithyphallic design was an unequivocal reminder to outsiders that fit, alert men were ready to defend the boundary, in the same way that baboon sentries will display themselves, with phallus erect, on the edge of their band's territory (Burkert 1979: 40). Whatever the reason, Hermes, the god of boundaries, later began to be depicted by painters and sculptors as a pubescent boy, once more, Burkert suggests, as a representation of the boundary between childhood and adulthood. Prior to this he had also been, and remained, the god of shepherds (dwellers on the boundary of the settlement), and in institutional religion his sacrificial animals were the shepherds' animals – the ram, the billy goat, and also the cockerel. A cockerel too is an animal of the boundaries: cockcrow marks the threshold between night and day. Speech, writing and travelling, which by late antiquity were the central rulerships of Hermes, also cross boundaries, those between one person and another. In myth, Hermes crossed another particularly awesome boundary as well. He was the only immortal who could journey from Olympus to Hades and back again, and so he became the messenger of the gods.

Hermes then was the personification of a fairly abstract natural feature, the boundary, but one which is common to animals as well as humans and was originally imaged in a pretty rough-and-ready form, as in tribal India to this day. As society developed in complexity, so did his cult, and the heap of stones became the ithyphallic guardian of a territory and then the subtly androgynous god of the mind, giving his name to hermetics and hermeneutics, without losing his essential natural significance as a liminal being. Divinities of nature, then, do not have to be primitive. The case of Hermes, like that of Janus, shows us how in Pagan iconography society itself is seen as a development of nature, an undoubted improvement on what was often thought of as the lawless world of instinct, but even in its most sophisticated form retaining powerful symbolic links with the natural world from which it has grown.

From northern Europe we have Woden or Odin, whose name means 'raging' and is cognate with the Latin word *vates*, meaning a bard or seer. Woden is the god of the raging wind, who in folklore became leader of the Wild Hunt, as well as of the raging delirium of intoxication and inspiration. The royal families of England and Scandinavia trace their genealogy back to him, in the European tradition which derives noble families from a divine ancestor, and several places in England are named after him: Wednesbury, Wornshill, the various Wansdykes, and one of the halls of residence at the campus where the 'Nature Religion Today' conference was held is called Wansfell – Woden's Mountain. For practical purposes of trance or inspiration, the practising European traditionalist would call upon Woden on a Wednesday (the day named after him) in one of the places which bear his name, possibly using a trance technique associated with him such as hanging, suspended between the worlds of life and death. Woden's sacred direction is the north, and so the worshipper would do well to turn in that direction too. In historical times, the Danish king Gotrik forced recently converted Christians to crawl into their churches through a specially low-lintelled north door, 'contrary to Christian custom' (*East Frisian Chronicle* II.225, quoted in Reuter 1934: 72), for which reason many north doors were walled up in the years following Charlemagne's Christian conquests.

Baltic Paganism personifies the sun as a radiant woman. *Saule Motul*, Mother Sun, has her special festivals at midwinter and midsummer, now preserved in folk tradition as Kaledos, when images of the sun are carried through fields and villages, and Ligo, when a bonfire is lit on top of a high pole and people dance and feast all night. Easter (spring equinox) is also sacred to her and to her daughter, Ausrine the goddess of dawn (who might be related to Bede's Saxon goddess Eostre, after whom Easter is named). The white flax is Saule's sacred plant, and women's traditional costume includes embroidered stars and sunbursts, and radiate head-dresses signifying the sun's rays (Velius [1981] 1989: *passim*). Further west, the Norse sagas describe beautiful women as 'sun-bright' (*Helgaqvida Hundingsbana* II.45) and 'brighter than sunbeams' (*Sigurdarqvida* 55). Sunna is the goddess or personification of the sun in the Norse Eddas. In Britain, the Easter custom carried on to this day in Scotland, of going before dawn on Easter Sunday to a high hill, then bathing one's face in dew that has been caught by the first rays of the rising sun, may derive from the worship of this North European sun goddess. Here again is a native tradition that in places has not died and elsewhere can appropriately be reaffirmed as part of modern Pagan worship.

This is a small sample of the many divinities which rule or personify natural forces, and of some of the traditions involved in their worship. For some reason they have not been widely recognised as what they are, and so ancient European religion, though well documented, is seen as being unutterably distant from modern life, and we are perceived as people without an indigenous Pagan tradition. Yet to construct a native European vision weekend from authentic traditions, as Catherine Albanese describes Sun Bear doing with his own Native American heritage, is easy enough, as will be shown later. Our question now is the extent to which the native tradition is active in modern life rather than having to be re-created from the past.

– III Survival or revival? –

Before dismissing modern self-styled Pagan ceremonies as romantic, imitative and inauthentic, it is important to consider what would actually count as genuine and what as inauthentic. Accusations of inauthenticity can be thrown about without careful thought, as can claims of age-old antiquity. We should recognise that foreign traditions were and are imported in Pagan societies past and present. Old traditions such as Pythagoreanism were revived in antiquity after lapsing for many years. New traditions were also invented, and syncretic reformulations, such as the reworking of Roman state religion by Augustus, or the creation of a national religion out of scattered tribal cults by the Lithuanian king Mindaugas in the early thirteenth century CE, took place in most societies complex enough to need them. Revival by itself is no argument for inauthenticity.

The paradigm case of authenticity would be the continuous existence of a Pagan religion with a priesthood, as in modern India. On the borders of Europe, we have this in Mari-El in the Caucasus, where the Kugu Sorta movement in the nineteenth century successfully resisted forced Christianisation and has continued its tribal religion to the present day. Further west, Lithuania reorganised itself from tribal to state Pagan religion in the early thirteenth century, incorporating a fully up-to-date contemporary social structure, only turning Roman Catholic through the political merger with Poland in 1387. In the sixteenth century, a visitor to Lithuania, Melletius, described the 'superstitious rites and idolatrous cults' of the Sarmatian tribe there, with their priests, called Vurschayten, and their many gods, invoked openly in traditional ceremonies two hundred years after the official adoption of Christianity. Generally, however, the Pagan priesthoods of Europe have disappeared.

A weaker version of authenticity is the survival of Pagan ceremonies without their priesthood, of which there are many examples in Europe, both ancient and modern. The ritual of the Coronation Stone in England has been noted. We are looking not just at ceremonies which were once as a matter of historical record blessed by a Pagan priest or priestess, but at ceremonies which are of the type which elsewhere were or are consecrated in this way. Door-to-door begging is a case in point. Walter Burkert calls it, less tendentiously, 'processions collecting gifts' (1985: 101). Perhaps someone should have used a similarly bland description to the Cambridgeshire police, who in 1960 stopped the traditional girls' Mayday procession under the Vagrancy Act. On May morning local girls would tour their village or town, carrying a May garland within which a May dolly was suspended, covered by a cloth, and revealed to householders who then rewarded the children with gifts or small change. This custom was stopped as constituting begging, as described in local newspapers of the time. Yet in ancient Rhodes on 1 March, according to Athanaeus (*Deiphon* viii, 360), boys would carry a carved wooden swallow around, singing a song to the effect that wealth was entering into the household, and begging gifts in return for the favour. Rather like modern trick-or-treaters at Hallowe'en, they would threaten householders with dire consequences if they refused – but no one did. Plutarch (*Life of Theseus* 22, 10) tells us that at certain festivals in ancient Athens children would parade around carrying an olive branch wreathed with fillets of wool and laden with first fruits and bread and flasks of oil. This branch was called the Eiresione (the 'Wool-Bearer'), and its attendants sang:

> The Eiresione brings figs and fat bread,
> Honey in pots, and oil to rub down,
> A cup of strong wine so you go drunk to bed.

In Ionia, according to Burkert (1985: 101f.), women would collect gifts, singing hymns to Opis and Arge, the Delian maidens, and the priestess of Athena in Athens used to go through the city on certain days, wearing the aegis of the goddess made out of woollen fillets, seeking out newly married women (who were presumably busy at their Athena-ruled task of spinning), and begging money from them in the name of the goddess of handicrafts. The ritual exchange of gifts or small change for the sight of a lucky talisman is thus part and parcel of the European tradition, although largely confined to unofficial and vernacular cults which are not supported by the state coffers. From the Sicilian herdsmen described by the scholiast to Theocritus, who would enter cities wearing antlers hung with bread in animal shapes, and carrying a wineskin and pouch containing all kinds of grain, to the modern Horn Dancers of Abbots Bromley in Staffordshire, who dance in formation, carrying their reindeer antlers, in and through all the houses of the village, we have a long tradition of processions bringing peace, good luck and health, demanding a small gift in acknowledgement. At Minehead in Somerset the Sailors' Hobby Horse is brought out by the lifeboatmen and dances all day, smacking lucky women with its tail to make them fertile (reminiscent of the Roman Lupercalia) and collecting money for the lifeboat fund: a ritual observance without a priesthood, yet evoking a kind of awe (or superstition), which is thoroughly integrated into the life of the modern community.

New Year's Eve rituals, never adopted by Christianity, are also of this sort; the giving of presents, the welcoming in of a dark-haired stranger carrying a piece of coal, the telling of fortunes. One of the fortune-telling rituals reported by Mellitus in the sixteenth century of our era is carried on in Lithuania to this day, when nuggets of hot lead are dropped into cold water on New Year's Eve, the resulting shapes depicting the caster's fortune for the coming year. But Potrimpus, the god who was once invoked at this ceremony, is now forgotten. Casting coins into wishing wells, tying pieces of ribbon onto lucky trees, giving a new-born baby a lucky spoon, are all customs which have documented parallels in fully Pagan societies. Pythagoras is said (by Diogenes Laertius, VII, 11, 7–9) to have remarked that at each stage of her life, a woman takes the name of a goddess. As an unmarried girl she is called maiden (Kore), on marriage she is a bride (Nymphe), and when she has children she is a mother (Meter). In English-speaking countries, with equal insouciance, the name of the Celtic fire goddess is given to a woman who is marrying: Bride.

Further from the paradigm case of authenticity, we have cases where Pagan ceremonies have been taken over by a Neo-Pagan priesthood, as is well documented in the cases of Christmas and Easter. All Souls' Day continues the customs of such ancestor-cults as the Roman Parentalia, when offerings of food and flowers were made at the ancestral tomb, something inveighed against by St Augustine. Feasting is generally part of Pagan ceremonies, by contrast with the fasting of Christianity. The ceremonial meal with ritual foods survives at Christmas (the boar's head for Frey, bringer of prosperity), and at the traditional funeral feast, where cold meats only are eaten. The Catholic Church took over almost wholesale a myriad of local ceremonies, from the crowning of the May Queen to blessing the village plough (after a day of dancing and processions) at the beginning of the year, and local saints, such as St Dionysius above, replaced local divinities and took over their functions. Remote corners of Islam furnish other examples.

To say, with Robin Lane Fox, that the Neo-Pagan context of these ceremonies 'changed their meaning entirely' or that those in the previous paragraph above 'were part of a "neutral technology of life"' (Fox 1986b: 22) without any religious importance is surely to miss the point. The European Pagan tradition has proved remarkably resilient in preserving and adapting its rituals for keeping human consciousness in touch with the world of natural forces. Sometimes adapting itself to Christianity, sometimes disguising itself as a 'neutral technology', it has fulfilled its age-old function of making human beings feel at home in the world around them.

It is sometimes assumed that because the Pagan priesthood disappeared with the advent of monotheistic religion, the practices once associated with organised religion now have no religious meaning. Yet these practices, existing in the ancient world as well as in the modern one, are examples of a basic underlying attitude to the sacred, which is surely the essence of religion. Ancient and not-so-ancient Europe sanctified many of these customs with a priesthood, or at least with dedication to a deity or semi-divine being. In ancient Europe, as in all complex Pagan societies, some rituals were carried on by the family or the community rather than by a priesthood as such, and modern Europe continues many of these traditions, sometimes with the help of a folk-spirit such as Father Christmas, sometimes in honour of a local saint. It is the same behaviour, directed to the same end, and it constitutes the European tradition in the present day.

We should also remember that some of our central modern values are of Pagan origin. Democracy, although it could have found a place in Christianity, which preaches the intrinsic worth of every human being, was in fact pioneered by the Athenians and reinvented by the Pagan settlers of Iceland in the tenth century. Science fought its battle with superstition in ancient Greece and reached a workable compromise there, being reasserted in the Renaissance, following the rediscovery of Pagan texts, only in the teeth of systematic opposition from the church. And the ideal of balanced humanity, the cultivation of a humane, well-rounded personality, contrasted with Christian humility when it was imported by the scholars of the Renaissance from the writings of the age of Cicero. The influence of Pagan antiquity upon the thought of the Age of Enlightenment was immense, and the institutions of Republican France and of the United States of America were designed in direct imitation of Greek and Roman originals. So in considering the European native tradition we are not simply fleeing to a primitive dreamtime of simple nature-worship, not even just following the Stoics (and the Cynics) in seeking to live 'in accordance with nature', but owning our inheritance of vast civilising influences.

– V The Tradition in modern times –

At the other end of the spectrum, though, to have a European tradition 'medicine wheel' weekend is not difficult. Such retreats are in fact carried on even now by women's groups in Germany. The elements of Sun Bear's celebration (Albanese 1990: 155ff.) find direct equivalents in the European tradition.

The medicine wheel itself is paralleled by the stone labyrinths found all over Northern Europe, used for dances and even races in historical times. At Sola, Norway, a megalithic 'medicine wheel' actually exists, a circle divided into eight, used in medieval times as a meeting place for the people of eight local districts.

The sacred number of stones composing Sun Bear's medicine wheel is illustrated in the Sola circle, composed of twenty-four main standing stones around its circumference. Multiples of eight and twelve are common in European tradition, and have their textual explanations as sacred numbers, deriving ultimately from Babylonian ritual cosmology.

Sun Bear's skull as centre marker would be replaced by a pillar representing the celestial axis or 'God's Nail', or by a sacred tree, an oak or especially a lime (cf. Wolfram, *Parzival*, III.162, and countless examples in German towns), or indeed by a stone, usually unhewn, as in the circle at Sola. Sacred colours of the quarters exist in several European versions, and the tobacco ties of cloth find their equivalent in the rags and ribbons tied to sacred trees, especially at well-heads, throughout Europe to this day. Purification by smudging has its European equivalents in bathing, fasting, sprinkling with consecrated water, and even perhaps running between two fires (this last recorded by Cormac in the ninth century for the purification of cattle). The pipe ceremony with prayers has its equivalent in the meeting cup of consecrated ale or wine, passed round the participants and sometimes poured as a libation.

Sun Bear's medicine wheel give-away has no direct parallel in European tradition. The feasts that follow Pagan ceremonies past and present, however, are occasions of sharing where the poorer participants can eat well despite only having contributed a small amount. The meditative ceremony of the sweat lodge is not exactly paralleled in the Nordic sauna, but there would seem no reason why this authentic tradition should not be used in this way, and perhaps once was by the prehistoric shamans of what is now Norway, Finland and Siberia where, after all, the Native Americans originated.

Crystal healing is a modern technique, but European traditions of trance and healing are well documented, from the *seidr* ceremonies of the Nordic *spákona* to the trance of the Delphic priestess. And the communal activities of drumming, chanting and dancing which take place in the medicine wheel ceremony find direct equivalents in European traditional dance and song, with the fiddle and pipes and drum to accompany them.

So the native tradition is alive and accessible, if modern nature religionists want to have a medicine-wheel-type retreat. But such a retreat, reconstructed in its American or European form from traditional components, offers spiritual experience only to a few, divorced from the context of their everyday lives. It is a kind of modern Eleusinian Mysteries, and as such it fulfils an important need. Here where we live on the sites of our own traditions, local customs are already woven into the fabric of the community, often honouring the spirit of the place which is so central to Pagan practice. Beating the bounds of one's village, Morris dancing on May or Midsummer morning, mumming plays at Yuletide, traditional processions for the May Queen, the Rose Queen at Whitsun, a local spirit like Snap the Dragon in Norwich, can all be reintroduced or supported by modern nature religionists. Local Pagan groups can go to clear their local holy well, look after a holy tree or other site – as when Odinists in Kent fought successfully to save the White Horse Stone from the Channel Tunnel Link – have open celebrations at festival times, and so on. Paganism within the community is a very real option here in Europe.

Small, dedicated groups in complex (not tribal) societies also follow their own deities and spiritual paths. The ancient world gave us the followers of Dionysos, of Isis, of the semi-divinised Pythagoras and so on. This is almost the norm in modern organised Paganism: groups of Witches, Druids, Odinists and others meet freely, if discreetly, and offer direct spiritual experience to those who take part. The origins of their deities in natural phenomena are never far from modern Pagans' minds, though I have had to draw attention to these when describing some divinities of the ancient world.

In tribal societies, individuals can follow the path of the Siberian shaman, Norse *spákona* or *völva*, Hungarian *táltos*, etc. Many modern Pagans follow such routes too, basing their practice on well-documented European originals. In the civilised world of late antiquity, when Pagan religion had been privatised into personal meditation under the persecution of the Christian church, the solitary magician or theurgist appeared – a well-known figure in modern Paganism. Maximus, the mentor of the emperor Julian, has more in common with Aleister Crowley or Alex Sanders than one might initially assume. The Hermetic current from Alexandria transmitted a highly condensed version of private worship and invocation, which was distilled down from the public practices of a more tolerant world and which surfaced during the Renaissance as an occult underground which has flourished to the present day (see Jones in Harvey & Hardman 1996: 39). Urban ritual magic might seem far distant from the peasant survivals documented by Frazer and his followers, but in it some very simple nature rituals as well as more abstract philosophical considerations reached their ultimate distillation in the ancient world as in the modern one.

– VI CONCLUSION –

All complex cultures tend towards a primitivist backlash, whether we are looking at Marie Antoinette playing shepherdess or at Seneca, tutor of Nero, complaining that everything was fine in the good old days when all Romans were farmers. In this chapter I have made two points about the primitivist trend described by Catherine Albanese. The first is that in Europe we have our own nature tradition to call on, well documented from the past, fully integrated into ancient society, and in many ways still flourishing in the present. Nature religion in Europe is not an invented reaction against an all-encompassing Christianity, but an independently existing tradition in itself. The second is that the Pagan framework (nature-venerating, polytheistic, and recognising deities of both sexes) within which the back-to-nature cult fits is not exclusively primitive but is both broader and deeper than its popular image would indicate, some of its images and attitudes being central to what we think of as the framework of western civilisation. It cannot easily be dismissed as a New Age fad.

CHAPTER 7

The Discovery of the Modern Goddess
RONALD HUTTON

– I INTRODUCTION –

My interest in this chapter is to trace the process by which the modern 'western' world came to have its most common image of a goddess. It is an image which has significant differences from those of the Pagan ancient world, where female deities were most commonly patronesses of cities, justice, war, handicrafts, the home fire, agriculture, love and learning; they stood for aspects of civilisation and human activity much more often than for aspects of nature. Furthermore, the overwhelming majority of ancient Pagans genuinely believed that the different goddesses were separate personalities. In only one text, the *Metamorphoses* of Apuleius, was the female deity declared to be the embodiment of all other goddesses, and represented by the moon and the natural world. Yet it is that, late, image which predominates at the present day. When did it come to do so, and how? The short answer is, only a couple of centuries ago.

– II THE GODDESS IN ENGLISH LITERATURE –

Throughout the Middle Ages and early modern period, the emphasis on Pagan deities, now used as allegories rather than worshipped, remained just where it had been in ancient times. A systematic survey of English literature written between 1300 and 1800 reveals that the most popular goddess for poets was Venus, patroness of love, followed by Diana, representing female chastity and (much more rarely) hunting, then Minerva, for wisdom, and Juno, symbol of queenliness.[1] A more impressionistic look at intellectual works shows Minerva, not surprisingly, to be apostrophised most often.[2] As a civic goddess, she also seems to appear most often in urban statuary from the Renaissance to the nineteenth century.[3]

It is true that in the early modern hermetic tradition there was a concept, derived from Apuleius and the ancient neo-Platonist texts, of a female figure identified with the starry heaven, who stood between God and the earth, and acted as a world soul.[4] The hermetic tradition was, however, very much the preserve of a minority of specialists. It is more relevant to our present interests that the ancient Greeks spoke of the earth as being female in gender and the sky as masculine (something which was not inevitable even in the ancient Levant, as to the Egyptians the reverse was true). As most western science was ultimately based upon Greek thinking, this language became embedded in it. The concept was developed by the mind-set of a patriarchal society such as that of early modern Europe, where the scientists were virtually all male; it was easy for them to adopt a language of male domination and exploitation of a female natural world.[5] Conversely, from the twelfth century onwards a few intellectuals and poets employed a female figure as an allegory of nature.[6] She was a rarity, however, in comparison to the familiar, 'civilised' goddesses.

This pattern was completely reversed by a movement which began partly as a self-conscious reaction to the mind-set of early modern scientific rationalism, and which is loosely termed Romanticism. In the form in which it took off in the late eighteenth century, it can be described as a tremendous exaltation of the natural and the irrational, those qualities which scientific language had come to identify as 'feminine'. It accompanied a recognition that humanity could at last be suffering from too much civilisation. For the first time in European history, mountains were seen as beautiful instead of frightening, and wild nature began to be valued over farms and cities, the night over the day, and the moon over the sun. These impulses only intensified as the nineteenth century wore on, and urbanisation and industrialisation spread across western and central Europe, and especially across Britain. In 1800 the overwhelming majority of the British still lived in the countryside; by 1900 the overwhelming majority lived in towns and cities. A mystical love of the natural world grew in almost direct relationship to the change.

The impact upon English poetry is very clear. Between 1800 and 1940 Venus and Diana (or Artemis) were still the two favourites. Juno, however, almost vanished, and after 1830 so did Minerva. They were replaced by Proserpine, as goddess of the changing seasons, and Ceres or Demeter, the Corn Mother. A reading of the texts discloses a much more dramatic alteration. Venus is often related to the woods or the sea, while Diana is no longer primarily a symbol of chastity or of hunting but (overwhelmingly) of the moon, the greenwood and wild animals.[7] Furthermore, the supremacy of Venus depended upon incidental references and metaphors. When a goddess was made the major figure of a poem, it was Diana who ruled, or a nameless female deity of moonlight, of the natural world.

The pattern was established clearly by the 1820s, showing prominently in those often-paired writers, John Keats and Percy Shelley. From his earliest poetry, Keats apostrophised the moon as a female deity, the 'maker of sweet poets, dear delight/Of this fair world'.[8] His first long and really ambitious work, *Endymion* (1818), had as its theme the love story of a mortal man and the moon goddess, containing such rhapsodic passages as:

> What is there in thee, Moon! that thou shouldst move
> My heart so potently? When yet a child
> I oft have dried my tears when thou hast smiled.
> Thou seemdst my sister: hand in hand we went
> From eve to morn across the firmament. . . .
> And as I grew in years, still didst thou blend
> With all my ardours: thou wast the deep glen;
> Thou wast the mountain top – the sage's pen –

The poet's harp – the voice of friends – the sun;
Thou wast the river – thou wast glory won;
Thou wast my clarion's blast – thou wast my steed –
My goblet full of wine – my topmost deed: –
Thou wast the charm of women, lovely Moon!'. (*Endymion* III: 142–69)

This shimmer of moonlight runs through the art of the early nineteenth century, from England to Prussia. It even gets into the music. When Vincenzo Bellini wrote the century's most famous drama about Druids, his opera *Norma* (1831), the libretto by Felice Romani made the heroine stand in a sacred grove and invoke the moon, in the most celebrated aria in the work:

Chaste goddess, who silvers these sacred trees,
Show your face to us without a veil,
Bring peace to earth as you have brought it to heaven. . . .

The other favourite way of personifying a goddess at that period was represented by Shelley. As a good classicist, he translated a series of Homeric hymns to various deities, but when he came to write an original one, he began:

Sacred goddess, Mother Earth,
Thou from whose immortal bosom
Gods, and men, and beasts, have birth,
Leaf and blade, and bud and blossom,
Breathe thine influence most divine. ('Song of Proserpine' 1–5)

By 1820 the dominant image of a goddess in the English poetic imagination was already emerging as the beauty of the green earth and the white moon among the stars. It was thoroughly internalised by the next generation. When the devout Christian Robert Browning tried his hand at a classical subject in 1842, he chose the goddess Artemis, and this is how he makes her speak:

Through heaven I roll my lucid moon along;
I shed in hell o'er my pale people peace;
On earth I, caring for the creatures, guard
Each pregnant yellow fox and fox-bitch sleek,
And every feathered mother's callow brood,
And all that love green haunts and loneliness. ('Artemis Prologizes' 4–9)

Even more remarkable is the case of Charlotte Brontë, who was born the daughter of an Anglican clergyman, chose to return to live in her father's rectory, and eventually married his curate. She always paid a passionate lip-service to Christianity, and made her most famous heroine, Jane Eyre, contemplate going abroad as a missionary. Emotionally, however, Jane operates within a cosmology by which a single supreme god has created nature to be a divine mother for living things. It is to this mother (and not to Jesus) that Jane turns for comfort when in serious trouble, and who at one stage appears to her out of the moon in a dream-vision, giving her advice (*Jane Eyre*, chs 27–8). It never seems to have occurred to Brontë that this view of divinity was not actually Christianity, a sign of how thoroughly the new goddess image had been internalised in the Victorian subconscious.

The final stage was to eliminate the creator god, leaving the composite goddess of nature as the single mighty source of all being, and this was taken by Algernon Swinburne in 1867, when he gave resounding voice to this deity under the German name of Hertha:

> I am that which began;
> Out of me the years roll;
> Out of me, god and man,
> I am equal and whole;
> God changes, and man, and the form of them bodily;
> I am the soul. . . .
> First life on my sources
> First drifted and swam;
> Out of me are the forces
> That save it or damn;
> Out of me man and woman, and wild beast and bird;
> Before God was, I am. ('Hertha' 1–15)

There, fully formed by the 1860s, is the mighty creatrix of later feminist Paganism. It would be easy but hardly necessary to follow this image later into English literature; to look for example at D. H. Lawrence's identification of eternal Woman with the moon, or at Robert Graves' *White Goddess*. For now it is sufficient to note how when organised Paganism does reappear, in the twentieth century, it takes its Goddess straight from this imagery; and no wonder, as Swinburne was one of the favourite poets of Aleister Crowley, Dion Fortune and Gerald Gardner.[9] I am, however, going to turn now to look at the impact of this concept of the Goddess upon fields which are normally regarded as more objective than literature or religion: ancient history and archaeology.

– III THE GODDESS IN ANCIENT HISTORY AND ARCHAEOLOGY –

It is necessary first to make one final retreat into the eighteenth century and to glance at a different sort of cultural phenomenon, a debate among European intellectuals over the nature of prehistoric religion. Crudely speaking, this was divided between those who suggested that primitive religious belief was a superstitious compound of ignorance and fear, and those who viewed it as an embodiment of sublime truths, which had degenerated and been forgotten amongst modern tribal peoples. The latter theory was especially popular among the German Romantics.[10] Like those British writers, John Toland, William Stukeley and Edward Williams, who had reconstructed Druidic beliefs to justify their respective notions of a supreme being, the Germans assumed that one of those eternal truths had to consist of monotheism.

They linked it to an instinctual understanding of the processes of nature and of human life.

In view of all the above, it makes perfect sense that in 1849 a German scholar, Eduard Gerhard, advanced the novel suggestion that behind the various goddesses of Classical Greece had stood a single great one, venerated before history began. As the century wore on, more and more classicists and ancient historians, in France, Germany and Britain, began to adopt this idea, drawing support for it from the assumption that the cultures of Anatolia and Mesopotamia were older than, and in some measure ancestral to, that of Greece.[11] Those cultures did contain some figures of pre-eminent goddesses, identified with motherhood or the earth. Such a tendency of thought was given additional impetus at the end of the century when excavation began to turn up figurines, many of them apparently feminine, on prehistoric sites in the south-east of Europe and the Levant. It was possible to interpret these as representations of the original single Goddess, and this is what sometimes occurred.[12] Among those who adopted this view were some very influential figures, such as Sir Arthur Evans' who rediscovered the civilisation of Minoan Crete.[13]

By the middle of the nineteenth century the image was already starting to combine with another, which had emerged from a debate between lawyers over the origins of human society and of the family. One of the sides in this debate, represented first by J. J. Bachofen in the 1860s, had argued that society was originally woman-centred. What was true in daily life had, logically, also to be so in religion. For my purposes the scholar who developed this notion most significantly was Jane Ellen Harrison, a Cambridge classicist who stood at the centre of an important group of academics in that university. In 1903 she published the view that prehistoric south-eastern Europe had been a peaceful and intensely creative woman-centred civilisation, in which humans lived in harmony with nature and their own emotions and worshipped a single Great Goddess. Harrison believed that this deity had often been venerated in three aspects, of which she identified the first two as Maiden and Mother; she did not name the third. This image was achieved by noting the common Classical Greek belief in triple deities (such as the Fates) and reconciling the otherwise incompatible attributes of virginal and maternal historic goddesses by declaring them to be aspects of the one; to somebody like Harrison, of course, brought up in a Christian culture and habituated to the image of the Virgin Mary, there was no difficulty in the reconciliation. Harrison believed that the Great Goddess had represented the earth, and that male deities had been lesser beings, both her consorts and her sons. This happy state of affairs, she proposed, had been destroyed before the dawn of history by patriarchal invaders from the north, bringing dominant male deities and warlike ways. Humanity, in her view, had never recovered from this disaster (Harrison 1908: 257–322).

All these ideas were opposed by other scholars over the same period,[14] but it must be noted that these other writers were no more distinguished or successful. In the last analysis the evidence simply did not permit of an absolute decision, and neither now nor later shall I propose one myself. I shall only suggest that the prehistoric Great

Goddess would not have been so apparent to many writers at this time had they not been already inclined to regard the divine feminine in this form.

All these theories, however, concerned only the Levant, the Balkans and the Mediterranean world. Experts in the emerging field of north-west European pre-history, and especially of Britain, reserved judgement on them. This was because their Neolithic looked so different. Its sites had failed to produce any of the female figurines which were such an important prop of the Great Goddess construct in the south-east. Instead, the western European Neolithic was characterised by a very widespread monumental tradition, of building megalithic tomb shrines, the structures commonly called dolmens, passage graves, and long barrows. It was true that by the 1920s prehistorians were starting to discuss the idea that these might have been the holy places of a single religion. It was also true that in some French tombs the figure of a woman was carved in the passage, indicating that a female deity was venerated there. The decisive evidence, however, was lacking, and experts refrained from reaching any conclusions as to the beliefs of the megalith builders.[15]

Popular writers, however, had no such inhibitions. A classic example of the contrast between the two groups is provided in the case of the long barrows of the Cotswolds, the first group in Britain to be systematically studied. In 1925 O. G. S. Crawford wrote a famous survey of them, in which he suggested that they represented the monuments of a single religion and then (once again) carefully left the nature of this open (Crawford 1925: 23–4). Seven years later Harold Massingham published a book about the Cotswolds. He was a mystic opposed to most aspects of modern life and famous for his romanticisation of the English countryside. In his description of the long barrows he followed Crawford right down the line, with a single difference; he declared confidently, and without discussion, that the deity of long barrows religion must have been the Great Mother Goddess, representing the sacred earth (Massingham 1932: passim).

All through the 1930s the experts continued to hold back, until in 1939 the vital piece of evidence seemed to be provided. At the bottom of a shaft at Grimes Graves, the big complex of Neolithic flint mines in Norfolk, the archaeologist A. L. Armstrong claimed to have found a female figurine, seated upon a crude altar, with a vessel for offerings placed before her. This appeared to be unequivocal proof of the worship of the Great Goddess in the British Neolithic as well. The figurine featured as such in successive publications upon the period in general and Grimes Graves in particular, and the Ministry of Works reconstructed its shrine on the site for visitors to see.

Ever since its discovery, however, rumours quietly circulated amongst the close-knit community of British archaeologists, to the effect that it was a fake. In 1986 Stuart Piggott at last broke ranks and became the first to print this suspicion, in the foremost journal of the profession, *Antiquity*.[16] Not until 1991 did it appear in a work designed for general readers, when I repeated it myself in a textbook (Hutton 1991: 43–4). In that same year a proper report upon the matter, based upon a full-scale investigation, at last appeared.[17]

This was provided by Gillian Varndell, who emphasised the following points. First, the excavation concerned had never been published. Second, Armstrong's site notebook stopped abruptly on the day of the vital discovery, without recording it properly. Third, on the day of the find, most unusually, Armstrong ordered all other experienced excavators to leave the site. Fourth, in comparison to the other worked chalk objects from the site, the 'goddess' and vessel looked suspiciously freshly carved; and fifth, somebody on Armstrong's team was an expert carver, because similar objects made from the same local chalk rock, like an Egyptian sphinx, were among his possessions from the dig.

Varndell concluded that as chalk objects cannot be scientifically dated, there is no absolute way of proving that these are fakes, but that they cannot be accepted now as reliable evidence. It looks, therefore, as if the Grimes Graves 'goddess' was like the Piltdown skull, a fraud perpetuated successfully upon the archaeological community because it represented so exactly what many of them wanted to find at that moment. The likelihood of this is increased by the fact that in the long years since not a single other figurine has been found on a British Neolithic sacred site.

Back at the time, however, the barriers were down for those who wanted to believe that the whole period had been Goddess-centred, and the most fervent of these was Jacquetta Hawkes. She was herself an expert in the Neolithic, who became a professional writer at the end of the 1940s and during the next two decades was one of the most popular authors upon European prehistory. From 1951 she developed Jane Harrison's view of it, with two important additions. First, she united the figurines of the south-east with the megalithic tombs of the north-west to produce a picture of the whole of Neolithic Europe as a single 'land of the Great Goddess'. It was guided by women, peaceful, creative and in harmony with nature. Second, she specifically identified the patriarchal invaders who destroyed it and brought in the ages of metal, warfare and abuse of nature as the Indo-Europeans.[18]

It is difficult to overstate the importance of Hawkes in this context. She was not only a best-selling author and respected scholar, but a figure in international cultural politics. The British government gave her the OBE, and she was one of only two British members of the United Nations cultural organisation, UNESCO, the other being the famous scientist Sir Julian Huxley.[19] Her example may well have helped to inspire three other giants of British archaeology, Gordon Childe, O. G. S. Crawford and Glyn Daniel, to declare in the mid-1950s that Neolithic and Chalcolithic Europe had been devoted to the worship of the Great Goddess.[20] Historians of religion and of art proceeded to incorporate the same idea into their own works.[21]

The most important fall-out from the shift of archaeological opinion, however, was among psychologists. They had come late to the issue. Freud had said nothing directly about it, although he had emphasised the universal importance of mother figures. Jung was very cautious, stating that the Great Mother was an important archetype but that her projection as a goddess was not of immediate concern to psychiatry because it was rarely encountered in the modern world; indeed, he seemed to imply that he only considered it because historians and prehistorians had made such a fuss about it.[22] It was left to his devoted disciple Erich Neumann, in 1963, to draw upon the apparent consensus among archaeologists to argue that the Great

Mother had been a universal religious archetype, representing a vital first stage in the development of the human psyche (Neumann 1963, 1964). A circular process was thus created, because the archaeologists had convinced Neumann, and could now, led by Jacquetta Hawkes, claim that Jungian psychology had proved that the Great Goddess was a universal human archetype, removing any remaining doubts about her worship in prehistory.[23]

This state of affairs lasted through much of the 1960s, and was brought to an end mainly by the work of two young archaeologists, Peter Ucko and Andrew Fleming. The former considered the figurines of south-eastern Europe, the latter the megalithic cultures of the north-west. Both suggested that there was in fact no decisive evidence that either represented the cult of a single deity.[24] They emphatically did not disprove the existence of one; they merely returned it to being an open question, and in this state of cautious agnosticism most experts in European archaeology have remained ever since. Some popular English writers like Michael Dames, however, failed to notice the new shift in expert opinion and continued to produce books about the Neolithic Great Goddess into the 1970s.[25]

– IV THE POLITICS OF THE GODDESS –

Behind the latter part of this story is a great unspoken fact; that many of the young archaeologists of the 1960s and 1970s were glad to see this Goddess depart. It is time for me to confront this fact directly, in the last section of this chapter, and discuss the politics of the Great Goddess. Her original image, as spirit of nature and the night sky, had been part of a radical language. At the time of writing about her, Keats Shelley, and Swinburne were all revolutionaries both in politics and religion. After the mid-nineteenth century, however, this pattern began to alter. Jane Harrison, for example, was a lifelong Tory and an opponent of the campaign to gain women the vote; she believed that politics was men's business, and that women should give themselves up to education and culture.[26]

This shift is very clear in the work of Harold Massingham, who hated modernity in virtually all its aspects, and declared that the finest institution in the present world was the Roman Catholic Church, because it resisted the modern age most strenuously. His ideal time was the Middle Ages, when (he believed) society had lived in harmony and everybody knew his or her place (Massingham 1943: *passim*, 1944: 49–109). This was exactly the language of Jacquetta Hawkes. She idealised a woman-centred Neolithic because she believed that women were the great forces for conservatism in the world. Her two great hatreds were science and socialism, and her favourite period was the eighteenth century, when the aristocracy lorded it over the land in beautiful houses and gardens and everything was kept in order.[27] Her sort of prehistory represented exactly the sort of reactionary sentimentality mirrored at the same time in the popular history books of Sir Winston Churchill and Sir Arthur Bryant, and the county guides of Arthur Mee. It was a Conservative government which decorated her.[28]

These attitudes were mirrored in archaeology. It was the proponents of the notion of the Great Goddess, Childe, Crawford and Daniel, who represented the traditional approaches to prehistory which the 'New Archaeology' of the 1960s was out to challenge.[29] This 'New Archaeology' aimed at drawing parallels from the new sciences of anthropology and archaeology to reconstruct models of ancient society. Nobody fought it more bitterly than Hawkes, who became the loudest voice of reactionary prehistory in the British scholarly community.[30] Some of the pressure applied to the young academics who questioned the old norms was both crude and direct. When Peter Ucko first aired his doubts about the conventional interpretation of prehistoric figurines, he received a furious letter from Margaret Murray, the famous Egyptologist and luminary of University College London, and author of controversial views about the nature of early modern witchcraft. She told him that he had no right to question the former universal veneration of the Mother Goddess, first because he was a man, and second because he was far too young.[31] The news of such tactics, filtering out among the junior staff of academic institutions, made some of them all the more determined to fight the Old Guard over the issue and to win.

This determination was the more pronounced in that to many young scholars in the 1960s and early 1970s, science and technology had emancipated ordinary working people from misery, while socialism, in the form of the welfare state, had given them dignity and security for the first time. The Neolithic Great Goddess had been made into the deity of the enemies of both. She could also be perceived as the enemy of female emancipation, for she stood for Woman as virgin, mother, grandmother, earth, nature and source of fertility. She never seemed to stand for Woman as company director, Woman as brain surgeon, Woman as politician, Woman as captain of industry, Woman as head of a government or a university department, or Woman as leading theoretical scientist; as some of the historic ancient goddesses, now being marginalised and trivialised by this theoretical 'great' one, had actually done. She accordingly had few or no friends among the young women making their way into academe at the time. The choice then did not seem to be between the Goddess and patriarchy, but between the Goddess and socialism. She was not the deity of Women's Liberation, but of the Mothers' Union.[32]

Many of the rising generation of British prehistorians between 1965 and 1975 were therefore glad to see her toppled from her throne. They were also glad to see the back of a sentimental pseudo-ecology which reverently lumped together genuinely wild landscapes, managed forests, and farmland which had been moulded by millennia of human cultivation, into the single category of 'Nature'. It was equally bracing to be rid of a psychology which created sexist stereotypes and then called them natural archetypes. One major feature of Erich Neumann's work was that it instinctually presupposed that the mass human psychology which was being created in his story was a male one, with the female symbols as auxiliaries to its development. It was a deeply sexist and restrictive language.[33]

Allied to the new prehistory was an anthropology which brought in huge quantities of new information about the way in which gender relations had been constructed in other human societies. It showed us the extraordinary range of possibilities which could be open to us and destroyed an insistence upon any essential female or male qualities in humanity. In 1975 the British anthropologist Shirley Ardener could pose the exciting question of whether our categories of 'men' and 'women' might not be entirely an intellectual creation which some day could disappear (Ardener 1975: xviii).

To many British prehistorians, therefore, it was a shock and a surprise when the old images and the old ideas came back to Britain from America in the late 1970s and 1980s, but this time as part of a radical discourse. Writers such as Mary Daly, Susan Griffin, and Adrienne Rich had taken up the old conservative idea of an essential female nature and simply reversed the sympathies, attaching a positive value to those qualities which the patriarchal language had defined as negative.[34] The most distinguished western scholar of eastern European prehistory, Marija Gimbutas, directly developed the work of Harrison, Hawkes and Neumann, but drew a liberationist instead of a reactionary message from it. She gradually came to reassert the notion of a woman-centred Neolithic Europe, devoted to a single goddess, but remoulded the figure of the latter to remove the concentration upon aspects such as motherhood and fertility and emphasise those of creation and universal capability.

In the process she carefully avoided contamination by the writers whose ideas she had appropriated by giving her works prefaces which suggested that her approach to the Neolithic was essentially her own original creation. In her first book on the Balkan figurines, in 1974, she did state that she was building on the work of others, and explicitly mentioned Neumann as the writer who had provided her code for the interpretation of symbols and designs. By 1989, however, feminist thought had turned against Neumann, for reasons stated above. It was necessary, therefore, for her to distance herself by attacking his work in detail while concealing the fact that her basic system of interpretation had derived from it. As for Jacquetta Hawkes and the old-fashioned British archaeologists, their books still appeared in her bibliographies, but in her prefaces and texts (and interviews), the Neolithic was treated as if they had never written. They had vanished from the story so that their ideas could be repackaged and expanded in a radical form.[35]

What had happened was that British and American radical intellectuals had dealt with the problem of the old stereotype in completely different ways. The British had deconstructed it; the Americans had reversed it. Both were excellent strategies in their own right; the problem was that they were completely incompatible. British archaeologists and historians of my generation had built up a whole series of excellent arguments for not believing in the Great Goddess of the conservatives. They were not able to drop them just because she had suddenly reappeared with an American accent and a new sort of politics.

In confronting this problem, one major defect in the 'new' archaeology and anthropology now became seriously apparent: that its proponents had mainly addressed professional colleagues. None of them had shown the interest in reaching a mass audience, and the genius for doing so, of a Jacquetta Hawkes, Michael Dames or Marija Gimbutas. Furthermore, the faith in science and technology which had underpinned many of the intellectual responses of the 1960s was now diminishing across the western world. The environmental costs of both were becoming alarmingly apparent, and lending a renewed force to the rhetoric of Mother Nature. As a result, the American ideas diffused very rapidly among British radical subcultures, and the more easily in that they actually preserved old and familiar models; they simply, as suggested, required people to change attitudes to them. When these subcultures collided with professional British archaeology, and found that the latter was unwilling to accept those ideas, the very academics who had supported the deconstruction of the Great Goddess in the name of socialism, feminism and radical reform found themselves being abused as patriarchs and reactionaries.

In the 1990s, however, the situation is starting to alter yet again, because of developments in the heartland of feminist theory, in America and Australia. Archaeologists such as Ruth Tringham are defining 'true' feminist archaeology as one which celebrates the ambiguity of the archaeological record and the plurality of its interpretation.[36] Feminist academics such as Carol MacCormack, Val Plumwood and Susan Heckman are once again questioning the validity of the idea of an 'essential' femininity. Val Plumwood could declare in 1993 that earlier American feminist theory had just replaced the myth of woman as 'the angel in the house' with the equally restrictive one of 'the angel in the ecosystem'.[37]

– V Conclusion –

In concluding this survey I would like to make a number of personal observations clear. As a man, I would not dream myself of defining what a 'true' feminist archaeology is or ought to be. I have also consistently avoided pronouncing upon whether or not the Neolithic was a 'civilisation of the Goddess'; I leave that question open, as I do the other one, of whether there is an essential femininity and masculinity among humans. I have furthermore carefully titled this chapter 'The discovery of the modern Goddess', instead of, in true postmodern fashion, the 'construction', the 'creation' or the 'invention' of the modern Goddess. In doing so I leave open the question of whether this Goddess actually exists. I am perfectly prepared to allow for the existence of divine currents, energies or even beings in the universe, to which human beings can relate in different ways at different times.

What I have tried to do instead is to trace the course of an extremely long and complex sequence of events, portions of which have often remained concealed from those who have been among the most fervent participants in the latter stages of it.

– Notes –

1 Smith (1984), and sources cited there under goddess names.
2 For example, by writers as different as Pierre Abelard in the twelfth century, Christian de Pisan in the fifteenth, and Giordano Bruno in the sixteenth.
3 This was based on a survey of public architecture in the following sample of cities: Venice, Paris and London.
4 Notable examples of it are in Fludd (1617) and Kircher (1652).
5 Examined in Merchant (1980).

6 Most vividly represented by Chaucer in *The Parlement of Fowles*, 11.295ff., where he cited as his source for the image the twelfth-century scholar Alanus de Insulis.

7 Smith (1984) and sources cited there.

8 'I Stood Tip-toe Upon A Little Hill', 116–22.

9 *Inter alia*, Crowley (1929 [1970]); Fortune (1935); Gardner (1959).

10 Especially in the *Werke* of Johann Herder, August and Friedrich von Schlegel, and Ludwig Tieck.

11 Harrison (1908: 262, n. 1); Ucko (1968), and sources listed there.

12 Ucko (1968: 409–12), and sources listed there.

13 Evans (1901, 1921).

14 Noted in Ucko (1968: 409–11).

15 Crawford (1925: 23–4); Childe (1925: 208–24, 1935: 22–105, and 1940: 46–118); Clark (1940: 103).

16 Piggott (1986: 190).

17 Varndell (1991: 103–6).

18 Hawkes (1951: 158–61, 1954a: 20–1, 189, 243–43; 1954b: ch. 6, 1962: 57–87, 1963: 204–344, 1968 chs 1–5).

19 Her career and decorations are listed in the current *Who's Who*.

20 Childe (1954: 64–5, 268, 1958: 21, 46, 58, 124–39); Crawford (1957: *passim*); Daniel (1958: 74).

21 James (1959: *passim*); Maringer (1960: chs 4–5).

22 Jung (1959: 75–102).

23 Hawkes (1968a: 260).

24 Ucko (1962: 38–54, 1968: *passim*); Fleming (1969: 247–61).

25 The first and most influential of these was Dames (1976).

26 Peacock (1988: *passim*); Africa (1991: 21–35).

27 Hawkes (1951: 143–201, 1954b: *passim*, 1962: 212–41, 1968a: 260; Hawkes and Priestly 1955: 277).

28 Led, in fact, by Churchill himself.

29 For a good-humoured view of the clash of generations, see Daniel and Renfrew (1988: 155–165).

30 Hawkes (1967: 174–80, 1968a: 255–62).

31 The now Professor Ucko preserves the letter in his possession.

32 Almost needless to say, you will find these attitudes recorded in none of the archaeological publications of the period, which ostensibly operated according to the strictest standards of scientific objectivity. They were, however, regularly aired in private conversation to the present author by the young archaeologists and historians who were his peer group and immediate seniors at excavations and in academe. Others of that peer group are welcome to disagree.

33 Pointed out first by Ruether (1975: 154–7).

34 The whole of this literature is reviewed in Heckman (1990: 135–51).

35 Gimbutas (1974: esp. 11–12, 238–9, 1982: preface to the new edition, 1989: esp. vii–xi, xiii–xxi, 316–21). For an example of her interview style, see Noble (1989: 5–7).

36 Tringham (1993: 196–7).

37 Heckman (1990: 111–19, 135–51); MacCormack (1980: 1–24); Plumwood (1993: 3–40, 196 – quotation from p. 9).

Chapter 8

The Nature of the Goddess: Sexual Identities and Power in Contemporary Witchcraft

Susan Greenwood

– I Introduction –

In this chapter I shall explore the issue of sexuality and identity in contemporary British witchcraft. British witchcraft was created by Gerald Gardner in the 1940s and it is widely viewed as a 'nature religion'. However, I argue that the practice is more focused on 'inner nature' and the power to define the self rather than 'external nature' or the environment. Contemporary witchcraft is seen by practitioners to be a spiritual path whereby a witch comes to find her or his inner self using what may be termed shamanistic techniques. Witchcraft is unique in the way that it associates femaleness and femininity with divinity: the Goddess represents the macrocosm – the cosmos. She is creatrix – and may be likened to what the theologian Paul Tillich (1951) has called the 'ground of being' – the ultimate reality connecting the universe in which all participate. She represents an avenue to authority for women which has been denied in mainstream orthodox religions: the Goddess shapes identity and sexualities through magical ritual and trance states.

Witchcraft ritual forms an important part of the practice and is an open terrain where sexual identities may be worked out in relation to the hegemony of the wider culture. The anthropologist Edmund Leach has pointed out how ritual serves to express a relation between the world of physical experience and an otherworld of the mystical imagination. The ordinary world is inhabited by mortal humans who are often powerless. By contrast, the otherworld is inhabited by immortal gods who are powerful. Ritual provides the channel of communication by which power of the gods is made available to humans (Leach 1976: 82). Using Leach's analysis of ritual as a channel of communication, I argue that witchcraft is a form of contemporary shamanic practice whereby the channel of communication between the ordinary world and the other-world is the means by which witches (re)negotiate their magical and sexual identities for self-empowerment. In this sense witchcraft is less a nature religion based on reverence for spirits of place and more an exploration of self or inner nature.

Witchcraft rituals are based on a reworking of the historical Christian notion that witchcraft is intrinsically evil. Contemporary witches claim that their rituals are a haven from the evils of a patriarchal society deeply influenced by Christianity, which has devalued and dominated women and nature. Thus witchcraft ritual offers a healing space away from the ills of the wider culture. In historical witchcraft women represented the forces of disorder and came to be associated with evil and the perversion of femininity. By contrast, contemporary witches say they are reclaiming these supposed occult powers and in the process they redefine and empower themselves.

– II WITCHCRAFT AS NATURE RELIGION –

Contemporary witchcraft is often described by witches and social scientists alike as a nature religion. This is largely due to the legacy of Margaret Murray's theory that European witches were practitioners of a natural fertility religion.[1] Although this theory has been discredited, her conviction that the witch cult of Diana was a pre-Christian fertility religion practised chiefly by 'the more ignorant or those in less thickly inhabited parts of the country' (Murray 1921: 12) has lived on and shaped contemporary ideas about witchcraft. Prudence Jones and Nigel Pennick argue, in *A History of Pagan Europe*, that the modern 'witches' who emerged in Britain after the repeal of the Witchcraft Act in 1951 were deeply influenced by Murray's view and saw themselves as 'rustic Pagans, following the inner Mysteries of a simple Nature religion which had been cruelly distorted by the black propaganda of the Church' (Jones and Pennick 1995: 217). Jones and Pennick, in a bid to resurrect indigenous Pagan traditions, seek to develop the view that modern Pagan practices are not new religious movements but are re-creations of ancient indigenous Pagan religions[2] which have a strong spirit of the sanctity of place and community.[3] Witchcraft is thus deeply associated with notions of nature religion.

However, it is my view that modern witchcraft is less a nature religion in its own right than a development of high magic, which in its later years, since the Hermetic Order of the Golden Dawn, has developed as a result of inner rather than external nature, the focus being on personal spiritual transformation and growth in association with the natural world rather than the worship of 'nature' as such (see Greenwood 1995, 1996a). Gerald Gardner had claimed that his nature religion was an ancient pre-Christian pagan fertility practice,[4] but the sources of his creation – that is, the magicians who influenced him – were largely inspired by Hermeticism, in particular the work of the Renaissance magus Paracelsus, who in turn was influenced by Ficino's talismanic and sympathetic magic rather than any folk tradition. It is probable that the essence of Ficino's natural magic filtered through to nineteenth-century occult revival writing, and was drawn on by Gardner when he invented witchcraft as a new magical practice some five hundred years after Ficino. Modern witchcraft has developed from high magic, and I shall suggest that the idea that witchcraft is an ancient pagan practice of the common people – the wise woman and cunning man – of the countryside is largely a romantic construction.

– III WITCHCRAFT RITUAL AND MAGICAL IDENTITY –

Since the Enlightenment western cultures have been associated with reason and rationality. Magical rituals provide a space devoted to the forces of 'unreason' –

whereby everything associated with femininity, emotion, intuition is valued. They form a theatrical space apart from the ordinary world in which the body is seen to be the locus of the forces (spirits, gods, goddesses, etc.) of the otherworld – as microcosm to macrocosm. For witches, ritual is a space of resistance to the wider culture with its rationalism and patriarchalism. Ritual is viewed as a space where a witch gains contact with the otherworld, which in totality is summed up as the Goddess as 'ground of being'. The Goddess is also a symbol of self-transformation – she is seen to be constantly changing and a force for change for those who open themselves up to her. Rituals are a special 'place between the worlds' which are entered 'in perfect love and in perfect trust', and they are believed to act as catalysts for self-transformation. The growth of the true magical self requires that the trappings of the patriarchal world be shed, thus enabling the practitioner to come face to face with her or his inner self or 'true nature'.

Self-transformation involves a negotiation of identity, and in witchcraft this is a two-stage process. Initially a witch must learn to open herself or himself up to the magical otherworld. This is sometimes accomplished with the aid of initiation rituals as rites of passage to the expansion of consciousness to the non-ordinary realities of the wider forces of the cosmos. In some forms of witchcraft, the first initiation induces the opening of consciousness, while the second is a descent to the underworld to discover the mystery of death. Opening up to the otherworld is a process which requires learning to interpret one's being within the wider magical whole – learning to see connections between the wider planetary forces and the self. This leads to a renegotiation of identity, the formation of the magical self, the identification of the self in relation to the wider whole; it also involves learning to communicate with otherworldly beings which in witchcraft are often anthropomorphic, as gods and goddesses of Celtic and classical mythology, or zoomorphic, as animal spirits or 'familiars'.

The second stage involves working with otherworldly beings, learning how to channel their energies within the microcosm of the body. Experience is gained through ritual and the calling in of spirits of the four quarters of the witchcraft circle: east, south, west and north. These correspond to intellect, will, emotions and body in the human microcosm. In addition, the witchcraft solar cycle of seasonal rituals, the 'Wheel of the Year', presents an opportunity to invoke different gods and goddesses who are appropriate to their season – for example Brigid, the goddess of fire, inspiration, healing and poetry, is associated with Imbolc, which is on or near 1 February, and Lugh, the Celtic sun god, is celebrated on 1 August as his power begins to decline before he is reborn at the winter solstice. Thus the emphasis in witchcraft is on communication with the otherworld, and witchcraft rituals may be examined as a form of western shamanism.

– IV WESTERN SHAMANISM AND TRANCE –

Shamanism is viewed by many as humanity's earliest and primordial religion (Eliade 1951; Bourguignon 1973; Noll 1985). 'Shamanism' is a term used to describe a particular form of behaviour associated with altered states of consciousness (ASC) and trance. Siberian shamanism is considered to be the classic form. In Siberian societies a shaman was a specialist in communicating with spirits and dealt with a community's specific problems, such as the whereabouts of food sources, and treating diseases. Geoffrey Samuel argues that the term 'shamanic' is a general category of practices found in differing degrees in almost all human societies. He defines shamanism as the regulation of human life and society through the use of altered states of consciousness 'by means of which specialist practitioners are held to communicate with a mode of reality alternative to, and more fundamental than, the world of every day experience' (Samuel 1993: 8). Since the 1960s and 1970s there has been a great deal of interest in shamanism in the west due to the drug counter-culture. In its western form, shamanism has been interpreted broadly to mean any magico-religious practice involving trance or altered states of consciousness (Harner 1980). It has become a spiritual alternative for western people estranged from major world religions (Atkinson 1992). Shamanism is seen to be a more authentic and original source of spirituality, uncorrupted by religious institution, dogma and power relationships. In addition, it is linked to various psychotherapies, and is, therefore, particularly interesting to contemporary witches who seek spiritual healing from many of the ills of the wider culture.

A link between shamanism and witchcraft has been made in the work of the historian Carlo Ginzburg. Ginzburg, while agreeing with other scholars that Margaret Murray's (1921) claim that those accused of witchcraft during the fifteenth to seventeenth centuries were practitioners of a pre-Christian fertility religion is disproved, nevertheless claims that Murray's work contains a 'core of truth'. He argues that it reveals a form of folk shamanic practice which is overlaid by an elite culture. Ginzburg argues that the historical stereotype of the witches' sabbat represented a fusion of two distinct cultural currents: of the learned culture as elaborated by inquisitors and lay judges based on the supposed existence of a hostile devil; and the other based on elements of shamanic origin such as the magic flight and animal metamorphosis, and the belief that some people, while in trance, could travel to other realms to bring healing or prosperity to the community (Ginzburg 1992: 307). While there is no direct link in the form of cultural tradition between those who were persecuted in early modern Europe and the contemporary practice of witchcraft, Ginzburg has argued that the ability to participate in different worlds in a state of trance is a human characteristic and basis of the historical witchcraft allegations. Similarly Erika Bourguignon suggests that the ritual uses of trance has ancient roots in human history and prehistory (Bourguignon 1979). Today's witches use ritual trance in a way which can broadly be termed a form of shamanism, in a practice aimed at incorporating experiences of the otherworld as part of a spiritual psychotherapeutic path to inner development and identity formation through the structure of a nature religion.

One important way of working with the forces of the otherworld is through sexual energy. In witchcraft sexual energy is seen to be sacred and a prime moving force of the cosmos. Sexual identities are shaped by different witchcraft practices (see Greenwood 1996b).

– V SEXUALITY AND GENDER TYPOLOGIES –

Susan Palmer (1994) has identified three major gender/sexuality typologies in her study of women's roles in new religions:

1. Sex polarity: women and men are seen to be unequal and different (for example, in ISKCON (International Society for Krishna Consciousness) women are seen to be on a lower scale of purity, while in Rajneeshism women are exalted over men).
2. Sex complementary: – women and men are seen as different but equal (such as in the Unification Church ('Moonies')).
3. Sex unity: sexual ambiguity is tolerated (for example, the Raelians).

Contemporary witchcraft embraces all three of Palmer's typological groups. Sex polarity is an underlying fundamental of all forms of witchcraft – women are exalted over men. This is exemplified in the notion of the Goddess as ultimate ground of being. Women are viewed as naturally more in tune with their bodies and the forces of nature due to the manner in which western cultures associate femininity with receptivity, emotion and intuition. These are attributes which are especially valued in witchcraft. There are two major forms of witchcraft: Wicca, which was, as previously mentioned, invented in the 1940s by Gerald Gardner, who claimed it to be an ancient pre-Christian practice; and a later feminist version, which was developed in the 1970s as a spiritual response to the new wave feminist movement of the late 1960s.

– WICCA –

In Wicca sex complementarity is a basic and fundamental working principle. As in yin and yang, men and women relate harmoniously together. The Goddess is not superior to the God but the feminine is valued because feminine energy is considered to be the 'impregnator on the magical and spiritual planes' – women are seen to be passive on the outer planes (the ordinary world) and active on the inner (the magical otherworld attained through trance states). Wicca has been heavily influenced by Jungianism, particularly the notions of *animus* and *anima* as contra-sexual psychological elements. In Wicca sexual identity is formalised by a third initiation process, 'The Great Rite', which is specifically focused on sexuality and the 'sacred marriage' on a physical level between priestess and priest, on a psychological level of *animus* and *anima*, and on a spiritual level between Goddess and God (Crowley 1989: 227). Sexual polarity is the basis of working Wicca. This is probably due to the fact that Gardner based his original idea on Murray's claims that witchcraft was an ancient fertility religion:

> In the Stone Ages man's chief wants were good crops, good hunting, good fishing, increase in flocks and herds and many children to make the tribe strong. It became the witches' duty to perform rites to obtain these things. This was probably a matriarchal age, when man was the hunter and woman stayed at home making medicine and magic . . . So the myth of the Great Mother came into existence and woman was her priestess. (Gardner 1988: 31)

Thus the emphasis in Wicca is on heterosexual dynamics as a means of raising energy in the circle. Most Wiccans I have spoken to, while stating that sexual polarity is the basis of their magical working, argue that the Wiccan circle may be used as an organising framework for alternative forms of raising magical energy. However, it appears to be a generally held belief among Wiccans that homosexuals and lesbians cannot work magic without sexual polarity. In practice I have not met many gays or lesbians who are attracted to Wicca; they often see feminist witchcraft as a more flexible medium.

– FEMINIST WITCHCRAFT –

In contrast to Wicca's sexual polarity, sex unity and tolerance of sexual ambiguity are evident in the feminist version of witchcraft. Broadly there are two forms of feminist witchcraft: liberal – mixed groups of women and men; and Dianic – those who tend to follow Z. Budapest's particular radical form of witchcraft, which is women-only and frequently lesbian.[5] Feminist witchcraft is shaped by feminist sexual politics and this has created an uneasy tension with Wicca. The certainties of gender polarity are questioned in the wider challenge of dominant cultural notions of femininity and masculinity. Feminist witches utilise magical practices to liberate themselves from what are seen as patriarchal social definitions. In short, sexual identity is not constructed in terms of a harmonic duality of femininity and masculinity but is more open and diverse and encompasses lesbianism and bisexuality. In feminist witchcraft sexuality is fluid and interchangeable and the practice offers the possibility for experimentation and change as the basis of spiritual awareness and transformation. At a workshop on women's and men's magic given by Starhawk, a leading feminist witch, the participants[6] 'visited' a 'Temple of Desire' in a trance journey. Starhawk took great pains to establish a magical ritual space free from any preconceptions about sexual orientation; it was a space which could be interpreted fluidly by heterosexual and homosexual witch alike. We journeyed to the Temple to find the place of our desire. At the threshold we met a guardian and those who did not want to pass the threshold could go to a 'Pavilion of Healing'. Starhawk visualised the Temple of Desire as a white, sacred enclosure which we entered and found within ourselves. After spending some time there – reflecting on our sexuality – the drumming increased and the energy reached a peak and was sent outwards and upwards. A cauldron of flames was actually lit in the centre of the circle and the participants took turns in jumping the flames before retracing steps on the journey back to ordinary consciousness.

I shall now turn to an examination of witchcraft as a process of shamanic identity (re)construction.

– VI MENSTRUAL BLOOD AS SYMBOL OF WOMEN'S INNATE POWER –

Witchcraft rituals function as a form of resistance to mainstream culture. The ritual space is where the feminine is specifically valued. The symbolism of femaleness *par excellence* is menstrual blood. Menstruation is said to be women's innate route to their shamanic, deeper, magical selves, and it is widely believed that women generally have a greater shamanic ability and that their experience is deeper because of their periodic rhythms. 'Dark moon' rituals have become increasingly popular for women to celebrate and reclaim what is seen to be the most feminine part of themselves. The dark moon is seen to be the 'time in the lunar cycle when the old moon dies and is then reborn again' (*Matriarchy Research and Reclaim Network* newsletter 63, Beltane 1990). The moon is often viewed as feminine in the way that it waxes and wanes and female witches identify with its rhythms. It is a time 'to come together in a sanctified women's space' (ibid.). The rituals start with purification and 'smudging' (a American Indian practice of burning a stick of incense). Post-menstrual and non-menstrual women are also included and find it an 'invaluable way' to mark their lunar rhythms. One feminist group I knew celebrated dark moon rituals by always wearing red clothing. On one occasion they stripped and covered themselves with red ochre to represent the blood of menstruation in a celebration of their synchronicity with the moon, menstruation and their foremothers.

Menstruation is often seen in witchcraft as the time when a woman is at her wildest, untamed by the forces of patriarchy, when she is in touch with her true, psychic, female self – her inner nature. This view of menstruation tends to view ovulation as the opposite phase, when a woman is said to be more attuned to 'the race' as a 'potential passer-on of the racial DNA codes' (Farrar and Farrar 1991: 163–4). Menstruation, for long the subject of taboo, has become a powerful symbol of female identity, a symbol for condensing and expressing a complex set of notions about women (Delaney 1988). In witchcraft, menstrual blood is an emblem of creative power and the fertility of the imagination. It has all the powers of the liminal, and is used to assert femaleness as a powerful source of identity. In addition, women are frequently seen as 'gateways into the mysteries' for men. This is because, as previously mentioned, often men are seen to be active on the outer planes but passive on the inner. Wicca draws extensively on Aleister Crowley's ritual writing and his emphasis on the female as 'altar' or gateway to the divine within.[7] In this sense, a man needs a woman to get in touch with the parts of himself which have been repressed. Thus in witchcraft rituals the physiological processes of women's bodies are used to construct a cosmos where male and female witches may connect with what is seen as women's ancient inner power.

– VII MAGICAL POWER AND SELF-IDENTITY –

The capacity for trance may be an innate function of the human brain, but the way that trance is interpreted is cultural. The anthropologist Erika Bourguignon distinguishes two broad types of altered state of consciousness: trance (of which shamanism is an example) and possession. Trance is a feature of small-scale, relatively simple hunter-and-gatherer societies such as the North and South American Indians; it is practised mainly by men and the experience is seen to be an end in itself – such as the North American vision quest as initiation into manhood. By contrast, possession trances are more common in societies dependent on agriculture and animal husbandry, and where the social structure is complex. In these cultures (typically sub-Saharan Africa) it is women who usually become possessed by spirits. Women are reared to be obedient and will not seek spiritual help to augment their own powers. Instead they become a vehicle for the spirits by calling on powerful otherworldly entities to act in their place by the impersonation of another personality. Bourguignon argues that both trance and possession are concerned with mastery, but the crucial difference is that the trance state enhances identity – power and knowledge of the otherworld are seen as special gifts bestowed by the spirits and structure identity – while in possession states the person in trance achieves the state by losing her own self and identifying with or making room for the more powerful self – she ceases to be herself (Bourguignon 1979).

At the heart of possession beliefs are fundamental claims about the essence of femininity. In a study of exorcism and the symbolic identity of women in Sri Lanka, the anthropologist Bruce Kapferer claims that it is cultural views of women which frame their possession. Kapferer draws on Sherry Ortner's well-known argument (1974) that it is women's cultural association with physiological processes of menstruation and reproduction which places them closer to nature. He claims that Sri Lankan women are culturally conceived as the nexus of culture and nature. This is symbolised by possession by demons, whereby the demonic is nature disordered and outside the order of culture (Kapferer 1991). The work of the historian Lyndal Roper (1994) on the European Counter-Reformation supports this view. Roper argues that Catholic exorcisms had a sexual logic: they were exclusively carried out on women because women were believed to be closer to the Devil and enslaved to their physical natures. Counter-Reformation Catholics believed that false religion was expressed physically – the body could be invaded by demons, and healing involved their expulsion.

Explanations such as those of Kapherer and Roper locate spirit possession with conceptions of nature and an innate femininity which has to be controlled. A different tack is taken by Janice Boddy (1994), whose work on the zar spirit possession cults in Sudan attempts to dismantle the category of spirit possession as an autonomous subject of inquiry and locate it in a wider sphere of human endeavour concerning self-hood and identity. In a similar manner, I maintain that the practice of contemporary European witchcraft is essentially concerned with the empowerment of self to (re)define self-hood and identity through the induction of trance states. Contemporary witches are in control of the trance and therefore the term 'possession' is not appropriate in this context. Women's nature is viewed in positive terms: the female blood cycle is affiliated with shamanism as a form of self-empowerment and it is celebrated. Ritual is used to exorcise the evils of patriarchal society and its malaise, which is related to masculinity, rationality and reason. Healing involves a connection with spirits, not through passive possession, but through an active process of communication which leads to positive identity formation.

– VIII CONCLUSION –

Contemporary witchcraft is a practice whereby a channel of communication between the ordinary world and the otherworld helps the (re)negotiation of magical and sexual identities. It is a process involving an active relationship with spirits, and is facilitated by seasonal and moon rituals associated with outer nature. Contemporary witchcraft is unique in the value it places on femininity. In Wicca, cultural stereotypes of femininity and masculinity are reinforced and naturalised but, counter to the mainstream, with a positive valuation of femininity.[8] Feminist witchcraft, being more fluid and open, forms a terrain where sexuality is explored, and this shatters to some extent the naturalised gender categories of masculinity and femininity. However, I argue that magic is still largely gendered through notions of innate femininity. This is seen especially clearly in the idea that women are shamanically dynamic on the inner planes due to their innate feminine power which is symbolised by menstruation. Both practices are fundamentally about the issue of control – the control to identify the self in a changing world. For witches, the power of the Goddess is brought into the everyday world through the ritual process. The witch as shaman is a specialist at communicating with spirits and this is the basis of her or his power to redefine the self. The emphasis in contemporary witchcraft is thus on the transformation of inner nature rather than the worship of external nature as localised spirits or the environment as such.

– NOTES –

Thanks are due to Pat Caplan, Annie Keeley and Ken Rees for reading and making critical comments and helpful suggestions on earlier drafts; I would also like to thank Elizabeth Puttick for valuable discussions. The research on which this work is based has been funded by the University of London Central Research Fund and the Economic and Social Research Council, to whom I am indebted.

1 Ronald Hutton points out four lines of influence on Murray: firstly, Jules Michelet's *La Sorcière* (1862), which portrayed the pagan witch religions as led by women, democratic and nature-loving (Michelet had also claimed that the Renaissance had been caused by the natural wisdom of the witch religion working its way upwards to artists and writers); second, Charles Godfrey Leland's *Aradia* (1899), which was directly inspired by Michelet and which purported to be the gospel of the Italian branch of Michelet's witch religion; third, Sir James Frazer's theory of evolution, in which surviving folk customs could be the fossils of old religions; and finally, Murray's association with the Folk-Lore Society (Hutton 1996a: 11, 12).

2 These ancient Pagan traditions are similar to Shintoism and Hinduism.

3 Jones argues in this volume that the Hermetic current is a condensed version which surfaced in the Renaissance and was a civilised urban model.

4 Hutton points out that Gardner was a Freemason, a Rosicrucian, a Spiritualist, a 'friend and probable member of the Ordo Templi Orientis', a member of the governing council of a Druid order, a 'very active member of the Folk-Lore Society' and a 'fervent admirer of Margaret Murray' (Hutton 1996a: 12).

5 In the US Dianic witchcraft tends to be interpreted more broadly as a magical practice based on the reverence of the goddess Diana.

6 I participated in this workshop as part of my anthropological fieldwork.

7 Aleister Crowley was influenced by Tantrism.

8 This raises the important issue, which space does not allow me to examine here, of whether this model of femininity is based more on male fantasies about women than women's empowerment as such.

CHAPTER 9

Goddesses and Gopis: In Search of New Models of Female Sexuality

ELIZABETH PUTTICK

– I INTRODUCTION: WOMEN AND SEXUALITY IN THE WORLD RELIGIONS –

The most fundamental duality in religion is that between body and spirit. It is strongest in the more overtly dualistic western religions, especially Christianity, but is also found in monistic religions such as Hinduism and Buddhism. Most organised religions and many new religious movements (NRMs) are ambivalent or condemnatory towards the body, particularly in terms of its sexual function. Furthermore, religious beliefs and practices regarding sexuality correlate with ideas about women and nature: both are perceived as inferior, subject to control and domination. These associations are particularly clear in monastic traditions, leading to a polarised model of (celibate) holiness as male and (sexual) sinfulness as female. Women are thereby perceived as fallen, fleshly, earthy, trapped in matter. As evil temptresses they are sinful innately, actively, and passively as objects of temptation. Women's bodies, particularly their sexual functions, are impure and polluted. Women are therefore prohibited from participating in sacred rituals, or even entering a place of worship, particularly during such taboo phases as menstruation or post-childbirth. Even where women are seen as spiritually equal (and in some religions they are held to have no soul or no capacity for spiritual advancement), their bodies 'represent the lower self of the bestial appetites and material, corruptible existence'.[1]

The transformation of anti-body attitudes into misogyny is a three-stage process. It begins with a view of the body as grossly material: our animal nature that connects us to the earth pulling us down from our lofty aspirations. In contrast the mind, and even more the soul or spirit, is perceived as our higher nature, drawing us away from the animals (and distinguishing us from them) upwards to the realm of angels and the divine. The mind–body split is arguable as a theory, but becomes problematic in the second stage when the dichotomy is viewed as oppositional, leading to the value judgement: body/sexuality = bad, mind/spirit = good; body leads to sin, spirit to sainthood.

The third stage arises from a social-soteriological inequality: organised religions are patriarchal constructions, male-created and male-dominated. They offer paths of salvation or enlightenment mainly to men, which consist partly or mainly in transcending the body including sexual desire. To achieve transcendence, celibacy is therefore a prerequisite, but it is hard for the normal human being to deny and suppress sexual energy. Eastern religion acknowledges the difficulties more than Christianity, tending to recommend celibacy for older, more experienced meditators and providing techniques to assist the process. However, the volatility of sexual energy ensures that even the most dedicated monk will have upsurges of libido, particularly in the presence of a woman. The woman may have no interest in the man, but the sight of her immediately arouses him, so she is blamed for pulling him down from his spiritual heights. And if no woman passes, the mind will create visions of beautiful women, such as the *dakinis* of Tibetan mythology, to tempt and seduce the monk. Women have already been disparaged as inferior to men on account of their perceived greater materiality. Now they are also demonised as evil temptresses, profane and polluting. Christianity portrays women as the Devil's gateway, while the Buddha liberalised the metaphor: 'It is better that your penis enter the mouth of a hideous cobra or a pit of blazing coals than enter a woman's vagina' (Stevens 1990: 32).

So patriarchal religion created the body/spirit split and the ideal of celibacy to heal the wound – which not only intensifies the problem but leads directly to misogyny. It is of course more extreme in monastic traditions, but versions of this morality are imposed on the laity. Religions play a major part in regulating sexuality through marriage ceremonies and restrictions on the permissible times, place and manner of sexual intercourse: (a) strictly for procreation; (b) joyless. It has also created taboos around purity and pollution such as the Jewish *niddah* laws of family purity and the *mikveh* (purification bath), as well as restrictions on clothing, adornment and the revealing of body parts.

The process may be observed in NRMs that promote celibacy. For example, since the Jesus Army has become influenced by a militant version of the men's spirituality movement its male members don combat gear as warriors for Jesus and worry about becoming feminised. Correspondingly, marriage is now viewed as the 'lower way', inferior to celibacy, which is now catching on among men, promoted by their 'inspirational bulletin' *Celibate Cutting Edge*.

ISKCON (International Society for Krishna Consciousness) has always been conservative and ambivalent towards women, but only became overtly misogynistic in the mid-1970s after men had been initiated as sannyasins (celibate renunciates). They tried to stop the initiation of women, which was now seen as problematic to their own spiritual advancement. Women were made to stand at the back of the temple, a practice that shocks educated Indians. Marriage improves the social and spiritual status of women but not men, who are held to be superior to women on all levels, particularly when celibate. Men tend to justify marriage as sacrifice for the good of the movement. This may lead to resentment against women as the cause of their fall in status, and even within the movement there are complaints of sex-related misogyny. A woman may be perceived as 'a temptress first and a devotee second', and excluded from sharing power with the men so as not to 'sexually agitate them'. The men themselves appear to be absolved from responsibility by the Vedic imagery of woman as fire, man as butter: 'When butter comes near fire, it melts'.[2]

Out of these attitudes and judgements arose the madonna/whore dichotomy and stereotype.

– II THE SEX GODDESS: THE SECULAR REBELLION –

The only solutions offered to women to redeem themselves from the sin of being female are to be reborn as a man or (in this life) to remain a virgin, particularly as a celibate nun. Of course sexuality cannot be altogether suppressed, and this would not be considered desirable on a wide scale by most priests, who are zealous in the expansion of their congregations. So religions tend to support women's reproductive role and sanctify motherhood. Christianity is unique in its attempt to have it both ways: the ideal of the Virgin Mother or Madonna. Only one woman has reputedly achieved this goal, but as an ideal it exerts a tyranny that helps to keep women submissively in their place.

Women who are not nuns, mothers, maidens or maiden aunts but are overtly attractive and sexual beings are liable to be labelled promiscuous or worse. Even thirty years after the 'sexual revolution' the predominant fear among teenage girls – the daughters of the revolution – is of losing their 'reputation' by being labelled a 'slag' or 'slut', which constrains their sexual and social behaviour. In some eras social attitudes have been more liberal, as in medieval courtly love, the Restoration, the Romantic movement, and the 1960s counter-culture. At such times female sexuality is celebrated and the Venus archetype predominates. Women are placed on pedestals and worshipped as sex goddesses, celebrated in art and poetry. Out of this veneration arose the myth of romantic love so fundamental to western culture.

However, there are various problems with this apparently positive model. First, it is selective and temporary. It applies to women who are young, beautiful, and successful at attracting admirers, and lasts as long as they remain so. It also depends upon their remaining elusive, unattainable – 'playing hard to get'.[3] The inherently temporary nature of romantic love partly explains why the great romantic myths and stories end in tragedy – separation or death – which at least preserves the intensity and illusion. Marriage, which raises a woman's social status, lowers her romantic desirability. Goddesses do not iron shirts.

The second problem is that the terms are set and controlled by men (though internalised by women). Poetry and passion create an illusion of power and status for women, but the adulation given can be taken away. The goddess can be dethroned if she does not fulfil the conditions, or if her worshipper tires of her. And a failed sex goddess becomes at best a mere mortal and at worst a whore. It is the fulfilment of a male fantasy, as are so many sexual and romantic images of women, including apparently strong models such as the dominatrix, which expresses a male fantasy of female domination. Significantly, this particular fantasy is a favourite among powerful male professionals such as judges and politicians who in real life dominate women and other men.

Third, romantic love begins in worship but ends in slavery. Balzac defined femininity as treating a woman as a slave while persuading her she is a queen. A more contemporary expression is the pithy 1960s feminist adage: 'It begins when you sink into his arms, and it ends with your arms in his sink.' It is a question not only of domestic exploitation but of psychological restraint, a process in which women collude. Women become dependent on worship, and fearful of falling off the pedestal, which is a somewhat restricted arena. Hence, romantic love becomes the psychological equivalent of St Simon Stylites' mortification on a pillar in the desert.

Altogether the model of the sex goddess is limited, constrictive, and fraught with perils. It is also dated and perilously close to parody, as demonstrated by the gay male enthusiasm for such self-parodying icons as Mae West, Marlene Dietrich and Madonna. On the other hand, at least romance can give women a first glimpse of their own divinity, mirrored through the worshipful eyes of a lover, thus restoring some of the self-esteem and empowerment that religion took away. At its height it expresses a fusion of secular and spiritual values where the woman embodies both, as in medieval courtly love and its derivatives ever since.

– III TANTRA: RESACRALISATION OF FEMALE SEXUALITY? –

Female sexuality has also been sacralised in a few minority religious traditions, particularly Tantra and Taoism in the east, and to some extent alchemy in the West. Tantra is often perceived and presented as a life-affirmative, body-positive path on which sexual passion is seen not as an obstruction but as our most powerful natural energy, which may be explored and transmuted into the great bliss of liberation. It is non-dualistic, immanentist: 'nirvana is samsara; the passions themselves constitute enlightenment'. Historically, Tantra has been dedicated to the female principle (Shakti), and Tantric myths and icons depict the erotic goddess as a life-giving force:

> Women are seen as earthly, or bodily, manifestations of goddesses, and this identity is reinforced by the patterning of male–female relationships upon the relationship between a devotee and a deity. The man's divinity is an accepted premise of Tantric metaphysics, but it is not given the same range of concrete expressions as the woman's divinity in this gynocentric context. (Shaw 1994: 69)

Women are worshipped, the male principle being complementary but subordinate: 'The female element is an embodiment of *prajna*, transcendental wisdom; the woman's *yoni* is the abode of pure bliss' (Stevens 1990: 63).

The main feminist debate around Tantra is whether the woman in a Tantric relationship was primarily a sex object for the man's enlightenment, or whether she was an equal partner. Miranda Shaw's detailed, meticulously researched book presents a convincing case for the empowerment of women not only as equal partners but often as superior, more skilled and capable, hence teachers to the male initiates:

Seeing one's partner as divine is the key to this form of worship. Having seen one's partner as a god or goddess, one naturally feels a sense of devotion . . . Although the man and woman recognise one another's divinity, implying complete reciprocity, the man is required to respond to the woman's divinity with numerous expressions of devotion, physical acts of homage, and a reverential, suppliant attitude. (Shaw 1994: 153)

However, other writers argue that women were exploited in Tantra. June Campbell argues in a recent study of female identity in Tibetan Buddhism that although historically women have been admitted as tantrikas in India and very rarely as tulkus in Tibet, the status of women in Tantra has now declined dramatically. She writes from personal experience of the inferior status and sufferings of the *songyum* (sexual partner of the lama), arguing that over the last 500 years or more 'there has been a degeneration of the teachings in general, which has resulted in women losing touch with their own powers and knowledge as Tantric lineage-holders' (Campbell 1996: 99). The problems are exacerbated in the case of lamas who outwardly maintain celibacy but secretly maintain a *songyum*, who is sworn to secrecy and threatened with all manner of punishments for indiscretion in this world and the next. It is only the Nyingma school of Tibetan Buddhism, in which the lamas are usually married, that the importance of women practitioners is acknowledged. Although many lamas have had consorts, there is no lineage of women teachers, and no women with any position of power. The very few women who are publicly recognised as possessing high spiritual qualities are the wives, mothers or sisters of lamas.

– IV Pagan sexuality –

One of the main progenitors of Pagan sexual practices was Aleister Crowley. He developed sex magick in his Rabelaisian Abbey of Thelema in Sicily, based on extensive experimentation with sex, magic and drugs to create altered states of consciousness, the results of which he published in a booklet *De Arte Magica*. It seems likely that Crowley was influenced by Tantra; some of the texts were available in translation, and there are Tantric elements in his Gnostic Mass.[4] His philosophy of sexuality also arose out of his channelled Law of Thelema: 'Do what thou wilt shall be the whole of the Law . . . Love is the law, love under will.' His community eventually collapsed amid lurid accusations, but has influenced various occult groups including the Temple Ov Psychick Youth, founded in the 1980s by the pop musician Genesis P. Orridge, which practises sex magick but moves straight into the final degree of heterosexual magic without passing through the previous seven degrees of initiation.

The main source of Pagan beliefs and practices is in the mythology of the Goddess, which affirms the female body and provides rituals for celebrating 'women's mysteries', particularly menstruation and childbirth. As Starhawk, the best-known witch and writer, expresses it: 'Sexuality is sacred because it is a sharing of energy, in passionate surrender to the power of the Goddess, immanent in our desire. In orgasm, we share in the force that moves the stars'.[5]

The English Wiccan high priestess Vivianne Crowley believes that the 'negative attitude to women displayed in Christianity has derived largely from negative attitudes to sex' (1996: 116), particularly following the glorification of celibacy. The resulting vilification of woman as temptress is bound up with another fear-arousing image: woman as witch. This is the term that goddess spirituality and Wicca are trying to revive in its positive meanings of wise woman and priestess.

Paganism may be seen as hedonistic but with provisos: Crowley's Law of Thelema is adapted to read: 'An it harm none, do what you will.' Vivianne Crowley: (1994: 163) describes Pagan sexual morality as simple:

> there are no barriers to sexual activity with other unattached adults; but we are expected to have regard to the consequences of our actions and to ensure that we do not cause unwanted pregnancy, spread sexual disease, or mislead others as to our level of commitment to the relationship.

Attitudes to homosexuality vary between different groups. In high magic groups where sex polarity is considered important homosexuality is discouraged. Wicca is mainly liberal, while some feminist witchcraft groups actively support lesbianism. Extra-marital sex is forbidden if it causes hurt, while rape and child–adult sex are 'anathema' (Crowley 1994: 163–4). The Pagan response to AIDS is compassionate, particularly as compared to Christian sects and NRMs, and is summarised by Starhawk:

> It is harder today, but perhaps even more necessary, to affirm the sacredness of the erotic . . . AIDS . . . has become an excuse for an attack on the erotic, especially on those forms that do not meet society's approval . . . If society valued the erotic as sacred, AIDS research would be a top priority, as would research on safe forms of birth control. (Starhawk 1979: 9)

Pagans are mainly uninterested in marriage as a legal institution, seeing it as a device to protect property and dominate women. However, a loving monogamous relationship is seen as a personal contract to be honoured. As Starhawk expresses it: 'Marriage is a deep commitment, a magical, spiritual, and psychic bond. But it is only one possibility out of many for loving, sexual expression' (ibid.: 27). There is an on-going debate between monogamy and 'free love' in Paganism, and Starhawk herself has caused some protest in the Reclaiming movement by changing to a pro-monogamy position now that she is herself in a monogamous relationship. Various Pagan groups have created colourful wedding rituals, sometimes called 'handfastings', which are often celebrated at a seasonal festival, such as the spring festival of Beltane. Alternative marriages are increasing in Britain at about 50 per cent a year, including among non-Pagans, in reaction to the perceived outdatedness and sexism of the Judaeo-Christian rituals and the unspirituality of the civil ceremony.[6] So this may be an indication of changing social trends.

The myth of the sacred marriage between king and priestess to ensure good harvests and control of the land is fundamental in Paganism, and its re-enactment is a recognition of the power of sex. It is the basis of the Great Rite: ritual sex between the high priest and priestess in pagan rituals, including the third degree of initiation in

Alexandrian Wicca. However, the evidence suggests that it is more often symbolic than actual, unless the participants are already partners. Some witches compare it to Tantra as a sacred ceremony to raise and release power, and channel it for the purposes of healing, consecration, creativity and inspiration. Witches do tend to worship 'sky-clad' (naked), but 'as a way of establishing closeness and dropping social masks, because power is most easily raised that way, and because the human body is itself sacred' (Starhawk 1979: 97).

– V SACRED SEX IN THE NEW AGE –

The New Age answer to the failure of free sex is sacred sex, a syncretistic selection from Tantra, Taoism, humanistic and transpersonal psychology, and clinical sexology. It began in America in the 1960s but did not take off till the 1980s, when various teachers and psychotherapists began leading courses. It is an influence on some NRMs, particularly the Osho movement and some Tibetan Buddhist groups, and is privately practised by some Pagans though not a formal part of the practice apart from the Great Rite. There are now many books and many teachers in America and Europe, of whom the best known is Margo Anand, author of the best-selling *The Art of Sexual Ecstasy*. She is a former Osho sannyasin who runs groups and trainings in 'High Sex' worldwide, and has set up SkyDancing Institutes in America and Britain. Her teaching emphasises 'intimacy as a subtle set of skills, an art that has to be developed before sexual union is considered' (Anand 1989: 94), a western requirement often ignored by eastern Tantric masters.

Other well-known teachers are Caroline Aldred, who teaches sacred sex via nine levels of orgasm, as learned from Shunyata (Robert Ferris), the 'Laughing Guru' based in Bali. David Howe, head of the Institute of Higher Sexology in South London, teaches a 4,000-year-old Seminal Ovarian Chi Gung. The best-known British teachers of sacred sex are Zek and Misha Halu, whose work is based on many years of study with Taoist masters in the east. They rose to media prominence as consultants for the video of the *Kama Sutra*, which attracted widespread media interest in their work, extending to other teachers of sacred sex. Although some of this coverage is predictably sceptical, prurient or sensationalist – they have been dubbed 'the Masters and Johnson of the New Age' by the tabloid press – the treatment is becoming increasingly serious and respectful. Like Margo Anand, they see sacred sexuality as a means of discouraging promiscuity, revitalising marriage and enhancing intimacy, hence a vital therapy for the age of AIDS.

New Age views on gender tend towards dualism, albeit a softer, more spiritualised version based mainly on Jungian psychology. Jung's theories of *anima* and *animus*, Eros and Logos, at least granted women a spiritual nature, but were still riddled with sexist assumptions:

> No matter how friendly and obliging a woman's Eros may be, no logic on earth can shake her if she is ridden by the animus. Often the man has the feeling – and he is not altogether wrong – that only seduction or a beating or rape would have the necessary power of persuasion. (Jung 1986: 172)

Another model of female sexuality which is popular in some New Age circles is one of the more bizarre offshoots of the women's spirituality movement: the sacred prostitute. Our knowledge of Pagan priestesses is minimal, but various women have written about the sacred prostitute as 'representing the vital, full-bodied nature of the feminine',[7] and let their imaginations run wild in fantasies echoing the current vogue for female erotic fiction, verging on soft porn. The following extract (the original runs for several pages) gives something of the flavour of the fantasy:

> She is a mystery, concealed by veils. We see her only dimly. Yet in the flickering light we discern her shapely feminine outline. A breeze lifts her veils to reveal her long black tresses. Silver bracelets adorn her arms and ankles; miniature crescents hang from her earlobes and lapis lazuli beads encircle her neck. Her perfume with its musklike aroma creates an aura which stimulates and enriches physical desire.
>
> As the sacred prostitute moves through the open temple doors she begins to dance to the music of the flute, tambourine and cymbals. Her gestures, her facial expressions and the movements of her supple body all speak to the welcoming of passion. There is no false modesty regarding her body, and as she dances the contours of her feminine form are revealed under an almost transparent saffron robe. Her movements are graceful, as she is well aware of her beauty. She is full of love, and as she dances her passion grows. In her ecstasy she forgets all restraint and gives herself to the deity and to the stranger. (Qualls-Corbett 1988: 21–2)

– VI God's gopis: religion and sexual abuse –

Another model of female sexuality that may be compared with the sacred prostitute and is widespread in religious groups is the gopi. Gopis are literally cowgirls but also sexual partners of the Hindu avatar Krishna. This could be termed the ultimate male fantasy: to be god and have 10,000 girlfriends dancing attendance. In this scenario women are the handmaids of the lord, and the perks of the lord's appointed: male charismatic religious leaders.

It is important to note that although sexual abuse in religion is often perceived as a problem of Asian gurus encountering more 'permissive' western societies, it is widespread within old and new religions, including Christianity. The most recent scandal in Britain featured the Anglican vicar Chris Brain, leader of the Nine O'Clock Service in Sheffield. His ministry was greatly admired by the Anglican establishment, who speeded up his ordination, but in November 1995 he resigned after admitting improper sexual relations with twenty of his female parishioners, known as the 'Lycra Lovelies'. Brain's theological justification for his behaviour was original and contemporary: 'discovering a post-modern definition of sexuality in the church'. The most widescale example of religious sexual abuse is in another Christian movement, the Children of God (now the Family). David Berg, the leader, abandoned his wife for another, younger follower, and then had multiple sexual relationships with other female followers. The practice for which the movement is most notorious is 'Flirty Fishing', a recruitment technique by which women brought in potential converts through prostitution, as a result of which they were dubbed

'Hookers for Jesus'. The practice spread throughout the movement's international communes, and women were working two to five nights a week, but it was eventually stopped mainly on account of AIDS. Berg justified Flirty Fishing in numerous letters to his followers as a legitimate recruitment technique:

> The 'fish' can't understand crucifixion, they can't understand Jesus. But they can understand the ultimate creation of God, a woman . . . Everyone of you girls who spreads out your arms and your legs on the bed for those men are just like Jesus, exactly like Jesus![8]

It is not always clear whether or how far sex is involved in these relationships, and if so how far it is considered abusive, particularly by the women themselves, but often in antinomian groups the women may be considered the group's sexual resources. Such favours may be hard to refuse. A Buddhist woman seduced by a roshi at 16 asked, 'What do you do when God makes a pass at you?' On the other hand, women may actively collude, competing for the attention of the leader via their sexual charms, but one might question the spirituality and ethics of teachers and organisations that encourage such power games: sex as a route to spiritual status and power, a function of unequal gender and power relations.[9]

Women in favour may well feel privileged and powerful, but their status is as precarious as that of the secular sex goddess. There is sometimes a belief that it is an honour and privilege to be God's girlfriend, and the women are offered special transmission of teachings or energy in return. But the qualifications for such favours may not be overtly spiritual. As one spiritual teacher, Andrew Cohen, remarked recently when asked about such relationships, 'Isn't it interesting how it's always the youngest and prettiest women who are chosen?' Such teachers often have short-lived, multiple relationships, and the results may be devastating to a woman believing herself 'special'. Research suggests that sexual abuse is one of the main reasons for women leaving NRMs, particularly when once-favoured women are rejected by a leader, and the ensuing feelings of bitterness, disillusion and betrayal may be devastating, worse than in a normal love affair, because of the unique nature and sensitivity of the master–disciple relationship and the trust invested in it.[10]

There are rumours of the abuse of power in Paganism, including some Wiccan covens, but no hard evidence. Shelley Rabinovitch has done extensive demographic research on Paganism in Canada and the USA, which reveals that an overwhelming majority had experience of severe childhood trauma and abuse. They came to Paganism seeking healing, but might be subject to repetition syndrome. She has come across some examples of sexual exploitation in covens – by women as well as men. She knows of one temple-based group where 'it's a long-standing joke that you only get your first degree if you sleep with the high priestess and/or the high priest'. The initiates did not necessarily take it as abuse but as an expression of Pagan morals as well as a prerequisite for getting initiated, and for some it was also an act of hero/ ine worship – though both priests now have 'feet of clay'. In her opinion these incidents are 'more indicative of dysfunctional upbringing than anything specifically wrong with the religion or its morals/ethics. We have individual instances of abuse, but none that seem to be systemic' (personal communication).

– VII CONCLUSIONS –

The Goddess is often held up as a positive model for women; there are clear potential benefits, particularly in a spiritual or religious context. However, the specific ideal of the sex goddess as a popular secular version of the divine feminine has become dated and dangerous as a female ideal. Myths of romantic love have failed us and are now being widely deconstructed, as the ending of the fairytale marriage between the Prince and Princess of Wales so poignantly symbolised.

Paganism provides a range of forms of the divine feminine, most pre-eminently in the earth goddess Gaia, which reverses the negative stereotypes of organised religion. In this mythology the earth, nature, the body, sexuality and woman are good, associated with positive attributes and virtues: nurturing, caring, feeling, compassionate, natural and empowering. Gaia is not specifically associated with sexuality, but other goddesses are, such as Inanna. Aphrodite, or Venus, has also been reclaimed as an archetype, from the bimbo of the popular imagination to her pre-Hellenic roots as a powerful and multidimensional form of the Great Goddess in her sexual aspect. It is interesting that both Inanna and Aphrodite were originally also embodied as the brightest star in the firmament.

Pagan forms of sacred sexuality allied with Goddess spirituality may work to empower women through the resacralisation of the body and sexuality, under certain conditions. First, women need to be self-determining, in control of our own sexuality including fertility – not enslaved to a lover or to a male sexual fantasy or to a sociobiological imperative of motherhood. A partnership of equals is essential in which both partners may embody the God and Goddess but ritually and symbolically. There is a time and place to be a Tantric *dakini*, but also for washing dishes – which may be equally divine but perhaps more in line with the Hera archetype. In other words, a more comprehensive and multidimensional model is needed to get away from the sexism and ageism of the sex goddess ideal. The Triple Goddess encompasses all the stages and processes of sexuality from menstruation to the menopause. Reclaiming the mother–daughter bond is important in Goddess spirituality, and the myth of Demeter and Kore serves this purpose. The third stage, the crone, still tends to hold little appeal for many women. Even feminist witches, who find it a powerful symbol in ritual, may be less enthusiastic about being expected to embody the crone in daily life. Vivianne Crowley (1996: 151) defines the third aspect of the Goddess not as crone but as Wise Woman and Woman of Power, terms more likely to gain wider currency in the endeavour to restore dignity, function and status to post-menopausal women. Native American society with its honouring of the Grandmothers as tribal leaders and counsellors provides a model: 'The older a woman becomes among the Sioux, the more powerful she is regarded to be, because her acquired wisdom is listened to and respected by all' (McGaa 1990: 9).

Androgyny is another way forward, blurring and undermining the assumptions on which the genderised body/spirit dichotomy is built. Within youth culture and to some extent the broader society in the west, the dualistic and stereotyped view of gender is now being undermined to allow more ambiguity, crossover – both biologically, through bisexuality, transsexuality, and the whole postmodernist questioning of sexual roles and stereotypes; also in a more psychological, total way through the concept of androgyny.[11] Androgyny is sacralised in Hinduism in the hermaphrodite god Ardhanarishvar, but there is some resistance and misunderstanding in the west, where it may be confused with bisexuality or unisex neutrality. There is a fear that by blurring the boundaries we lose the charge, the excitement, the dynamic attraction of polar opposites. The greater the distance and difference, the greater the magnetic attraction – but also the more misunderstanding and conflict. To become whole we need to heal the wound, the split within and between men and women, through healing the inner male and female.

Most of the support for holistic spirituality, in all religions, is from women, and it may be that body-positive immanence is inherently more female, celibate transcendence more male, as believed by many Pagans and feminist theologians among others. Restrictions and denial of female sexuality by male theologians, priests and religious leaders in the name of morality and spirituality clearly arise from misogyny, particularly when accompanied by explicit doctrines of female sinfulness. What is clear is the need for women – as well as men – to be in control of their own sexuality and emotional life. After 500 years of belief in the myth of romance and happily ever after, we are now in a transitional state of postmodern, post-romantic experimentation. But there are signs of a way forward, beyond the ruins of romance, without reverting to a backlash or the seclusion of the monastery. It is possible to integrate sexuality and spirituality, and in so doing heal the wounds of femininity – and masculinity.

– NOTES –

1 Ruether (1983: 218); see also King (1989); Bednarowski (1992).
2 Cited in ISKCON's official magazine *Back to Godhead* (1991), issues 1 and 2, in which a selection of women devotees express their views. These attitudes and practices were also confirmed in my own fieldwork. See Knott 1995 for an extended account of women in ISKCON.
3 A currently best-selling relationships book on both sides of the Atlantic, *The Rules* by Ellen Fein and Sherrie Schneider, blatantly advocates a systematic strategy of subterfuge and unattainability as the time-honoured way for a woman to catch her man and marry him.
4 Geoffrey Samuel discusses the possible influences of Tantra on Crowley and Wicca in his comparison of Paganism and Tibetan Buddhism (see following chapter).
5 Starhawk (1979: 208). For other accounts of Pagan sexuality and women's healing rituals see Plaskow and Christ (1989); Neitz (1990); Noble (1991); Shallcrass (1996b).
6 This trend has attracted media attention in national newspapers and magazines, for example 'Pagans of Suburbia' in *Elle* (February 1994), and articles on alternative weddings in the *Independent* (13 February 1995, 24 December 1995). Even *Hello!* magazine has featured a celebrity handfasting. Graham Harvey has written on handfastings (1996).
7 Qualls-Corbett (1988: 14), see also Deena Metzger in Zweig (1990); Noble (1991).
8 Letter written in 1978 by Mo (Moses Bag, leader of the Family) and cited in Melton (1994), who gives the fullest account of sexual practice in the Family.

9 Peter Rutter gives a psychological account and explanation of sexual abuse in his groundbreaking work *Sex in the Forbidden Zone*, interpreting it as 'an epidemic mainstream problem that reenacts in the professional relationship a wider cultural power-imbalance between men and women' (Rutter 1990: 2).

10 Janet Jacobs (1984) carried out extensive research on the abuse of women by male religious leaders and how these experiences led to 'deconversion'. Boucher (1988) gives a trenchant analysis of sexual abuse in Buddhist communities in a chapter entitled 'The Problem of the Male Teacher'. See also Butterfield (1992). My own book gives a more general overview of sexual abuse and the abuse of power throughout religion (Puttick 1997).

11 The most comprehensive presentation of androgyny from a psychological perspective is in two papers by Sandra Bem (1974, 1979).

CHAPTER 10

Paganism and Tibetan Buddhism: Contemporary Western Religions and the Question of Nature

GEOFFREY SAMUEL

– I INTRODUCTION –

The growth of paganism or neo-paganism[1] and of Tibetan Buddhism[2] are two of numerous religious responses within western societies to the contemporary world. Both seem to have something significant to say on the question of our relationship to 'nature', taking that term in a wide sense. Here I shall examine how Tibetan Buddhism and Paganism deal with this relationship to 'nature', both in the sense of our physical embodiment as part of nature and in the sense of our connection with our natural environment. I hope to use the contrasts between these traditions to clarify how each deals with this vital relationship.

It should be said to start with that there is no one 'Tibetan Buddhist' position on nature, and certainly no one 'Pagan' position. Tibetan Buddhism in its traditional Asian context was not consciously an environmentally aware religion, but it employed various ritual and symbolic resources to deal with the relation between human beings, nature and the environment. Some of these resources have been taken up by western Buddhists, others have been ignored, and new modes have developed as a self-consciously Buddhist environmentalism has grown up (cf. Harris 1995). There are many different Tibetan Buddhist groups and organisations within western societies today, most of them linked to one or another living or recently-dead Tibetan teacher (Samuel 1995a).[3]

Pagan groups are even more decentralised and variable than Tibetan Buddhist organisations. In this chapter, I shall be looking mainly at Wiccan and Wiccan-derived groups from both the UK and the USA. The British material is mostly from the Gardnerian and Alexandrian Wiccan traditions, including Gerald Gardner's own writings and those of Doreen Valiente,[4] those of Janet and Stewart Farrar, Vivianne Crowley and Prudence Jones.[5] The American material comes from Starhawk,[6] the Church of All Worlds (CAW),[7] and Circle Sanctuary.[8] These US groups are better described as Wiccan-influenced rather than Wiccan in any strict sense, but they share a central core of symbolic material with the Gardnerian and Alexandrian covens, including, for example, the idea of the ritual circle, the elemental associations of the four directions, and the cycle of eight Sabbats.[9]

– II SIMILARITIES AND CONTRASTS BETWEEN THE TWO TRADITIONS –

In the UK, the USA and similar societies, both Tibetan Buddhism and Paganism belong to the general context of 'new religious movements'. Both came to public notice and began to grow at around the same time, in the 1960s onwards. Today, Paganism and Tibetan Buddhism have roughly comparable numbers of followers, and comparably diffuse and decentralised organisational structures. There are also at least some indications of an overlap between memberships of the two religions.[10]

There are also, I think, relationships between these two religious traditions at a less superficial level, and here it is perhaps useful to say something about the specific character of Tibetan Buddhism as compared with other Buddhist traditions. Tibetan Buddhism in Asia has in common with other Buddhist traditions a central ideological orientation towards the attainment of Buddhahood. Buddhahood, *bodhi* in Sanskrit, usually translated as 'Enlightenment' in English, is a radical transformation of our ordinary lives which, though described in many ways and in any case by definition incommunicable in words, involves a withdrawal from ordinary attachments to the world. Tibetan Buddhism also shares with other Buddhist traditions a deep concern with questions of death, mortality and the radical unsatisfactoriness of everyday life in the world. I shall return to these points later.

However, Tibetan Buddhism differs from other Buddhist traditions in its much more direct involvement in rituals and practices aimed at this-worldly ends. These practices, as in most parts of Asia, are conceived of in terms of relationships with the local deities and the spirits of the environment.[11] In other Buddhist societies in south and south-east Asia they are performed for the most part by lay people, and by priests and religious practitioners who are explicitly not Buddhist (cf. Spiro 1967 for Burma, Tambiah 1970 for north-east Thailand). In Tibet, while lay people do carry out regular rituals to local deities, much of the on going business of dealing with these forces is carried out by lamas, monks and other specifically Buddhist practitioners, using the ritual techniques of Vajrayāna Buddhism (Samuel 1993).

This brings us to the subject of Vajrayāna Buddhism, or Buddhist Tantra, which is an important component of Tibetan Buddhist practice. Vajrayāna or Tantric Buddhism had its origin in India, where it seems to have been practised, at any rate in its earlier period, say the fourth to eighth centuries CE, by small initiatory cult groups. The central ritual of these groups was the *gaṇacakra*, a night-time sacramental circle, usually outdoors, often in a cremation ground or similarly spooky and 'powerful' location, with distinctly antinomian elements. These included the ritual use of sexuality, although it is not clear how far this was performed literally and how far symbolically. The *gaṇacakra* involved possession, dancing and singing, and also magical procedures. It was seen as an occasion to enter a non-ordinary state of consciousness.[12] Similar rituals, called by a related term (*cakra pūja*) were performed by Śaiva and Śākta Tantric practitioners, in other words followers of various forms of the Hindu deity Śiva and his consort the Great Goddess, known variously as Durgā or Kālī and under other names (Bharati 1965; Gupta *et al.* 1979; Sanderson 1988).

The similarity between these ancient Indian 'circle' rituals and the modern Wiccan circle is striking. Wiccans too meet at night in a ritual circle, invoke a kind of possession by the God and Goddess, dance and perform spells for magical purposes, and make ritual use of sexuality, although again this is generally symbolic in the context of the coven meeting. The circle too is an occasion for a non-ordinary state of consciousness. The similarities, which were noted many years ago by the Wiccan writer Doreen Valiente, one of the founders of modern witchcraft (Valiente 1978: 136–41), are surely not coincidental.

In part, no doubt, they arise because both kinds of group are or were acting out a widespread human stereotype. The idea of witches who meet at night to carry out illicit magical rituals is found in an extremely wide range of cultures. In both cases, Indian Tantra and Wicca, the fantasy has been inverted. The participants are not working evil magic but transcending the limitations of ordinary human behaviour for the good of the community as a whole.[13] In addition, Wicca developed in a context where Indian Tantra was known; the books of Arthur Avalon (Sir John Woodroffe) introduced the English-speaking public to Hindu Tantra at the beginning of this century, and were popular in occult and esoteric circles (e.g. Avalon 1952, 1956). Direct borrowings are not impossible, and indirect influence is virtually certain through intermediary figures such as Alastair Crowley, who had visited India and was influenced by Hindu Tantra in his own writings.[14] Wicca, however, presents itself as a revival of ancient western tradition, not as a borrowing from the East.[15]

Whatever the historical connections, Wicca today is in some respects a modern recreation of something rather like the Indian precursors of Tibetan Buddhism. Both modern Wicca and ancient Indian Tantra were based on initiatory cult groups; both placed a strong emphasis on ecstatic and trance states; both had small group rituals where participants undertook behaviour that was unconventional and disapproved of in the wider society. In both cases, too, this rejection of and by the wider social context seems to be at least part of the point of the exercise. People are not on the whole attracted to Wicca out of a desire to be good conformist members of society, nor, one imagines, were they attracted to Indian Tantra for that reason.

At the same time, it is possible to see these elements within Wicca as incidental and historically contingent, and to see Wicca as developing over time into, as it were, simply another mainstream religion; less patriarchal and more life-affirming, perhaps, than conventional Christianity, but not essentially different. Paganism, after all, in the sense of Classical Paganism, was once a perfectly respectable, state-endorsed religion, and could be again. Paganism could be as respectable a religious choice as Presbyterianism, within a society little changed in other respects. Yet Paganism today is still some way from a mainstream religion, even by comparison with Buddhism. Part of the attraction of Paganism remains its rejection of conventional social norms and attitudes, and much of US Paganism in particular is associated with radical social criticism of one kind or another. Thus Starhawk's recent novel, *The Fifth Sacred Thing*, the most sustained attempt I know of to imagine a society where Wicca has become the dominant religious tradition, envisions a society which has been radically remade in a decentralised, ecologically balanced and egalitarian mode (Starhawk 1993).

Tibetan Buddhism became a mainstream religion, of a kind, long ago. Tantric practices initially arrived in Tibet in the seventh and eighth centuries. Over the following twelve hundred years they were gradually normalised and regularised, though unlike in most other Buddhist societies, they were never eliminated from the 'official' practice of Buddhism.[16] Tibetan society was in certain ways made over on a Buddhist model, but Vajrayāna Buddhism was in the process itself radically reshaped, initially into a set of magical techniques employed by hereditary village shamans, and later into more clerical and monastic forms (Samuel 1993, 1995b). The lineages of initiation into Tantric practice continued, and today they can still be traced back to the Tantric masters of ancient India, but the present context of Tantric performance is different from that which seems to have been the case in India. Much though certainly not all Tantric practice is done by monks and nuns committed to vows of celibacy. Tantric initiations or empowerments (abhiṣeka) in Tibet are often large-scale occasions, but many of those attending are there primarily for the associated 'blessings' (byin rlabs). In fact, serious Tantric practice is generally seen as appropriate for a small minority only. The ancient Indian gaṇacakra, the circle ritual I discussed before, is far in the past.[17] In Tibetan practice it has long been replaced by the gaṇapūja (Tibetan tshogs), a considerably tamer affair, still involving a sacramental meal but normally performed indoors and without possession or dancing.[18]

The Tibetan Buddhism that came to the west was the end-result of these processes, and as I have already said it is quite varied in its forms, with a general continuum stretching between what I have elsewhere labelled the 'shamanic' and 'clerical' extremes (Samuel 1993). While Wiccan initiation is generally linked to becoming a member of an active coven, Tantric empowerments in the west do not necessarily define tightly bound initiatory cult-groups. Initiations are into one or another Tantric cycle with its associated ritual practices, and involve being introduced to the specific deities of that cycle. There are hundreds of different Tantric cycles, however, and many thousands of empowerment rituals. In fact, it is not unusual for western Buddhists to collect multiple empowerments from several lamas without necessarily becoming deeply involved in doing any of the related practices, although any on going practice group will have a series of core practices which members perform regularly.

The tshogs ritual remains important within many western groups, where it serves its classic function of periodic reaffirmation of the unity of the community of practitioners, but the ecstatic elements are played down, and many of those who perform it are probably unaware of its relationship to the ancient Indian Tantric gaṇacakra.[19]

On the whole, while westerners involved in Tibetan Buddhism may initially be attracted by the dramatic imagery of the Vajrayāna, including the famous yab yum deities in sexual embrace, they soon find themselves in a context in which the magical, ecstatic and antinomian elements of Tantra have been drastically down-played and marginalised. These elements are emphatically not a central part of how Tibetan Buddhism presents itself to its western followers.[20] Vajrayāna Buddhism, from the beginning, and in contrast to Hindu Tantra, took place within the context of Mahāyāna Buddhism, with its strong emphasis on altruistic motivation (Samuel

1989). All Tibetan Buddhist practice is explicitly oriented towards the practitioner's achievement of enlightenment in order to free all living beings from their suffering, even when a ritual has an immediate this-worldly purpose such as healing or protection. This altruistic motivation (*bodhicitta*) is the normative orientation of all rituals and all forms of meditation, and it sets a rather different tone from the basic Wiccan ethical formulation, 'An it harm none, do what ye will.'

The rather complex relationship between Wicca and Tibetan Tantra could perhaps be put in another way; both religions have historically been involved in a move towards greater respectability and wider social recognition, and this move has involved various degrees of tidying up and normalising in each case. For Tibetan Buddhism, however, all this happened long ago in the Tibetan case, while it is only in its early stages for Wicca. It is true, of course, that while the Vajrayāna attained respectability in Tibet, being a Vajrayāna Buddhist is a less normal religious commitment within western society. Becoming a Buddhist is nevertheless a slightly different undertaking to becoming a witch.

That is most of what I want to say by way of general comparison, since I want to move on to look at attitudes to nature in a number of key areas. One final issue, though, needs mentioning, since it relates to much of what follows, and that is the question of gender and patriarchy. Much of the appeal of Wicca is its emphasis on the primary role of the Goddess. Many cultures, Tibet included, associated the earth, nature and the biological aspects of life with the feminine (cf. Volkmann 1995; Samuel 1994), and valued them less highly than predominantly male-associated religious practices. While the Buddhist tradition on the whole had a less negative attitude to women than many others, the ambivalence of Buddhism to women is well known (Sponberg 1992; Keyes 1984; Kirsch 1985). The rejection of nature, and the assertion of power over nature, is thus often linked to the subjection of women.

Tantra in general, and Vajrayāna in particular, can be seen as a partial reintegration of those aspects which had been dismissed by male-centred religious traditions, but the extent to which Tantric traditions in practice have managed to avoid recreating the patriarchal order is very much open to question. In India and Tibet, Tantra at least in theory allowed women new and significant roles within what had been male-dominated religions, both as female partners in Tantric practice and as autonomous female Tantric practitioners. In practice, women often became little more than accessories to men's quest for magical power or transcendence.[21] The issue of gender remains a critical one in the comparison between Wicca and Tibetan Buddhism, although a full treatment of it would require much more space than I have here.

– III ATTITUDES TO PHYSICAL EMBODIMENT: LOVE, PLEASURE AND ECSTASY –

I move on now to look explicitly at attitudes to nature within the two religions. I start off with attitudes to everyday life and our physical embodiment, because I think these underlie much that follows. I say 'physical' (or organic) 'embodiment' rather than simply 'body', since most Wiccans, like Vajrayāna Buddhists, see mind, body and spirit as a unity.[22]

Gerald Gardner was clear from the outset that Wicca was a life-affirming, ecstatic religion. The Charge of the Goddess, perhaps the most widely known of all Wiccan texts, declares that 'all acts of love and pleasure are my rituals' (Kelly 1991: 53; Farrar and Farrar 1989: 43). Already in his first publication on witchcraft, the 1949 novel *High Magic's Aid*, set in England in the early thirteenth century, Gardner has one of his characters declare that 'Witchcraft is . . . a rival religion to Christianity, a religion of love, pleasure and excitement. Therefore does the Church suppress it' (Gardner 1994: 19). This life-affirming orientation seems to have its background in Gardner's own connections with naturism and other radical and alternative currents in the 1930s and 1940s (see Wilson and Medway 1995), and also in the Murrayite view of witchcraft as a survival of pagan fertility cults (see e.g. Hutton 1996b). Whatever its origins, it was built organically into Gardner's basic Wiccan rituals, and these set the direction in which Wicca has continued to develop.

Almost thirty years after *High Magic's Aid*, Starhawk explicitly counterposed witchcraft and Buddhism in *The Spiral Dance*, one of the classic texts of the Pagan revival:

> Witchcraft does not maintain, like the First Truth of Buddhism, that 'All life is suffering' . . .
> Suffering certainly exists in life – it is a part of learning. But escape from the Wheel of Birth
> and Death is not the optimal cure, any more than hara-kiri is the best cure for menstrual
> cramps. When suffering is the result of the social order or human injustice, the Craft
> encourages active work to relieve it. Where suffering is a natural part of the cycle of birth and
> decay, it is relieved by understanding and acceptance, by a willing giving-over to both the
> dark and light in turn. (Starhawk [1979] 1989: 41–2)

This marks out a straightforward contrast: Wicca is life-affirming, Buddhism is life-denying. In fact, matters are a little more complex than this on both sides. Paganism, and witchcraft in particular, in practice devotes a perhaps surprising amount of attention to darkness and to death. This is hinted at in Starhawk's comments on the 'natural cycle of birth and decay'.[23] Buddhism, too, can be less negative than the stereotype suggests. The Four Noble Truths and the idea of escape from *saṃsāra*, from the Wheel of Birth and Death, are certainly not the only things that Buddhism in its more developed forms has to say on the matter of suffering and the meaning of life.

It is nevertheless true that Buddhism is not primarily a path of the affirmation of 'all acts of love and pleasure' for its Tibetan followers, nor is it for its modern western practitioners. Though blissful states may be a by-product of the Buddhist path, they are an accidental by-product, and attachment to them is definitely to be avoided. Buddhism was and is a path to enlightenment, and enlightenment has a complex and in many ways negative relationship to the everyday world. Attachment to *saṃsāra*, the everyday world, symbolised in particular by the family, marriage and children, is to be rejected and avoided. Tibetan Buddhism allows rather more room for lay householders to be active Buddhist practitioners than is offered by other traditions of Buddhism, where the primary involvement of lay people was traditionally to provide material support for the monastic community. However, the ideal remains that of the lama, the monk or nun, the lay yogi or yogini who withdraws radically from involvement within the world or at least from attachment to it.

The influence of celibate monasticism within Buddhism is perhaps particularly noticeable if we look at attitudes to the body itself (e.g. Sponberg 1992). Here Buddhism is ambivalent, whereas Wicca tends to be celebratory. For the early Buddhist schools, meditations on the repulsive characteristics of the body were standard techniques for reducing attachment. Since the meditator was generally assumed to be male, the stress is specifically on rejecting attachment to the female body, although the idea is certainly applicable in reverse to the minority of meditators who were female. This was part of a general ethos of rejection of everyday life.

For the Vajrayāna, the stress is on transformation rather than rejection of attachment. In Tantric practice, the 'body' (along with 'speech' and 'mind', the other components of the Tantric trinity) can be transformed into the body, speech and mind of a Tantric deity. Yet the point of this transformative meditation is really to access the enlightened qualities of the Tantric deity rather than to learn to see our ordinary human bodies in a positive light.[24]

The modern Pagan tradition has always taken a more positive orientation to the body, which is perhaps hardly surprising for a tradition where rituals are often performed 'sky-clad'. The body and its natural functions, above all those of sexuality, are given spiritual value and celebrated. Here again this is made explicit in the central rituals of Gardnerian Wicca, such as the wording of the Fivefold Kiss in Drawing Down the Moon.[25] How this works out in terms of more general attitudes to embodiment differs between Pagan groups, with some of the Americans perhaps tending furthest to the celebratory end. Thus Vivianne Crowley in *Wicca: The Old Religion in the New Age* says:

> Like other religions, Wicca accepts that there is a non-material as well as a material reality, but it does not believe the non-material is superior to the material and it does not seek to deny the material world or the stages of existence between the physical and the divine. Matter is not regarded with horror and the emphasis is on the joy of the flesh rather than the ascetic's view of flesh as sin. This is not to say that Wicca is hedonistic, but rather that we are followers of a middle way. Our time in physical incarnation is a gift from the Gods which is to be enjoyed and we should appreciate the joys of sensory experience of the world around us. However, we must also seek the spiritual growth which expands our consciousness and allows us to live on levels beyond the physical. (Crowley 1989: 13–14)

This is, as the perhaps Buddhist-inspired reference to a 'middle way' suggests, at the moderate end of the spectrum. For a more extreme view, we might look at an essay by Moonstorm (Harlan White) of the Church of All Worlds. White sees sacred sexuality as one of the six major principles of the church (the others are pantheism, polytheism, nature worship, seasonal ritual and neo-tribalism) and writes that:

> [a]ntithetically to most Christian churches, in which the physical body and its pleasures are viewed at worst as diabolical and at best as unworthy, CAW celebrates the body as a divine

vehicle through whose pleasures God/dess itself experiences joy . . . CAW encourages the classic Wiccan practices of ritual nudity and sexual activity as a celebration of the divine as well as to encourage acceptance of the body as something natural and beautiful rather than shameful. One author has described a key goal of Paganism as being to achieve 'an erotic relationship with life' – a rich, sensuous, playful enthusiasm for all of existence. (White n.d.)

There is another side to the Pagan orientation towards physical embodiment, and that is the question of healing. Healing is important in modern Paganism, and much Wiccan and other Pagan ritual is about healing. Many Pagans are practitioners of other healing or healing-related techniques such as massage, counselling or aromatherapy. So, in fact, are quite a few Buddhists. There is a close relationship between the traditional Tibetan medical system and Buddhism, and some Tibetan Buddhist teachers (e.g. Akong Rinpoche, Sogyal Rinpoche, Tarthang Rinpoche) have been involved in healing and medical work in the west. Empowerments for health and long life practices are frequently given, often with the justification that good health and long life are a necessary basis for the attainment of enlightenment.

This brings us back to a more general point I have already made. Tibetan Buddhist philosophy, along with much Buddhist meditative practice, is premised on the transformation of everyday life, but much Buddhist practice is directed towards this-worldly ends. Buddhism in Tibet survived because it found ways of meeting the needs of a population most of whom were oriented more towards ordinary life than the ultimate goal of enlightenment.

Buddhism in the west is in a less clear-cut position. Western Buddhists tend to be more oriented towards the ultimate goal of enlightenment than are most Tibetans, at least in terms of conscious motivation, or they would scarcely have turned to Buddhism rather than other religious or secular options. Yet they too are concerned with health and this-worldly goals, and share many of the general counter-cultural and alternative interests of Wiccan practitioners.

In practice, some Tibetan techniques for achieving this-worldly goals have been relatively widely accepted, while others are less available or less easy to integrate into the western perspective. Thus there has been a wide interest in the traditional Tibetan medical system, a herbal-humoral system with historical connections to Greek medicine, Arabic medicine and Ayurveda, but considerably less interest in, for example, Tibetan astrology, Tibetan divination methods, or the local deity rituals.

– IV THE ENVIRONMENT –

Some of these complexities and ambivalences recur in connection with relationships with the natural environment. As I mentioned above, in most Buddhist countries, everyday life is the preserve of a parallel religion to Buddhism – pagan, polytheistic, and focused on deities and spirits whose responsibility is for this-worldly success and misfortune. People in Thailand or Burma are not either Buddhists or spirit-worshippers. They are, for the most part, both, and turn to whichever religion is appropriate for the situation they find themselves in. Spirit-worship, for the most part, deals with this life and its problems, while Buddhism deals with death and future lives.

Matters were handled rather differently in Tibet, in part because Buddhism in Tibet was less an official, state-endorsed ideology than a religious tradition which developed organically within the life of a largely decentralised agricultural and nomadic society. In practice, the majority of Tibetans continued to live lives within the secular world, and Tibetan Buddhist practitioners were constantly involved in ritual action to affect things in this world. Deities were and are regularly being evoked for this-worldly ends, whether healing, prosperity, or defence against malevolent spirits, on behalf of the individual practitioner, the community of practitioners, or the village community as a whole (Samuel 1993). These rituals derive in form if not in detail from the Vajrayāna Buddhist rituals of India, and many of them involve transactions of various kinds with gods and spirits. They are a central part of Buddhist practice in Tibetan societies.

Most significant here are rituals addressed to the various regional and local deities (*yul lha, sa bdag* etc.), which are generally associated with prominent geographical features such as mountains, lakes and rivers. The entire landscape of Tibet is pervaded by associations with local deities and spirits. The most important of these are specific, named gods and goddesses, personified in ritual texts and represented in religious art. They are held to have been bound to the service of the Dharma through the activity of Padmasambhava or other great sages of the past. They can be helpful to human beings, and are given regular incense-offerings by lay people in domestic and village ritual, but they can easily be provoked by accident or neglect and cause illness or misfortune. In specifically Buddhist ritual they may be invited and given offerings, but they are treated as very much inferior to the Buddhist Tantric deities and Guardians, and they can be threatened with magical punishment if they do not co-operate. In ritual, the Tantric deities and the Guardians are regularly invoked in order to keep the local deities, and through them the lesser spirits, in order.

Tibetan practice, in other words, is directed towards making sure that local deities and spirits behave positively toward the Tibetans, that, for example, they do not cause illness or misfortune, that they do not cause inappropriate weather conditions or other problems in what is in any case often a difficult and threatening environment. While Tibetan lay people may make offerings to local deities to try to ensure their favour, Tibetan Tantric practitioners invoke the more powerful deities of Tantric Buddhism to compel the obedience of the local gods and spirits.[26] A key metaphor here is that of taming (*'dul ba* in Tibetan), a word that is used in a variety of contexts: the binding of the local deities by the eighth-century Tantric culture-hero Padmasambhava and other great lamas so that they are obedient and subservient to the Buddhist teachings; the training of monks by obedience to the monastic discipline; the training of disciples through the Buddhist teachings; the bringing of wild land under cultivation.

In the western contexts, the Tantric Buddhist deities, *yi dam* and *chos skyong*, are regularly invoked in practice sessions by western students, but there is little attention given to the question of the local gods and spirits. One could imagine this changing, since the Tibetan lamas themselves deal with the western environment in terms of local gods,[27] and a few lamas teach practices relating to them to their students.[28] However, it is difficult to imagine a major shift away from an approach based on taming and control.

On the Pagan side, while relations with local spirits and deities certainly formed a significant part of pre-Christian Pagan traditions throughout Europe, they are of limited significance in Gardnerian or Alexandrian Wicca. Covens vary in the specific names by which they invoke the Goddess and God, but as far as I know specifically local gods are rarely if ever invoked as the primary identity of the deity. Thus Gardner's Charge of the Goddess begins 'Listen to the words of the Great Mother, who of old was also called among men Artemis, Astarte, Dione, Melusine, Aphrodite, Cerridwen, Diana, Arianrhod, Bride, and by many other names' (Kelly 1991: 53). Some of these names were perhaps not Goddess-names originally, but none refers specifically to deities of a particular locality.[29]

However, in the wider context of the western 'earth mysteries', contact with local deities and spirits is often actively pursued, and the idea of practising at 'powerful' places such as stone circles and other old sacred sites has grown up, contributing towards a general sensitising towards the natural environment as having significance and power apart from its direct utility to human beings. In some North American Wiccan-derived traditions, ideas of contact with local spirits, often seen as elves, fairies or devas,[30] are quite extensively developed. These spirits are often associated with specific plant or animal species as well as with specific locations.[31] The relationship is phrased in terms of co-operation and learning, and never of control.[32]

More generally, Wicca has been associated all along with a positive attitude towards the natural environment. In a recent interview with Doreen Valiente, she was asked what Wicca meant to her when she first encountered it. She commented that:

> It meant the world of nature. At that time, you must realise, all the feeling for ecology which we have today was practically non-existent. I'm talking about the days when the invention of DDT was hailed as a great British triumph . . . The countryside was being destroyed at a great rate. People who opposed this sort of thing were still regarded as cranks. People who cared about preserving the forest for preserving animals, or anything like that, they were thought to be just out of touch with the modern world. (Valiente 1995: 21)

Asked if that was the ethos in Gardner's coven, she replied: 'The ethos of ecology and caring about natural things like the forest[,] of nature and the seasons: that was there in the coven. Yes, it was' (Valiente 1995: 22). Valiente's comments are less surprising in the light of recent suggestions of connections between Gardner's coven and groups such as the Woodcraft Folk and the Order of Woodcraft Chivalry.[33] Here too we can look at Gardner's basic Wiccan rituals, not only the Charge, in which the Goddess describes herself, significantly, as the 'beauty of the green earth', but the cycle of seasonal rituals.

The cycle of eight seasonal rituals or Sabbats, taking place at the solstices, the equinoxes and the four quarter days, was one of Gardner's masterstrokes, apparently derived from or worked out in conjunction with his friend the Druid author Ross Nichols.[34] Directions for the eight rituals are given in Gardner's *Book of Shadows*, although not in great detail (Kelly 1991: 67–70, 116–19). They have been elaborated variously by subsequent authors, most notably by Janet and Stewart Farrar in their *Eight Sabbats for Witches* (Farrar and Farrar 1989). The Farrars wove the rituals into an annual cycle based on the myth of the dying and reborn God, an idea which has been taken up by subsequent writers.[35] As an example, I quote from Rae Beth:

> Each of the eight Sabbats in the year celebrates a phase in the relationship between the Goddess and the Horned God, Mother/Father Nature, according to season. [At Imbolc] it is early spring. The very first of fresh new growth is just beginning. The Goddess is young again, virgin, and the God, reborn at the winter solstice, now appears as a young man. Their love promises all fulfilment, growth and fertility. (Beth 1992: 20)

For the anthropologist, there is something curiously self-conscious about the Wiccan ritual cycle. Rituals in traditional cultures are rarely so transparent in their meaning, so obviously constructed along with their interpretation. Yet there is no doubt that they have been enormously successful, and they have been generally adopted within the wider Pagan community.[36] Along with the lunar cycle of Esbats, less important ritual meetings celebrated ideally at the time of the full moon, they translate the Wiccan perspective on life into a meaningful construction of the passing of time (Wales 1996). In particular, this is because of the way they tie in to the annual cycle of the seasons, in a society where people feel increasingly divorced from nature. They also provide occasions, as in the Janet and Stewart Farrar rituals, for incorporating all kinds of traditional material into Wiccan ritual, since most of the Sabbats[37] correspond to dates of traditional festivals in various parts of the British Isles (Hutton 1996c).

– V Environmental ethics and being part of Gaia –

I now move on to the more general question of environmental ethics. Earlier I cited Starhawk's contrast between Wicca as life-affirming and Buddhism as life-denying. Certainly Buddhism, in the west, has a much more ambivalent relationship towards this life and this world. This has consequences when it comes to the question of attitudes to nature. It is possible, and consistent with at least one aspect of the Buddhist tradition, for a Buddhist to say that any attempt to deal with environmental issues or any other this-worldly problem is a superficial distraction from the real job of attaining enlightenment. In practice, few modern Buddhist teachers or writers have taken so extreme a position in public, though Ian Harris cites the Japanese writer Noriaki Hakayama as one example (Harris 1995: 176 and n. 18).

In many ways, despite Hakayama, Buddhism provides a natural basis for an ethic of interconnectedness and mutual responsibility. Buddhism after all was throughout its history the doctrine that denied the self, that was centrally concerned with counter-ing and eliminating our ordinary perceptions of ourselves as separate, independent and autonomous, and replacing them with a view of mutual interdependence. This is constantly reaffirmed in rituals; Tibetan Buddhist rituals are performed for the benefit of all sentient beings.

Yet there are problems here. 'Sentient beings' are human beings, animals, gods and demi-gods, hungry ghosts and hell-beings. Trees, plants and the vegetable world are not included, and there is little doubt that they are seen for the most part in terms of their utility to sentient beings – in practice, to human beings.[38] As we saw in relation to the local deity rituals, Tibetan Buddhism in its native Himalayan context is quite explicitly concerned with controlling nature for the good of human beings. One maintains good relations with the environment, but for the sake of human beings, not for the sake of the environment. This goes back, at least in part, to the ambivalent conceptualisation in some Tibetan myths and legends of the earth as a goddess or demoness who has to be held in place and controlled (Samuel 1993: 168, 222).

Harris suggests that it is difficult to ground a radical environmentalist conscious-ness – as opposed to compassion for other living beings – coherently in Buddhist philosophy. The most plausible lines of argument, which derive from the idea of the Buddha-nature (tathāgatagarbha) within all beings and all phenomena, or from the related idea of the mutual interpenetration of all phenomena found in the Ava-taṃsaka Sutra, would seem to imply as much tolerance towards pollution, nuclear weapons and destructive viruses as towards trees, animals and human beings (Harris 1995: 176–7). This is a problem not only for Buddhist environmentalists, but for all environmental ethics based on universal tolerance: the influential 'deep ecology' tradition runs into similar difficulties.

Nevertheless, many Buddhist authorities in recent years have made statements in favour of a positive environmental ethics, and Buddhists in the west and in Asia have been involved in environmentalist activism. Yet it seems to me unlikely that many people have become environmental activists because they are Buddhists. It is more plausible that in some cases people have become Buddhists because, in part, they are environmental activists. Buddhism is rightly viewed as a tradition which enjoins non-violence and harmlessness in our relations to other living beings, and which stresses our interconnectedness, and while these themes do not by themselves amount to an environmentalist position, they are compatible with one.

Here, it seems to me, Paganism is in a stronger position, both because of its much more consistently life-affirming stance, and because of its much more personalised conception of the earth as Goddess. Gaia, after all, has some say in the matter. She may choose to prefer peace to war, trees to viruses. In the remaining sections of the chapter I want to look at the question of environmental activism and of the personification of nature in contemporary Paganism.

The modern ecological concept of Gaia is usually traced back to the work of the British biochemist James Lovelock, in the mid to late 1970s, but it apparently developed independently in the USA, where Tim Zell (now Oberon Zell), the founder of the Church of All Worlds, 'had a vision of the unity of the Earth's planetary biosphere as a single organism on the evening of September 6, 1970' (Melton et al. 1990: 183). In an article in the CAW journal Green Egg the following year he referred to it as Terrabia, a name which perhaps fortunately was soon forgotten. To quote the *New Age Encyclopedia*, 'his message was not widely received outside the Neo-Pagan community . . . due to the limited circulation of his writings' (Melton *et al.* 1990: 183).[39]

In more recent years, the CAW has become strongly committed to the concept of Gaia. To quote a recent CAW statement:

> The Church of All Worlds is an organisation of individuals who regard the Earth and life on it as sacred. Living in harmony and understanding with life's myriad forms is a religious act. While we prescribe no particular dogma or creed, our commonality lies in our reverence and connection with Nature and with Mother Earth, seeing her as a conscious living entity. We are not only her children, but evolving cells in Her vast, organic body. (Church of All Worlds 1995)

Perhaps the most fully developed basis for ecological activism can be found in the works of the Californian writer Starhawk, whom I have referred to several times already. Starhawk and the Wiccan-derived groups she has worked with participated in a series of non-violent actions against nuclear power and nuclear weapons in the early 1980s. These were clearly formative experiences for her; they are referred to at length in her books *Dreaming the Dark* (1990a: xxix–xxx, 43, 95ff., 112, 119ff., 151ff.) and *Truth or Dare* (1990b: 151–3), along with her later experiences with the Greenham Common Peace Camp (e.g. 1990b: 248–52).

I do not have space to discuss this material at length here. One of its most striking features for me is the way in which Starhawk develops the theme of anti-structural power within witchcraft: the ability to set limits to authority, to say and do what the censor (external or internal) forbids, to create non-authoritarian social structures. The decentralised affinity-group structure of the anti-nuclear campaigns, developed initially at the 1977 Seabrook action, and the theme of non-violent direct action associated with the campaigns against nuclear weapons and nuclear power, seem to underlie much of her work in this area. Starhawk has also clearly been influenced by the growing ecofeminist movement witnessed in books such as Carolyn Merchant's *The Death of Nature* (Merchant 1980). Starhawk's second and third books, *Dreaming the Dark* and *Truth or Dare*, are both deeply political, and thoroughly committed to a transformation of American society in the direction of ecologically sustainable modes of living and of radical equality across boundaries of gender and race.

Starhawk's style of witchcraft is often, correctly, described as feminist, but I think it is important to note that it is also anti-racist, environmentalist and generally aligned with a radical critique of contemporary western society. As I mentioned earlier, her novel, *The Fifth Sacred Thing*, provides a visionary picture of what a transformed future society might look like, and how it might deal non-violently with the opposition it would undoubtedly encounter (1993).

It is difficult to know the scale on which ideas like Starhawk's are spreading, but the combination of Wiccan-derived ritual, anti-hierarchical politics, ecofeminism and environmental protest clearly makes an attractive mix. In Britain, there are signs of similar modes of Pagan-inspired environmentalist protest in the 1990s, in the series of campaigns against the Criminal Justice Act and against road-clearance schemes at Twyford Down, Newbury and elsewhere (McKay 1996: 138–9). Even the relatively staid and conservative Pagan Federation now organises annual rituals for Earth Healing Day, and organisations such as the Dragon Environmental Network have become an accepted and significant part of the Pagan scene.

I do not want to imply that this is the only way that Paganism can develop an adequate response to the environmental, social and political crisis the planet is facing. There are, I think, many kinds of activity that can contribute towards a more positive outcome. However, I think it is worth pointing to the potential within contemporary Paganism to generate and facilitate this kind of radical environmental and social activism.

– VI Conclusion –

For my conclusion, I return to the comparison between Paganism and Tibetan Buddhism. To what extent might either or both of these traditions provide a basis for an appropriate contemporary understanding of our relationship to nature and our biological embodiment?

It is difficult – at least for anyone who has a certain cynicism towards and distrust of authorities and their usually self-interested strategies – not to sympathise with the Pagan and Wiccan approach. Pagans assert and sacralise the joy of living. If a real transformation towards ecological consciousness is to take place, it will need that joy and sense of sacredness to motivate and sustain it. Paganism is well adapted to energise and orient such protests; the Goddess who is 'the beauty of the green earth' is an ideal symbol for the planet we need to protect and preserve, because without it we ourselves cannot survive.

The question of whether our relation to the local environment should be seen in terms of co-existence or control is a complex one, and not only for Pagans. Communing with nature on an equal basis is intuitively attractive, but I wonder if it ever will or should be the totality of our relationship to our environment. Perhaps it is more appropriate, and more realistic, to recognise that there may always have to be elements of control as well as harmony. As Monica Sjöö has pointed out, the emphasis on harmony, sweetness and light at places such as Findhorn can have a very dark underside (Sjöö 1992).

On the more general question of our physical embodiment, it is difficult not to feel that both Buddhists and Pagans have a point. 'Life is joy, celebrate it' and 'Life is suffering, overcome it' are not such polar opposites as they may at first appear. In a way, they are two sides of the same coin. Buddhism may not sell itself as a path to ecstasy, but its final goal is also, in its way, celebratory. Yet the Buddhist solution undoubtedly appeals at different times and in different situations to the Pagan solution. At times when our physical embodiment breaks down through ageing or illness, or when we are forced to live in an environment which has also radically broken down and deteriorated, Buddhism has the language and resources to respond. In all Buddhist countries, death and rebirth are the specialities of Buddhism, and there is no doubt that Buddhism has developed deep and meaningful responses to the darker sides of the human condition.

I am not suggesting that Wicca and other forms of Paganism are not capable of responding themselves to such situations. Wicca has from its earliest stages approached these realms too, through the rituals of Samhain, the various crone aspects of the Goddess, and the degrees of initiation. Wicca remains after all an esoteric cult, and its initiates are priestesses and priests of the Mysteries. As with the Buddhists, this involves, sooner or later, a confrontation with death and the dark. We can I think see distinct signs in recent Wiccan and Pagan writing of attempts to develop a theology and an approach to life that can cope with the times when a simple assertion of love, pleasure and ecstasy is no longer enough.[40]

Yet it seems that it is in these areas that western Paganism is most likely to turn to Buddhism and other Asian traditions for inspiration. Perhaps a natural complementarity may develop between Buddhism and Paganism in the west, as it has done in Asia where, as I pointed out, Buddhism is almost always associated with a life-affirming, lay-centred 'pagan' religion. Tibetan Buddhism in Tibet incorporated much of this kind of religious attitude within itself, but so far little of this aspect of Buddhism has been transferred to the West. Wicca and the other forms of western Paganism point, perhaps, towards a developing western version of a life-affirming, lay-centred religion, while Buddhism in the West as in Asia continues to sound a deeper counterpoint, pointing to the ground on which we encounter life's tragedies and integrate them into our total experience. Perhaps we need to bring their insights together.

– NOTES –

1 Both terms have been widely used, but members of these groups in the UK on the whole prefer 'Pagan' to 'Neo-Pagan' and I follow their usage here.

2 Tibetan Buddhism is of course only one of the forms of Buddhism which has come to the west. My discussion here is restricted to it, since many of the issues dealt with here are approached differently in other Buddhist traditions.

3 Thus in the UK major groups include the Samye Ling network, directed by Akong Rinpoche; the FPMT, founded by the late Lama Thubten Yeshe and his student Thubten Zopa Rinpoche; the New Kadampa, headed by Geshe Kalsang Gyatso; the Dechen network, directed by the British lama Ngakpa Jampa Thaye (David Stott), himself a student of the Tibetan lama Karma Thinley Rinpoche; Rigpa, directed by Sogyal Rinpoche; the Dzogchen Community, directed by Namkhai Norbu Rinpoche; the network directed by the British lama Ngakpa Chögyam; etc. Some of these are based in the UK, others are local branches of international networks.

4 For Gerald Gardner (1884–1964) and Doreen Valiente see e.g. Valiente (1989), Kelly (1991). A general survey of the history of modern Wicca in England is given by Julia Phillips (1991).

5 Janet and Stewart Farrar (Farrar and Farrar 1984, 1989); Vivianne Crowley (Crowley 1989, 1990, 1994); Prudence Jones (Jones 1992). See Phillips (1991).

6 Author of *The Spiral Dance* (Starhawk 1989), *Dreaming the Dark* (1990), *Truth or Dare*

(1990b) and *The Fifth Sacred Thing* (1993). Starhawk's early training was with Sara Cunningham and with Victor Anderson, teacher of the 'Faerie tradition' of Witchcraft. She became a major figure in the US Pagan scene from the early 1980s onwards. See Melton *et al.* 1990: 432–3).

7 The Church of All Worlds was founded in 1967 by Tim Zell (a.k.a. Otter G'Zell, Oberon Zell); see Adler (1986: 283–318, Melton (1992: 780–2).

8 Circle Sanctuary (under its earlier name, Circle Farm) is discussed in Melton (1992: 782–3 and Orion (1995). It was originally founded by Selena Fox and Jim Alan in 1975, and is now directed by Selena Fox and her husband, Dennis Carpenter.

9 Other significant influences on Starhawk and the CAW include Victor Anderson, whose Faerie or Feri tradition incorporates Hawaiian Kahuna and 'shamanic' practices, and in the case of the CAW, Robert Heinlein's cult novel *Stranger in a Strange Land*. For Anderson see Adler (1986: 78ff. Anderson (1994).

10 The well-known US Pagan magazine *Green Egg* devoted a recent issue (no.116, Nov. Dec. 1996) to 'Buddheo-Pagans'; see also Webster (1996).

11 And also, in some regions, including Tibet, in terms of strengthening and recovering spirit-essences (separate 'souls', e.g. Tibetan *bla*) within the individual. I omit this complex subject here, although it does have implications for the individual's relationship to the environment (cf. Samuel 1993: 263–4, 438–9).

12 The only article devoted specifically to the *gaṇacakra* is that by Lalou (1965). However, references to the *gaṇacakra* may be found throughout the literature on Vajrayāna Buddhism (e.g. Snellgrove 1987; Samuel 1993), and the extant Tantric texts include directions for these rituals (e.g. the Hevajra Tantra, Farrow and Menon 1992). Interesting Tibetan descriptions are available in Kun-dga' grol-mchog's life of Krsnacarya (see Templeman 1994: 26–27) and gTsang-smyon Heruka's life of Marpa (Trungpa 1982); I thank David Templeman for allowing me to see his draft translation of Kun-dga' grol-mchog's life.

13 On this reversal in the Wiccan context see e.g. Hanegraaff (1995).

14 The contacts between Crowley and Gardner are quite well known but evaluated differently by various commentators (Valiente 1989: 57–9; Kelly 1991; Greenfield 1992; Wilson and Medway 1995). Modern Hindu Tantric practice varies from the very tame and entirely respectable to the realms of black magic and sorcery well known from the Hindi movies. Some Hindu tantrics, however, undoubtedly do still practice private *cakra* rituals with a decidedly antinomian flavour (McDaniel 1989; Dehejia 1986: 11–13, 62–3; Marglin 1985: 217–28; Gupta *et al.* 1979: 155–6).

15 Several Wiccan writers have drawn on Hindu and Buddhist Tantric material either to supplement Wiccan techniques, as in references to the system of *cakra* within the body by Vivianne Crowley (1989: 89–93) and Starhawk (1990: 52), or to make equations between Wiccan and Tantric initiation (Jones 1992: 17, 30), though without implying any historical connection. The *cakra* within the body are in any case very widely used in modern western esoteric traditions, probably because of their adoption by the theosophists.

16 Outside Tibet, Buddhist Tantra survived to a more limited degree among the Newars (in Nepal), in Japan and in Bali (Indonesia). Elsewhere it was purged from official Buddhism, though Tantric procedures survived in various unofficial forms throughout Asia.

17 Although there is still a tradition of lay yogic practice in dangerous and 'powerful' places such as the charnel grounds where dead bodies are exposed, particularly in relation to the Chöd (*gcod*) practice.

18 Though it is worth noting that possession by the Tantric deities still forms part of the Newar Tantric consecration (Gellner 1992) and that ritual dances remain important in the context of monastic festivals in Tibet (Samuel 1993; Cantwell 1995).

19 Though some teachers (e.g. Namkhai Norbu Rinpoche) do refer to the gaṇacakra, and emphasize the importance of the gaṇapūja being carried out in a non-ordinary state of consciousness (that of the Tantric deity).

20 The nearest perhaps is the Buddhist shamanism of the western Buddhist teacher Ngakpa Chögyam (Chögyam 1990). Ngakpa Chögyam has a valid lineage from recognised Tibetan lamas, but his approach is eccentric by the usual standards of Tibetan Buddhism in the west. Some other teachers from the rNying-ma-pa/rDzogs-chen end of the Tibetan spectrum, such as Namkhai Norbu Rinpoche and Chagdüd Rinpoche, have taught Chöd (n. 17) to western students, but Chöd does not explicitly involve possession or ecstatic states.

21 Two important recent contributions referring to Tibetan Buddhism are Klein (1995) and Campbell (1996); see also Volkmann (1995) and Shaw (1994), though the latter probably over-argues the case for the high status of women in Indian Vajrayāna. In relation to Hindu Tantra, Bharati (1976) argues for its being generally exploitative of women, while Denton (1992) discusses contemporary women Tantric practitioners, and McDaniel (1992) argues that the Bauls of Bengal constitute an example of gender equality.

22 For Vajrayāna Buddhists, see Samuel (1989). Rejection of the mind–body dichotomy is common in the Pagan literature, e.g. Starhawk (1989: 116, 157).

23 Her next book was in fact called *Dreaming the Dark* (Starhawk 1990).

24 This is a rather complex point. Technically, the meditator practises replacing his or her ordinary, impure karmic vision with the 'pure vision' of an enlightened Buddha.

25 'Blessed be thy feet, that have brought thee in these ways. Blessed be thy knees, that shall kneel at the sacred altar. Blessed be thy womb, without which we would not be. Blessed be thy breasts, formed in beauty. Blessed be thy lips, that shall utter the Sacred Names' (e.g. Farrar and Farrar 1989: 40–1). The wording is slightly altered when given by a woman to a man.

26 There is a pervasive ambivalence to the local deities, as illustrated, for example, by a contemporary Tibetan writer: 'The worship of mountain gods and burning of incense on hilltops [bsangs] are pervasive customs followed by most Tibetans . . . According to the fundamental view of Buddhism, taking refuge in worldly deities is against the precepts of taking refuge in the three jewels. Therefore, it is strongly discouraged . . . However, the practice of ritual deity invocation and the purification rite of incense burning, which were derived from the Bon [pre-Buddhist] religion, didn't stop even after Bon was officially banned. Instead, Guru Padmasambhava subdued several of these worldly deities and made them the protector deities of Buddhism . . . some aspects of this custom, such as raising prayer flags, burning incense and circumambulating hills, have never degenerated and remain intact even today' (Chabpel 1991: 1, 9–10, 13).

27 Thus at Samye-Ling, the Tibetan Buddhist centre in Scotland founded by Chögyam Trungpa Rinpoche and now directed by Akong Rinpoche, there is a shrine in the river adjoining the centre to the *naga*-spirit of the river, and a notice asking visitors not to smoke within fifty yards of the shrine since this irritates the *naga*.

28 E.g. Namkhai Norbu discusses relationships with local deities in his teachings. Groups of his students in different countries recite specific verses to the particular Tibetan classes of deities to which the local gods are held to belong, and also carry out *bsangs* (fire-offerings of fragrant wood, incense and other 'pure' substances) to the local deities.

29 The actual list is occasionally altered and augmented in later versions; thus the Farrars add Athene and Isis and substitute the Irish form Dana for Diana. They also suggest in a footnote 'If you have a local Goddess-name, by all means add it to the list' (Farrar and Farrar 1989: 42 and n. 10).

30 'Deva' is the standard Sanskrit term for 'god'. Its use here is I think a borrowing from the Findhorn Community in Scotland (on whom see e.g. Melton *et al.* 1990: 171–4).

31 See the 'Faeries and Deva' issue of the CAW journal, *Green Egg* (111, winter 1995) for several examples.

32 Jo Pearson has pointed out to me that in the ritual magic tradition control over spirits is an important theme, and traces of this remain in contemporary Wiccan ritual, such as the summoning of the elementals (spirits of the four elements).

33 Wilson and Medway (1995: 12–15); Hutton (1996b.) On John Hargrave, the Woodcraft Folk and the Order of Woodcraft Chivalry, see also Rosenthal (1986: 244ff.); Webb (1991: 84–94).

34 Nichols is supposed to have broken away from the main Druid Order as a result of their failure to accept his suggested expansion of the ritual cycle to the eight-fold cycle we know today (Wilson and Medway 1995: 15).

35 They say of the original rituals 'They were like eight little tunes, pleasant and separate, when what we really wanted was eight movements of one symphony' (Farrar and Farrar 1989: 21). While the detailed cyclical interpretation in terms of the death and rebirth of the God (for another version of this, see Crowley 1989: 189) is thus a later development, the idea of seasonal rituals as fertility rituals linked to the annual cycle can already be found in *High Magic's Aid*: 'We did all the wicked and beautiful things, knowing that they must be done if we were to have health and happiness and good crops . . . What else were our rites for but to bring rain when needed, and dry days for harvest? When the sun was at its lowest, did we not have a Dance of the Wheel, when all danced in a circle with torches to show the sun the way to come back and conquer Winter: To rise high and bring back summer?' (Gardner 1994: 15).

36 See for example Gwydion Pendderwen's cycle of songs for the eight festivals (Pendderwen 1995: 2–15), or Rae Beth's festival rituals (Beth 1990: 20–40, etc.).

37 Imbolc, Beltane, Midsummer, Lughnasadh, Samhain, Yule.

38 A recent statement in favour of ecological responsibility by the leader of the Tibetan Buddhist government in exile, HH the 14th Dalai Lama, includes a poem, 'The Sheltering Tree of Interdependence: A Buddhist Monk's Reflections on Ecological Responsibility', including several verses encouraging people to preserve and plant trees (Dalai Lama 1994; I thank Keith Milton for bringing this poem to my attention). The poem is symptomatic of the current shift towards environmentalist orientations by Tibetan Buddhist leaders (cf. Huber 1991) but at the same time it illustrates the lack of any substantial basis in the tradition for environmental preservation; the arguments are almost all in terms of the utility of trees to other living beings.

39 This article was presumably written by Aidan Kelly.

40 Much of Starhawk's later writing moves in this direction, as do some British Wiccan writers (e.g. Crowley 1989; Jones 1992). The concept of initiation is used by all three of these authors as a way of dealing with the negative sides of existence (cf. the Myth of Inanna in Starhawk 1990b, and the treatment of the three Wiccan initiations by both Crowley and Jones). There seem to me to be interesting convergences with Buddhism as each author deals with this material (explicit in Jones 1992).

PART THREE

Nature Religion in Practice

CHAPTER 11

Feminist Witchcraft and Holy Hermeneutics
JONE SALOMONSEN

– I INTRODUCTION –

'Reclaiming' is an anarchist and feminist Wiccan community in San Francisco, founded in 1980 by Starhawk and her friends. It is not a commune but a networking, urban community in which 150 people are cross-related through a variety of activities: teaching witchcraft weekly in classes and at retreats; publishing of newsletters, tapes and books; facilitating public rituals according to the Wheel of the Year; participation in direct political action, social work and experimental living. Reclaiming is an affluent community and during the course of a year, a thousand people may have gone through its 'school' in witchcraft. Its success is primarily due to its inclusive, anti-hierarchical structure and to Starhawk's influential books, such as *The Spiral Dance* (1979), *Dreaming the Dark* (1990a) and *Truth or Dare* (1990b).

'Feminist witchcraft' as practised in Reclaiming is, to a certain degree, different from its non-feminist kin, in regard to symbolism, ethics and organisation. While Gardnerian-type witchcraft tends to reclaim a religion, feminist witchcraft tends to reclaim a spiritual path and to give final authority to individual, mystical experiences. Feminists also tend to organise in mono-sexual, anti-hierarchical circles rather than in traditional mixed covens led by a priest(ess)hood. Finally, feminists explicitly emphasise the Goddess as representative of divinity, often on behalf of the Horned God and other male, Wiccan deities. Reclaiming witches are, in addition, consciously eclectic. They search cross-culturally for powerful female imagery with which they believe they may create new conceptual frameworks, both for religious worship and for liberating feminist world-viewing today. The aim of this chapter is to describe and analyse this new feminist conceptualisation as a specific hermeneutical endeavour.

Since Wicca is a cultural product of modernity, scholars have tended to ask modernist questions of the material, such as 'how can highly educated and rational people find magic persuasive?' (cf. Luhrmann 1989). My point of departure is not sociology and the rationality debate but theological hermeneutics and the 'indigenous' quest for truth and meaning. I will, therefore, approach the phenomenon according to its own claims, that is as a genuinely religious movement with emancipatory goals. In fact, feminist Wicca represents a new version of a very traditional form of religiosity, namely the *Unio Mystica*.

Having chosen this angle, I shall proceed by analysing how Reclaiming witches interpret 'reality', how they define 'religion', how they contrast 'experience' and 'symbols', and how they incorporate the realms of magic into their interpretative language. My goal is eventually to display how the ethno-hermeneutics of Reclaiming witches is organised spatially as a dialectic between the 'horizontal magic of everyday life' and the 'vertical magic of ritual'.

The present study is based upon my own fieldwork in the Reclaiming community. It was conducted in 1989–90 for a doctoral dissertation in theology and social anthropology. Since my empirical data are strictly community-based they should not be read as a general description of witchcraft but rather as a particular representation of feminist Wicca as conceptualised and practised in Reclaiming.

– II THE TRUTH OF EXPERIENCE: THE TRUTH OF SYMBOL –

Sofia is one of the founders of Reclaiming. When I asked her why she became a witch, she referred to a religious experience she had in 1974 (when 23 years old). She lived by the ocean and used to walk on the beach in the evenings. One evening she suddenly felt a presence. She looked around and saw nobody. She finally looked at the moon, and felt an intense stream of communication, almost as if she merged with the moon. She heard a voice from inside the moon, talking to her, telling her that it had saved her and protected her from all kinds of danger throughout her life:

> What happened was that I was being picked out by the Goddess to hear her message. She told me to meditate every full moon and said I would start meeting women that would show me what I needed to know. The Goddess also asked me to take back Sofia, my birth name – which also is one of her names – and told me her creed, the 'Charge of the Goddess'. It almost had the same form as the traditional one.

This extraordinary experience changed Sofia's life. She believed she had been elected as a subject for divine revelation, and from that day she started meditating every full moon, while waiting for the women who should teach her to show up. First she met Z. Budapest in Los Angeles, and through her she was (in 1977) introduced to Starhawk. Sofia learned that the Goddess who had revealed herself at the beach was exactly the same divinity who was worshipped in the religion called 'witchcraft'. She then, of course, joined this religion, and is presently still a witch.

This story is not unique to Sofia, and among many Reclaiming witches it is fairly common to refer to one's religious path as some kind of selection, a waking up or even 'conversion', sparked by an extraordinary experience or revelation. Francesca, a friend of Reclaiming, told me that:

> the sheer physical presence of the Goddess captured me and changed my being. You get chosen, yes, Goddess kidnaps you, that's it, and that's how I have experienced a lot of my path. But I cannot tell you that this is objective reality. We do not believe in such a concept. If you are going to understand something, you get involved with it. You get involved with your whole being, with your god spirit, with your sacred animal nature, with your passion – you bring all parts of you and experience it. If you bring that being to your observation of nature, you will truly see nature for what it really is. You will see the Goddess in it, and understand her mysteries. Anybody can find her mysteries if they just look with their whole being and live it. Witchcraft is not a belief system which you adopt intellectually. It is rather our understanding from being alive and interacting with things.

One of the functions of stories like this is to assure the believers that their religious path is not made up, in a fictitious sense, but refers to something real. My informants would repeatedly tell me that, 'Even though we make up this religion, the goddess is not made up. She is more than a chosen metaphor; she is real and she is alive.' 'Experience' becomes a key concept to explain the existence of goddess and her religion. To Francesca, experience means total involvement and is a fundamental hermeneutic principle to 'read' reality. Francesca's reference to experience resembles the Aristotelian notion 'empeira', meaning knowledge received from interacting with things, being involved and skilled, in opposition to 'theoria' which means knowledge from looking at, observing at a distance, as when astronomers study the planets.

To Sofia, the concept of 'experience' is a way to legitimise the possibility of living with a consciousness of inventing religion but not of making up that which religion is essentially about: the experience of divine reality. Witches 'invent', while at the same time insisting on the religion's 'truthfulness'. In Sofia's religion, people have decided that the moon is one of the normative symbols of female divinity, and the core understanding of the essential being of this divinity has been expressed in a creed called The Charge of the Goddess. This creed was originally written by Gerald Gardner and Doreen Valiente, but most witches – among them Starhawk – claim it to be both ancient and traditional (cf. Starhawk 1979: 76–7). This information, as well as the whole discussion on whether a religious element is ancient or modern, whether it is a chosen metaphor or a true expression of reality, is irrelevant to Sofia's conversion narrative. She invokes another reality, in which the moon itself speaks and tells the truth directly to her. Like Francesca, she regards her own experience as her highest authority, and according to this experience the creed is authored by goddess herself. It may also be true that it was written down in the 1950s, but in her opinion this information is only true in the reality of science and visible facts.

To cope with multiple realities and several concepts of truth, the Reclaiming witches depend upon an implicit hermeneutic distinction between what they understand to be pre-symbolic experiences and cultural symbols. This 'indigenous' distinction between 'truth' and 'cultural invention' is crucial to an understanding of their self-proclaimed authority and cultural mission, as well as their world view in general. Witches may disagree strongly on certain beliefs, but they all agree on method: to contrast experienced reality continuously against representations of reality.

However, the witches themselves do not claim the notion 'hermeneutics'. It is solely an etic category which I utilise in order to develop a descriptive terminology and to come to terms with presumably confusing, interpretative strategies and multiple realities invoked by Reclaiming witches. To be able to do so, we must start by delimiting 'hermeneutics' as a theoretical concept, and then proceed to contextualise the ethno-hermeneutics of witchcraft in relation to the ways in which prevailing academic theory reads reality and its signs. My presentation of hermeneutics is based on Daniel (1986), White (1987) and Ricoeur (1988).

– III Religion and hermeneutics –

The word 'hermeneutics' is derived from the name of the Greek god Hermes. He was believed to be the carrier of divine messages from the gods to the humans. Later he also became the mythical inventor of writing. Hermeneutics, then, was originally the art of understanding the messages from the gods as these were revealed directly and experientially to a human medium; that is, of bridging between the divine and the mundane. It was a tool to mediate between two kinds of reality, to overcome the gap between divine speech and human reality and make them one (a vertical inter-pretative move), while its contemporary meaning has become the art of interpretation in general (a horizontal interpretative move).

In the Classical period hermeneutics was developed further as the art of inter-preting divine discourse which was already encoded in sacred text. The sacred text in Classical Greece was the Homeric Epic. But Homer's anthropomorphic portrait of the gods was considered all too human and amoral for the Classical taste. The solution to this problem was not to question the authority of the narratives as such, and write new sacred texts, but to find an interpretation that was not literal, but which created another, more acceptable meaning. This 'translation' is a metaphorical interpretative process, a prototype of horizontal hermeneutics.

The tension between direct experience (revelation) and encoded message (text) in medieval times was expressed via the imagery of god revealing god-self through two kinds of books: the 'Book of Nature' and the 'Book of Scripture', representing respectively an immanent and a transcendent aspect of god. Each of 'the Books' was true, or carried truth. The way for human beings to understand both divine (macrocosm) and human (microcosm) reality was to interpret these books, the one by means of the other. This 'reciprocal' interpretation was possible because the human microcosm was believed to be a reflection of the divine macrocosm. Accordingly, the goal was not only to read the 'sacred Books' but to be read by them.

The duality between nature (revelation) and scripture (text) eventually received a this-worldly interpretation in Romantic hermeneutical theory. The duality inside god was transferred to human psychology as a duality between direct experience (nature/revelation) and indirect reflection (scripture/text); in fact, the duality itself came to be understood as the basic dilemma in all religious discourse. A Romantic theory of religion, going back to Schleiermacher and Goethe, invokes several, parallel realities. It regards fundamental religious experience as mystical, since it belongs to a reality beyond language. According to Thomas Aquinas' brief definition, mysticism is '*cognito dei experimentalis*', '*knowledge of god through experience*'. But mysticism is also bound to the paradox of language. The mystical knowledge, which cannot be told, must be spoken and symbolised to have meaning. Romanticism acknowledges both the power of language and that of experience, but it does not subsume the one under the other.

In post-Romantic hermeneutic theory this is exactly what happens. The duality between the realities of experience and language/reflection, between 'nature' and 'scripture', is synthesised and reduced to a secularised one-ness. The most influential historical figure in this process was Feuerbach. First, he transformed metaphysics to naturalism by merging the 'Book of Scripture' with the 'Book of Nature' into one, sacred reality immanent in the profane world. Second, he completely merged the sacred with the profane, with the consequence that the notion of 'the immanent sacred' got lost in time. Third, he proclaimed the institution of religion, and the elevation of the sacred to another reality, to be a human projection.

Feuerbach's unification of heaven and earth has been essential to the sociology of religion. In the positivist, empirical tradition going back to Comte, the unified sacred-profane reality was reduced to empirical daily life. Durkheim proclaimed religion to be nothing but society writ large, and Mauss described the hermeneutics of sociology as completely horizontal: first a description of facts, which are people's actual beliefs in spiritual beings; second an interpretation of these beliefs by placing their entire foundation in social organisation, not in a meta-human reality.

In the symbolist neo-Kantian tradition, reinterpreted by Durkheim and later developed through influence from literary criticism, the formula 'human projection' became a norm for all kinds of cultural phenomenon. The interesting approach to religion was no longer to see it as a human illusion (which it is, *de facto*, also to a symbolist) but to regard it as a system of symbols conferring meaning upon human reality. The context is still human sociality, but the focus has changed from social facts to social meaning.

In contemporary post-Romantic hermeneutical theory, in social sciences as well as in the humanities, we still find these two major positions. From a Romantic point of view, they are both reductionist. The empiricists emphasise ordinary experience and claim to study the empirical reality of daily life. The symbolists emphasise language and cognition and claim to study the symbolic reality of human culture. To the empiricists, language is not part of reality but simply a medium to represent experienced reality. To the symbolists, language itself is the problem. They regard language and signs as fundamentally arbitrary in relation to reality. Language never represents reality; it creates reality and interprets reality. Consequently, there is no non-linguistic reality available for direct experience. While the empiricists ultimately interpret meaning to understand reality, the symbolists have totally given up on the concept of reality.

Symbolists regard the Romantic distinction between direct experience of reality and indirect linguistic reflection both as illusion and as a simplification of the socialising power of language. To them there is only figuration and no privileged position within language from which cultural language can be questioned. There is no true 'meaning', only infinite alternative 'meanings'. Symbolists also dismiss the empiricists' hermeneutical principle in which social facts are believed to be interpreted through a study of social organisation. 'Interpretation', according to them, cannot show the foundation of social facts (as religious beliefs) in social organisation or social reality, because this reality is just as fictitious as the text/the sign itself. Analysis can only be a metaphorical translation from one universe of meaning to another.

Paul Ricoeur is a Romantic symbolist, known to have extended the literary notion of text, as a system of signs, to encompass all sign systems, from religious activities to sport. He is a Romanticist when he describes the goal of hermeneutics as the transformation of something foreign to something familiar by the 'bridge-building' act of interpretation (cf. Ricoeur 1988). The existential condition sparking the hermeneutical process is, in other words, an experience of alienation. The crucial question then is: what needs a bridge? What is to be united? According to Ricoeur, the unification process in religious hermeneutics is a translation of presumed divine reality to make it relevant to this world of ordinary, daily life, overcoming the split from a human being's point of view. He turns into a symbolist when he goes on to interpret this bridging as a metaphorical, horizontal process in which language is discontinuous with the things (that is, divine reality) it represents. Acceptable meaning, to him, is created solely through interpretations and new names, by metaphorical translation of one universe of meaning to another.

None of these post-Romantic hermeneutical strategies is able to encompass Sofia's sensory experience of being addressed by extraordinary divine reality without reducing it to a non-sensory, symbolic representation within ordinary reality. In order to develop a descriptive language for witches' ethno-hermeneutics which may comprise the magical and experiential aspects claimed, we need to go back to an older notion of hermeneutics, extending the one unification axis to include two. In addition to a horizontal, metaphorical interpretative process on a cultural level, witches may be said to operate with a second unification, which is vertical, magical and individual. This axis is about the unification of supernatural and natural, of sacred and profane, of extraordinary and ordinary, the merging of real substances in the experience of a single person beyond ordinary language and narrative. Reshaped through this transformative experience the individual is now (ideally) made capable of invoking a magical language of action, not only of signification. This magical language is not only symbolic but indexical as well: it is conceived as continuous with the things it represents (just as smoke may be continuous with fire).

We may say that the ethno-hermeneutics of magical religion unifies both horizontally and vertically. But in order to name reality and position religion it also comprises symbolic and empirical positions. This presumed inconsistency is due to witches' non-synthetic, plural concepts of reality. Let me make this explicit by presenting their dualist definitions of religion, which eventually lead to a third notion: magical reality.

– IV RELIGION AS SYMBOL, EXPERIENCE AND MAGICAL REALITY –

As stated earlier, witches confess to a Romantic distinction between pre-symbolic experience and cultural symbol. This is incisive to their acclaimed cultural mission and to their argument concerning why it is worthwhile to recreate dead or dormant traditions and invent religion. One argument is existential, the other political and pragmatic. As existentialists, they are focused on what is true. As politicians, they are concerned with strategies and necessities and firmly believe that it is not possible to change western culture without changing western religion. Therefore, it is only in accordance with a differentiation between existential (what is true to the individual) and political (what is necessary to create a better society) that we may say that witches separate functionally between religious experience and religious symbols. Experience is viewed as authentic and true in a pre-linguistic sense, symbols and forms as secondary inculturations of those experiences. When defining religion on a cultural level they adopt symbolic anthropology, embracing among others Clifford Geertz and Victor Turner. When defining religion existentially they adopt an esoteric version of Romanticism. Thus they operate simultaneously with (at least) two different concepts of religion. In Starhawk's recreations of witchcraft, this duality becomes rather visible.

First, Starhawk relies on Clifford Geertz and maintains that religion is constitutive of culture because it creates a cultural ethos which defines the deepest values in a society, and in the persons living there. Religion, in Starhawk's language, is (empirically) 'the soil of culture – in which the belief systems, the stories, the thought-forms and all other institutions are based' (Starhawk 1990a: 72). She claims that there is no way to accommodate cultural change without changing religion: not rejecting it, but replacing it with another symbol system and structures that evoke other values. At this argumentative level Starhawk accepts that religion as form is a human projection or construction. But it is a most powerful and necessary construction. The question, then, is not whether this construction is an illusion or not; it is whether the construction is life-affirming and nourishing to human beings or life-negating and oppressive. Metaphysics is measured with ethics. What is considered true 'dogmatically' cannot be true 'in fact' if it does not liberate people and sanctify all of life. The explicit goal of witchcraft at this level is to unite spirit and politics, to unite the values attributed to divine reality and the values circulating in social reality: to realise religion as social utopia.

Second, Starhawk depends upon esoteric Romanticism and opposes Geertz and symbolic anthropology. She states that religion is constitutive in human life not only due to the power of symbols but also because it deals with substance, with real power, life-generating powers, that actually can be 'tapped' by the art of magic (such as ritual invocations, prayer, meditation). When talking about religion inside this realm of 'real power', Starhawk defines religion essentially (not empirically) as 'a matter of re-linking, with the divine within and with her outer manifestations in all of the human and natural world' (Starhawk 1979: 186). Divinity is ultimately defined as 'life-generating powers' in a very literal sense, even though 'Goddess' also can be symbolised conventionally as deity. Divine reality is not divided between immanence and transcendence but between visible reality, as experienced in ordinary life, and invisible reality as experienced extraordinarily, abruptly as in 'revelation', in ritual space or in altered states of consciousness (trance). Correspondingly, we find two fluctuating meanings of the concept of 'experience'. One refers to ordinary life, the other to a mystical, extraordinary experience.

The double floor in Reclaiming witches' conceptualisations of reality and the two-fold definition of religion place them in the category that sociologist Peter L. Berger calls 'inductive strategy' in the renewal of religion: going back to experience and, from there, assessing tradition. In *The Heretical Imperative* (1980), Berger displays a Romantic theory of religion which, to a certain extent, 'echoes' witchcraft. It is based on the thesis that the individual experience of the 'supernatural' is not co-extensive with the social phenomenon of 'religion': 'Religion can be understood as a human projection because it is communicated in human symbols. But this very communication is motivated by an experience in which a metahuman reality is injected into human life' (Berger 1980: 52). Berger claims that the distinction between experience and reflection is crucial if the study of religion is to become something more than a history of ideas and if we are to have any chance of understanding the strong energies playing in religious fields or, say, new religious movements. From there he defines religion empirically (but not essentially) as a human attitude that conceives of the cosmos, including the supernatural, as a sacred order (Berger 1980: 53). Both the 'sacred' and the 'supernatural' must be present for Berger to call a phenomenon 'religion'.

If we apply Berger's terminology to the witches, 'sacred' refers to a horizontal interpretation of unity between self and cosmos, in which the Goddess is experienced metaphorically as visible, ordinary reality itself, meaning that she is manifest and present in all life forms in a non-personal form. 'Supernatural' designates, according to Berger, 'the radically overwhelmingly other', referring to an experience of something being 'out there', as 'having an irresistible reality that is independent of one's own will' (Berger 1980: 42). Applied to the witches, 'supernatural' refers to a vertical, invisible reality in which the Goddess may be experienced as substance, as 'life-generating powers' or, personally, as 'the other', as deity.

However, this is not all there is to say about the Goddess. She is also believed to 'exile' herself from transcendent supernaturalism and materialise in a magical sense: to incarnate and descend into people – an act named 'sacred possession' by Starhawk. In order to understand how language is used for such a possession to happen and to grasp the symbolic complexity of witchcraft, we need to deepen the Romantic theory of religion summarised above and linger with the fact that Wicca is also a magico-mystical religion within western esotericism. As such, it attempts to restore a magical worldview and to seek extraordinary mystical experiences. A simple differentiation between experience and cultural symbol does not fully comprise the 'possessiveness' of the Goddess and this 'other' magical reality. Within a more esoteric frame of reference, witches no longer understand the function and meaning of symbols exclusively as signifiers, as the 'clothing' of experiences into cultural languages. In addition, symbols are, in themselves, regarded as literal vehicles and pointers to other realities. Within this magical-mystical framework we may ask: how do they now 'read' signs? How do they comprehend 'magical reality' and 'position themselves' in relation to a more 'realist' view of language?

Just as Starhawk operates with two concepts of religion so she assumes, simultaneously, two corresponding sign-theories. One is metaphorical, nominalist and horizontal, suiting her feminist, post-Romantic symbolic programme. The other is magical, realist and vertical, suiting her personal-spiritual transformation agenda and occult lineage. On the one hand, Starhawk claims that language, as such, is basically metaphorical and arbitrary, irrespective of whether it is expressed through explicit metaphors (poetry) or implicit metaphors (scientific concepts): 'Scientific knowledge, like religious knowledge, is a set of metaphors for a reality that can never be completely described or comprehended . . . Religion becomes dogmatic when it confuses the metaphor with the thing itself' (Starhawk 1979: 190). On the other hand, Starhawk adopts esoteric 'realism'. In order to grasp the mystical meaning of symbols, she recommends that 'as part of an initiate's training, she is taught to visualise symbols, to meditate on them and play with them in her imagination until they reveal their meaning directly' (1979: 81). The 'meaning' referred to here is not metaphorical and arbitrary, but 'archetypal'. Archetypal knowledge is eternal knowledge that 'inhabits things', independently of the human subject, but it may become known to the subject through her active involvement, play, emotionality and meditation.

But then, at a certain point in the sign process, divine knowledge and the question of semantics (whether archetypal or metaphorical) abate altogether, whereas the symbol as a mediator for divine substance, for power in a realistic sense, takes over. Within this linguistic framework, very different from metaphorism, Starhawk maintains, 'The symbol tells us, look at this. Experience this thing; become this thing; open a channel so the power can flow through you' (1979: 74). In this context, the symbol is 'of the object', the transcendent has become indexically present as 'real forces', and the symbol acquires a literal, almost material, magical character.

The sign theory confronted here is derived from esoteric neo-Platonism, according to which language itself is constituted by cosmic, divine law and activity, not by human creativity. Platonic language theory maintains that some phonic archetypes are eternal, constituting a realm of 'phonic ideas' which underlies the phenomenal reality. Such a 'realist' view of language is necessarily part of all magical world views, because of the very fact that magic originates from belief in cosmological correspondences: that there are real, invisible physical or energetic relationships between the elementals of nature as well as between words and things; that is, between symbols of people and people, between sacred symbols and that to which the symbols refer. According to Starhawk, magic opens the door to a 'reality' which is just as valid as the 'tangible, visible world'; only it has a different quality:

> The tangible, visible world is only one aspect of reality. There are other dimensions that are equally real, although less solid. Myths and metaphors are maps to other dimensions. Tir-Na-Nog, the Land of Youth in Irish mythology, is not a metaphor nor an archetype, it is a real place that can be visited. But its reality is not a physical one and the visits do not take place in the physical body. Beings also exist in those other realms, for the gods are more than symbols. They are real powers . . . When we reach for Goddess, she reveals herself to us. (Starhawk 1990b: 25)

In order to integrate a notion of 'multiple realities', Reclaiming witches have developed a corresponding concept of 'multiple selves' in the individual: a divine 'Deep Self', an emotional 'Younger Self' and a rational 'Talking Self'. The structure of human consciousness is also believed to be organised according to these three selves: the ordinary consciousness of the Talking Self; the unconscious or dream state of the Younger Self; and the extraordinary consciousness of Deep Self. While Younger Self experiences the world, Talking Self structures it by arranging, categorising, classifying and giving names. Deep Self, however, is 'the Divine within, the ultimate and original essence, the spirit that exists beyond time, space and matter' (Starhawk 1979: 22), and is only accessible through Younger Self. It is not the rational 'I' that communicates with the divine (although this 'I' may communicate about the divine), but the intuitive 'self'. The content of this 'communication' cannot be categorised as 'rational knowledge' but is rather a spontaneous awareness, a discernment of the way things really are.

In *A Rumour of Angels* (1970) Peter Berger indirectly supports the Wiccan position when he argues that reality never is experienced as one unified whole, either by ancients or by modern people. Rather, it is perceived as multiple, as containing zones or strata with greatly different qualities. The realities that differ from being wide awake in ordinary, empirical reality he calls sub-universes and points out that these may be based on physiological processes, such as the dream state, or they may be experienced as a radical rupture from daily life, such as in ecstasy. Starhawk's conscious rotation between different modes of being, then, is not a sign of irrationality or regression. The fact that these sub-universes are questioned at all Berger ascribes solely to the process of secularisation: the social plausibility structures supporting magical beliefs are weakened or gone. But secularisation does not mean that the consciousness of modern people has changed and developed *en bloc* from irrational to rational.

In order to approach 'magical reality' and the literal qualities of language, I shall combine Berger's concept of 'sub-universes' with the Wiccan concept of the 'three selves', and investigate the magico-ritual framework for the experiential category of entering realms like 'Tir-Na-Nog' and 'reaching for the Goddess'.

– V TRANCE INDUCTION: REMEMBERING TIAMAT –

As elaborated by Starhawk, the sacred can be perceived and experienced at two different levels: either as an awareness of divine presence immanent in the visible reality of empirical daily life, or as an extraordinary experience within a 'less solid', invisible sub-universe of the presence of divine reality. Witches make use of ritual trance techniques in order to induce an extraordinary consciousness of divine presence. Trance is a controlled form of hypnosis which alters the ordinary consciousness to a mode close to the dream state (Goodman 1988: 6–7). It is, in fact, to enter the dream state while being awake. In Reclaiming this is regarded as a major magical tool. It 'helps' a person to 'leave' the sensual body and travel somewhere else in her consciousness. This journey is believed to take place on the 'astral plane', a place beyond time and space and the limits of the corporal body. In 'dream state' a person can journey to a mythological universe, 'enter' the narrative and become simultaneous with narrative time.

In shamanic traditions this journey to another world is often induced by strong sensory stimuli: fasting from food and drink, flagellation, exhausting dancing or – most commonly – the monotonous and steady beat of a drum. The essence in trance work is not the drum, but 'guided visualisation'. The medium is taken to another reality by a narrator's voice. The body position of the medium is that of lying down on the floor or walking slowly in the room, in both cases with her eyes closed. She is taken into an altered state of consciousness, into the dream state of her Deep Self, by letting her mind follow the guidelines of the narrator. The experiences in trance are considerably heightened if the 'dream state' is built to a level of ecstasy. This is most commonly done by ecstatic techniques such as exhausting singing and dancing. According to Reclaiming witches, 'letting oneself trance' requires deep trust in the narrator as well as in one's fellow ritualists.

This mental journey to a place where historical time and space dissolve into mythical present is possible because witches believe that some part of them, some part of their Deep Selves, actually reaches back to the beginning of time in an unbroken line. The memory of the 'beginning of time' is literally stored in their DNA cells and can be called forth in every new reincarnation of a human being. Trance is an aid to healing and becoming depossessed from oppressive culture and imagery, and it is a means to dispense with time and remember through the body, as Starhawk puts it, 'that goddess lives in us as we in her as in each other' and that she has been incarnated in humans since the beginning of time. Ritual trance may, therefore, also help the participants to remember their former lives, for example as hunters and gatherers in prehistoric Africa or as witches burned during the inquisition. In trance, the history of evolution and all time lags can be merged into the memory of a single person.

Let us now enter the witches' ritual space to explore how trance can be used. The following example is from Witchcamp in Vancouver in 1989, a one-week intensive retreat organised by Reclaiming. At Witchcamp, the Goddess was invoked by this method and the trance work was jointly led by Starhawk, Raven, Deadly, Cybelle and Pandora. Approximately one hundred people participated. The ritual sequence lasted probably about half an hour.[1]

The ritualists are asked to move slowly clockwise in circle with their eyes closed. Starhawk enters the centre of the circle, while beating a certain rhythm on her doumbec drum. Raven moves counter-clockwise at the circle's edge, also beating his drum. After a while Deadly starts speaking, slowly and evocatively:

> Long ago, there once was a time when people knew that the earth was a living being and that all of life was holy. They knew the Goddess and they worshipped her as Tiamat, as Inanna, as a Goddess of many names and guises. This harmony was interrupted when her sons all of a sudden wanted the power. They came together in Babylon, cut her body into pieces and made the world as we know it today, dismembered and scattered . . . Now, we who are alive in her as she in us as we are in each other will go back to this time and remember Tiamat. We shall re-member the Goddess, shed her old skin and recreate her anew.

(Starhawk now starts singing, and people follow:)

> Snake Woman, shedding her skin, Snake Woman, shedding her skin,
> Shed, shed, shedding her skin. Shed, shed, shedding her skin.

(The song is repeated again and again, building up energy. Then it fades and ends, and only the drumbeat is heard. After a while, Starhawk continues the trance induction:)

> Remember how we who are alive in her as she in us were fettered, beaten, raped, tortured, burned, and poisoned. Remember how we were dismembered and scattered, almost

destroyed. Remember the feeling of being lost and lonely, how you are hurt and wounded by other people. Remember the times when you feel that you fail, how you hurt and wound others . . . Breath deep, feel the pain – where it lives deep in us (as salt), burning. Flush it out! Let the pain become a sound, a living river on the breath. Raise your voice – cry out. Scream. Wail. Keen and mourn for the dismembering of the world.

(As the ritualists start to embody the images and the sound of the narrating voice, they cry out, wail and mourn. After quite a while, Starhawk continues:)

Remember, there is a place within us all, deep within, where we still are whole and can feel the wholeness, before we were cut into pieces. Now, reach for that sacred place, which always has been there. Reconnect with Deep Self and remember that you are a whole being and always have been.

(The song starts again, builds up and fades:)

Snake woman, etc.

(After a while Cybelle continues to talk:)

We are remade; we are whole; we are healed. You do not any longer feel lost or scattered. Feel that place of peace and rest deep within, stretching back in time, and make a vision for the future . . . Now, imagine that every child on this planet is fed and cared for. Imagine that we cultivate the land in harmony and respect for its internal balance. Imagine a city in which women can walk the streets in peace, without any fear. Imagine a culture in which the Goddess again is worshipped and sanity restored . . . What is your challenge to recreate the world? . . . Listen to your inner voice; what do you hear, what is your challenge?

(The song starts again, and energy is slowly built into an ecstatic state, raising what witches call 'a cone of power'. This energy is meant to actualise and give an energetic 'form' to the vision created by Cybelle, transforming it from image to reality on the astral plane, which again can manifest on the mundane. Pandora continues to talk:)

Reach out and feel the energy in the centre of the circle. Place your hand on the lower part of your belly, and feel the place deep within where the Goddess is re-membered . . . Now, bend and place your hands on the ground and give back to the earth the energy you do not need. Reach for your challenge and keep it in your hand . . .

When you are ready, return to this room. Stamp your feet hard on the floor. Open your eyes and look around you. Clasp your hands three times, and say your own name out loud . . . Find two other people in this room, and form groups of three. Share your experience of dismemberment, of wholeness and of your challenge.

The mythic imagery used in this trance work is taken from *Enuma Elish*, the Babylonian creation epic. It tells the story of how the cosmos was created by defeating chaos, symbolised as the goddess Tiamat, the primeval snake. In fact, the myth portrays how the world as we know it came into being when Marduk dismembered his mother Tiamat's body. He cut it in two pieces, like a crabshell. One part of her body became heaven; the other became the dry land.

Starhawk does not read *Enuma Elish* as a creation story but as a symptom of the displacement of a prehistoric Goddess religion and the subordination of women by male warriors. As observed in the ritual above, the participants are asked to investigate and 'experience' the mythical event by entering the sub-universe of mythical time and becoming Tiamat, the snake woman; they are asked to unweave history by depossessing or shedding their skins and being reborn; they are asked to remember what they possibly cannot remember, the deep centre of their being which never was cut in pieces and destroyed by Marduk's 'priests', and to reconnect with it. They are asked to remember the time before men where rulers and gods were champions, to remember that women's bodies and sexual power are the oldest imagery used to symbolise divine creation. It is taken for granted that the Goddess is a power manifesting in Deep Self, and that merging with the Goddess 'who is alive in us as we in her as in each other' is conducive to healing a common cultural heritage as well as to psychological healing of individuals. The word 're-member' has double meaning; it refers both to 'recall' and to 'putting something together'. This 'putting together' within a ritual context not only is a symbolisation but is considered a magical act with real impact upon people and the state of affairs in this world. But, for healing actually to take place, it is obviously equally important to leave the trance state of collective merger and undifferentiation, to re-enter the ordinary reality of separation and individuality, and then to complete the healing process by re-experiencing it at this level through the acts of sharing and putting into metaphorical language.

The 'energy' experienced and 'raised' in ritual trance belongs to rhetoric as well as to the field of 'psychophysical' emotional exercises. 'Energy' is set in motion by the compelling force of symbolic language and its semantics. But it is also affected by the 'materiality' of language itself: since 'the word' is voiced it becomes a bodily 'thing', not only a rhetorical 'sign'. In addition, the symbolic figure Tiamat is perceived by witches as a living entity concealed simultaneously, so to speak, as linguistic tropes in the mythical text, and as a virtual being in the Deep Self. When retelling the myth as a ritualised trance induction, witches maintain that the Goddess becomes alive within the experience of the trance mediums; they meet her as substance, as 'the great powers' taking possession. In accordance with a world view of living nature and cosmological correspondences, witches believe in the possibility of real (although invisible) relationships between 'words' and 'things'. Therefore, as the transcendent 'becomes' present as real forces in the subject, the 'narrative of Tiamat' no longer operates as pointer to the 'thing' (that is, divine reality) but emerges as an indexical symbol: Tiamat is contiguous with the divine object; the made-up sacred narrative is 'of the 'thing': it is the material and medium through which the Goddess takes possession of Deep Self.

– VI CONCLUSION: HERMENEUTICS OF SPACE –

In the above I have tried to show that the way in which witches systematise reality is by operating with plural states of human consciousness, corresponding to a 'multiple self' and to plural meanings of 'symbol', 'experience' and 'religion'. Since they take an interest not in developing a consistent meta-theory, but rather in creating a symbolic universe in which the existence of multiple realities can be true, their ethno-hermeneutics appears to be paradoxical.

There is, nevertheless, an elementary 'order in the paradox' in terms of an implicit interpretative matrix constituted by the 'hermeneutics of space': symbolic movements from one level of reality to the next according to a vertical and horizontal axis, resonating with the 'horizontal magic of everyday life' and the 'vertical magic of ritual'. Starhawk's Romantic theories and arguments develop along this axis as four successive hermeneutical steps. The very same steps also correspond to witches' 'internal maps' when they undertake magical journeys of growth and transformation, as well as to the deep structure of magical ritual itself. Within this spatial, non-synthetic framework we may include the hermeneutical characteristics of Wicca described above.

Starhawk's four hermeneutical steps are as follows: (1) she starts in the visible, ordinary reality of the Talking Self. Here language has the status of metaphor because it can only grasp reality indirectly. This is Starhawk's nominalist and symbolic position. Her Nietzsche-inspired criticism is that metaphor in our culture has turned into dogmatic concept, confusing the metaphor with the thing itself. To cut loose from this language 'trap', the only way out is to 'dive' experientially into (2) the source of invisible, extraordinary reality, that is, into the Deep Self and the life-generating powers that convey real truth. The path to Deep Self goes through Younger Self. It can be found in ritual, and the status of language is now magical. This is Starhawk's magico-empirical, or realist, position. After knowing truth from 'diving' into the source, she returns to (3) visible reality and Talking Self, where language again is metaphorical. She now chooses new metaphors for this reality dependent upon the values implicit in names, not because they are true in a conceptual sense.

This whole process I place on a vertical axis. At this point Starhawk is ready for (4), the horizontal movement in the world to practise the magic of everyday life, where 'talk' is equivalent to 'walk'. In this ordinary reality, she constantly moves between an empirical-experiential and a symbolic position. Still, she is not outside the realm of the sacred, which is believed to be immanent and ever present. She has only changed consciousness. In magical reality the divine encompasses her completely; in ordinary reality she carries the divine inside as Deep Self and confronts it in 'the other'.

– NOTE –

1 The actual ritual was not taped, and my retelling of it is primarily based on fieldnotes and my memory. Even though not all the words may be exact, I choose to write in the present, as if I were quoting the ritual process word by word, to give a better impression of 'trance journey' as a magical method. A substantial part of the words 'said' by Starhawk, I have copied directly from *Truth or Dare* (1990b: 28–31).

CHAPTER 12

A Priest of the Goddess

PHILIP SHALLCRASS

– I INTRODUCTION –

In this chapter, my own experience as a priest of the Goddess is used as a framework on which to hang some general observations about the nature of priesthood, of deity and of the two Pagan traditions of which I have most firsthand knowledge: witchcraft (Wicca) and Druidry.

Although initiated a high priest of Alexandrian Wicca in the late 1970s, I consider myself primarily a Druid, more specifically a Pagan Druid, a distinction that has to be made since many Druids are avowedly not Pagan. Pagan Druidry as practised now is a relatively new and rapidly evolving phenomenon that emerged in the 1970s when instinctive Pagans such as myself, often with Wiccan training, began to think of ourselves as Druids, inspired, in my case at least, partly by images of Merlin and Gandalf, but mainly by the aura of mystery surrounding those semi-legendary priest-magicians of ancient Europe: the Celtic Druids.

The way in which I practise Druidry is primarily as a priest of the Goddess. The term 'priest' is widely used in witchcraft, but shunned by many Druids, who maintain that Druidry has no priests. In some Druid groups this may be true in theory, but in practice there are people within the Druid community who perform priestly functions. There is, however, almost universal agreement among Druids that pre-Christian Druids did perform priestly functions. This is adduced from classical authors such as Julius Caesar (*De Bello Gallico* VI, 13, quoted in Kendrick 1927: 77), who stated: 'Druids . . . are concerned with divine worship, the due performance of ritual, public and private, and the interpretation of ritual questions', and Diodorus Siculus (*Histories*, V, 31, 2–5, quoted in Kendrick 1927: 82–3), who wrote that:

> [The Gauls] have philosophers and theologians who are held in much honour and are called Druids . . . It is the custom of the Gauls that no one performs a sacrifice without the assistance of a philosopher, for they say that offerings to the gods ought only to be made through the mediation of these men, who are learned in the divine nature and, so to speak, familiar with it, and it is through their agency that the blessings of the gods ought properly to be sought.

Why, then, the ambivalence towards the term 'priest' among modern Druids? By contrast, the first-level initiation into Alexandrian Wicca ends with the declaration that one 'has been consecrated priest, Witch and hidden child of the Goddess'. In

Wicca, priesthood is conferred on every initiate and seen as empowering the individual. Many Druids see the term as elitist, as taking power away from the individual and giving it to an intermediary. To me, a priest is one who mediates, focuses or channels divine power on behalf of a group or individual. There is an apparent contradiction here, since one way in which Paganism is perceived to differ from more centrally organised religions lies in the fact that each Pagan makes her or his own contact with spiritual forces, without the need for an intermediary.

In practice, however, there are often individuals within Pagan groups whose contact with the spirit world is recognised to be significantly different, clearer or stronger, and such persons are often given, whether by conscious design or unconscious agreement, leading roles in bringing spiritual energy into the group's workings. This is not elitist, it is simply an observation of the way things are. In education, there are those who teach and those who learn from them, drawing on the teachers' acquired knowledge. There is no implication that those who teach are superior to those who learn, they simply fulfil complementary roles in the process of education. Similarly, the role of Pagan priest is one not of superiority but of service. We do what we do because we can, because people wish us to, and because our Gods and guides call upon us and enable us. The concept becomes even less elitist if we allow that a fundamental role of the Pagan priest is to assist individuals actively to form their own spiritual connections, rather than doing the connecting for them. A Pagan priest may have many roles, operating as initiator, teacher, counsellor, healer, ritualist or diviner, but these functions, though important, are secondary to, and to a large extent dependent on, the ability to channel spiritual energy.

– II SPIRITUAL ENERGY –

At this point, we need to address what we mean by spiritual energy. In Paganism each of us constructs her or his own model of the universe. In common with many Pagans, my model has developed through direct experience and through study of a number of religious and philosophical traditions and is continually evolving. My current understanding is that the fundamental nature of divine reality is unity. A similar view is expressed in one the Triads composed by the eighteenth-century scholar, literary forger, Unitarian Christian, and Druid revivalist, Edward Williams, better known by his Bardic name, Iolo Morganwg. He wrote: 'There are three Primeval Unities, and more than one of each cannot exist: one Deity, one Truth, and one point of Liberty where all opposites conjoin.'

One problem with this definition is that absolute unity is difficult both to attain and to conceptualise. Other traditions have encountered this difficulty and adopted various ways of dealing with it. Taoism resorts to metaphor and paradox, as in these lines from the Tao Te Ching (Lau 1963: 70): 'Its upper part is not dazzling; its lower part is not obscure. Dimly visible, it cannot be named, and returns to that which is without substance. This is called the shape that has no shape, the image without form.'

Having conceived of a supreme, non-dual reality and dubbed it Brahman, Hindu philosophers realised it was not accessible to the human mind and personified it as Ishvara, Creator and Lord of the Universe, viewing all other gods as manifestations of aspects of Ishvara. The name I give to non-dual, ultimate reality is Celi, a Welsh word meaning 'creator', or 'deity.' I see each of us as containing a spark of this essential spirit, a spark that connects us with all the rest of creation, for every other being also contains this same undifferentiated spiritual essence. And here I refer not only to human beings, but to all our relations, animal, vegetable, mineral and spiritual. In common with many Pagans, I am a pantheist, seeing spirit in all things.

Another problem with the concept of unity is that it is, by its nature, static, allowing no possibility of action and reaction. For creation to occur, there must be interaction, and the minimum requirement for this is a duality of forces which may be characterised as Yin and Yang, male and female, light and darkness, sun and moon or God and Goddess. However we perceive them, these two polarised forces provide the necessary dynamic for creation to take place. To some extent, then, I am a dualist. There are two related ways in which I characterise this creative interplay of forces. One is as an eternal dance, or sexual union, of God and Goddess. The other is the image of two intertwined serpents. In Celtic folklore, snakes are said to copulate on the eve of Midsummer, producing the magical talisman called the Glain Naddair, or Serpent's Egg. Druids themselves were referred to as Neiddred, 'adders', and the egg is a widespread symbol for the nascent universe.

Ultimate unity is, of necessity, beyond good and evil, which makes it difficult to conceive of it taking any interest whatsoever in human affairs. I regard the merging of the individual spirit with this cosmic unity as the ultimate goal of all spiritual paths, and yet, when I commune with deity, I usually do so through that half of creative duality that I call the Goddess. Perhaps I can best explain what I mean by the Goddess by explaining how my understanding of her has developed, and something of the process by which I became her priest.

– III How I became a priest of the Goddess –

My first memory of the Goddess is also my first memory. I was about six months old and sitting in a pram. The sky was a brilliant turquoise blue. Apart from it, the object that filled my sight was huge, warm and powerful. My infant mind recognised it as the supreme source of nourishment and love. It was my mother: she who fed, clothed and bathed me, and who taught me to read and write at the age of 3. It is hardly surprising that I came to relate to the figure of the Goddess as nurturer and giver of wisdom. What surprises me is that the whole world is not full of Goddess-worshippers. Freudians may note that I had a difficult relationship with my father and other authority figures, who tended to be male, perhaps explaining why the idea of a male God had less appeal. When I learned that the Judaeo-Christian God was an angry man, given to inflicting ghastly plagues on his followers for relatively trivial misdemeanours, I went off the idea even more. Even so, I was not entirely opposed to the notion of male deities. Reading Thor comics as a teenager I found it easy enough to relate to the gods of Norse tradition. They displayed a humanity lacking in the wrathful but utterly distant All-Father of the Hebraic Old Testament, whilst retaining more power to inspire than the rather limp figure of Jesus portrayed in school religious education. Reverence for the Goddess was not, then, inevitable. Furthermore, I was brought up as an atheist and scientific rationalist by parents who saw all spiritual beliefs as nonsense. I always had a sense that there was more to life than the physical.

My childhood experience of the spirit world came largely at night, in dreams or out in the open, beneath the moon and stars. I would sneak out of the house while my parents slept and walk the moonlit seashore, mentally following the path of the moon's reflection out across the water. I fought armies of demons who flew in through my bedroom window, wielding a visionary sword of light until the last of them was defeated. In many tribal cultures, the future medicine man, witch doctor or shaman is marked out by being a weird kid. I fitted this pattern well, being utterly incomprehensible to my parents, teachers and other children. I became a pacifist and anarchist at the age of 4. I was a loner who preferred to walk along the beach at night, or roam the streets with the local cat population, rather than play football with my contemporaries. In the jargon of social psychology, I would doubtless have been described as dysfunctional. It seemed to me at the time, and still seems now, that the lack of desire to join gangs, fight, bully smaller children, or become obsessed with football, cars, racism and obscenity were rational responses to a dysfunctional society.

The next step for a would-be medicine man is to undergo a physical or mental crisis. True to form, I suffered a nervous breakdown at the age of 18, brought about by mental, physical and emotional stress, and natural sensitivity exacerbated by hallucinogenic drugs. The breakdown came complete with suicidal urges, virtual catatonia, dislocation of time and space, and vivid hallucinations. Having annoyed a Freudian psychiatrist by telling her that my problems had nothing to do with childhood bed-wetting, I was left to construct my own recovery programme; to fit the pieces of my own shattered mind back together. This was an interesting experience and one which, I suspect, taught me far more than if I had relied on psychiatry to do the job for me. The process of crisis and catharsis associated with mental breakdown and recovery has close parallels with the process that rites of initiation seek to emulate within the safety nets of tradition and peer group support.

My first conscious step towards reverence for the Goddess came in 1974, when I read Robert Graves' *The White Goddess* (1961). Graves was a fine poet, an unreliable historian and an idiosyncratic mythographer, influenced by Sir James Frazer's *The Golden Bough*, with its theories about dying and resurrected gods and folk survivals of ancient religion. Despite its errors of fact and interpretation, *The White Goddess* remains an extraordinary work, dealing, in essence, with the Goddess as poetic muse. Graves clearly expressed his concept of the Goddess in his dedication to the book:

All saints revile her, and all sober men
Ruled by the God Apollo's golden mean
In scorn of which I sailed to find her
In distant regions likeliest to hold her

Whom I desired above all things to know
Sister of the mirage and echo.

Green sap of Spring in the young wood astir
Will celebrate the Mountain Mother,
And every bird-song shout awhile for her;
But I am gifted, even in November
Rawest of seasons, with so huge a sense
Of her nakedly worn magnificence
I forget cruelty and past betrayal,
Careless of where the next bright bolt may fall.

During the early 1970s I had explored ritual magic through the writings of Israel Regardie (1971) and others. In the rites of the Hermetic Order of the Golden Dawn, gods and goddesses seemed to be little more than extras, or even props, in elaborate theatrical performances. The contrast between this and Graves' love for his White Goddess, made manifest through his mortal muses, was a stark one.

The White Goddess draws heavily on Celtic tradition, and my interest in this inspired me to look for a Druid group to join. The one that might have interested me, the Order of Bards, Ovates and Druids, fell silent in 1975 following the death of its founder, Ross Nichols. However, the image of the Druid had taken hold of my psyche and I began to think of myself as a Druid and wonder how I might become the image. Failing to find a Druid group, I eventually joined a newly formed Wiccan coven in the late 1970s.

The Wiccan way of working with Goddess energy is dramatic and powerful. During Wiccan rituals, the priestess becomes the Goddess through the process known as Drawing Down the Moon, during which the priest invokes the spirit of the Goddess into the priestess with these words:

O Great Goddess, Mighty Mother of us all, bringer of all fruitfulness; by bud and stem and root, by leaf and flower and fruit, by life and love do I invoke thee and call upon thee to descend upon the body of this, thy servant and priestess.

During this invocation, if all is working well, a transformation takes place within the priestess. She holds herself with greater confidence, her voice may deepen, she may appear to gain in stature, and the ambient level of light in the circle may increase, as if radiating from her body. Members of the coven treat her differently, for she has become more than human. The priest recognises the change in her, saying:

Hail, Goddess! From the Amalthean Horn
Pour forth thy store of love; I lowly bend
Before thee, I adore thee to the end,
With loving sacrifice thy shrine adorn.
Thy foot is to my lip . . . my prayer upborne
Upon the rising incense smoke; then spend
Thine ancient love, O Mighty One, descend
To aid me, who without thee am forlorn.

From this time on the priestess speaks as the Goddess. Her first act is to invoke her power into the priest who is her working partner. She then speaks the Charge, 'the words of the Great Mother'. This, in its most widely used form, was written by Doreen Valiente and Gerald Gardner, drawing on a variety of sources including the writings of Aleister Crowley and the Isis speech from Apuleius' *The Golden Ass*. The following version is the one my coven used, rewritten by me from Robert Graves' translation of Apuleius (1950: 228–30). Celtic Goddess names are substituted for the Classical ones in the original. First, the priest says:

> Listen now to the words of the Great Mother, she who our ancestors worshipped as Don, Mother of the immortal Gods; Arianrhod of the Spinning Castle; Rhiannon of the flowing mane; Branwen, daughter of Llyr; Olwen of the White Track; Blodeuwedd, maiden of flowers; Gwenhwyfar, beloved of Kings; Penarddun, Modron, Creurdylad, and many other names.

Then the priestess speaks:

> Behold I am come in answer to your prayers. I am Nature, the Universal Mother, Mistress of all the elements, primordial child of Time, mightiest of the Divine powers, Queen of the Dead, Queen also of the Ever-living; the single manifestation of all Gods and Goddesses that are. By my nod I command the shining heights of Heaven, the wholesome sea breezes, and the mournful silences of the world below. Though I am worshipped in many aspects, known by countless names, and propitiated with all manner of varied rites, yet the whole round Earth venerates me. The true Grove of the Druids of the Isles of Britain, who excel in ancient learning, call me by my true name, Ceridwen, Patroness of Bards. I have come in pity of your plight, I have come to favour and aid you. Mourn therefore no more, lament therefore no longer, for the hour of thy deliverance, shone over by my watchful light, is close at hand. Give heed then to my commands. Above all, have faith: do not think that my commands are hard to obey. Only keep these words of mine ever in your heart: that from this day forward till the last day of your life, you are in my service. It is only fitting to devote your whole life to the one who makes you whole. Under my protection you will prosper, and when at the destined end of your life you descend into the Land of Ghosts, there too you shall adore me as the Realm of Annwn's Queen, shining through the darkness as moonlight's gentle gleam.

When I first heard a version of this Charge spoken in a consecrated circle, in 1978, I was asked: 'Shall you obey this Charge?' Having said that I would, the priestess said:

> Then you shall be taught to be wise, that in the fullness of time you shall count yourself among those who serve the Gods, among those who belong to the Craft, among those who are called the Mighty Dead. Let thy life, and the life to come, be in the service of our noble Lady.

Even at the time, I realised the awesome responsibility implicit in those words. It was an oath I felt bound to honour, and I have tried to do so, aided by the Goddess, who has a habit of kicking me should I wander too far from the path. In retrospect, making that commitment was a major turning point in my life, which is, of course, what initiations are supposed to be.

Our coven became increasingly Druidic in its working, so we decided to stop calling ourselves a coven and call ourselves a grove instead. This Mother Grove represented the first incarnation of what later became the British Druid Order. As is the way of such things, the members of our group eventually went their separate ways, leading to a moment of doubt. The transformation of our priestess during the rite of Drawing Down the Moon had increased my awareness of the Goddess as a real and living presence, yet I still wondered if I was following the right path. One night, I stepped onto the balcony of my flat and looked up at the stars, asking for a sign that the way of the Goddess was right for me. I asked for a specific sign: a shooting star. No sooner had the thought formed in my mind than a brilliant meteor sliced across the sky directly overhead. That settled it. Not long afterwards I had a vision of the Goddess. She walked into my bedroom dressed in a floor-length, black, hooded cloak. She drew back the hood, and I saw that she was black, about 25 years old and very beautiful. She held me in her gaze for a few moments, then turned and passed back through the closed door. I got up to look for her, but she had gone. Since then she has appeared to me in many forms, by no means all of them human.

After our Mother Grove drifted apart, I reverted to solo Druidry, occasionally working with one or two others, but more spontaneously, in the open, in woods, by sacred springs or on the seashore. I began to appreciate the Goddess as Mother Nature, bathing in the beauty of moonlight as I had as a child. And I began to do something that had not been part of my Wiccan training, which was to practise Drawing Down the Moon alone. I used a simplified version of the ritual to call the energy of the Goddess, directing it into my heart centre, as a way to contact Goddess energy without an intermediary. I visualised this energy as a silver stream of moonlight. A male equivalent of Drawing Down the Moon, called Drawing Down the Sun, was published by Janet and Stewart Farrar a few years later in *The Witches' Way* (1984: 67–70), but I was attuned to moon energy, winter and night. Drawing Down the Moon in this way I never felt myself to be becoming the Goddess, as would a priestess, but opened up the connection with her that I saw as essential to ritual.

In about 1990, I contacted the newly revived Order of Bards, Ovates and Druids, now under the leadership of Philip Carr-Gomm. By one of those odd coincidences that liberally sprinkle the path of the Druid, the first OBOD Grove I attended took place at Imbolc, the primary Druidic festival of the Goddess. Before the ceremony, Philip asked me to read something to the assembly. To my delight, it was the Isis speech from Apuleius' *The Golden Ass*. It made me feel quite at home.

Throughout all this, a major problem in communicating with the Goddess remained my rationalist upbringing. Not only were my parents atheists, but I was brought up in a largely secular society. So, in spite of my weird childhood, growing connections with the Goddess, and the evidence of my senses, it took me nearly twenty years to convince myself that she existed outside my own mind. I adopted a Jungian approach for a while, believing that gods were archetypes of the collective unconscious, until I realised that the phrase is virtually meaningless. Jung's theory that our unconscious minds are all linked in some way is intuitively attractive, but

Jungian analysis is based on a series of such philosophical theories that are impossible either to prove or disprove, but are often mistaken for scientific statements.

The dowser and field archaeologist, Tom Lethbridge, in his book *Ghost and Ghoul* (1961), proposed the theory that negative ion fields created by, among other things, running water are capable of storing mental images and that, if enough people empower such images, they might take on an independent existence, becoming resident spirits, or even gods. Has anyone measured ionisation levels at Lourdes? This splendid theory appealed for a time, even though it suggests that communing with the Goddess is like holding a conversation with a hologram. But so much of the way of the Goddess lies beyond the rational that all efforts to pin it down under a satisfying scientific theory are, I now realise, doomed to failure.

– IV THE REALM OF MYTH: AWEN –

A widespread Pagan axiom maintains that 'All Gods are one God, and all Goddesses are one Goddess'. I have stated my own belief in an ultimate divine unity, yet one need only look briefly into the realm of myth to find deities behaving in such contradictory ways that it is hard to believe they are really one. My own experience of the Goddess is that she appears in many forms, and yet I still refer to her as 'the Goddess'. Rather than denoting a single entity, I use this as a convenient shorthand for a Goddess energy that manifests in many different ways. I see this energy as equivalent to the Hindu Shakti, defined in Chambers' *Dictionary of Beliefs and Religions* (Chambers 1992) as:

> The female energy or power of the Hindu god Shiva. Whilst Shiva is regarded as passive consciousness his consort, Shakti, is the power whereby he performs the five acts of creation, maintenance and destruction of the universe, bestowing grace on devotees and concealing himself from them. Shakti is personified in Shiva's wives . . . in orthodox texts, but is particularly important in the . . . Tantras . . . She is personified in various gentle or ferocious forms [and] becomes more important . . . than Shiva in many Tantric traditions. In Hindu Tantra Shakti is not only a cosmic power, but also a power within the body in the form of Kundalini who, once awakened through yoga, causes liberation.

In the Druidry I practise this energy is called Awen, literally a 'fluid essence', or 'flowing spirit'. Awen is associated with the Pagan British Goddess, Ceridwen, whose name means 'Crooked Woman', or 'Bent White One'. Medieval Welsh Bards referred to her as patroness of their order, and the inspired poet was said to have drunk from her cauldron containing Awen in liquid form. The three gifts traditionally conferred by Awen are poetic inspiration, prophecy and shape-shifting, powers equated with the three main areas of Druidic practice: poetic inspiration for the Bard, prophecy for the Ovate, and shape-shifting for the Druid. Awen, Shakti and the Christian Holy Spirit are each held to be the power whereby deity carries out the act of creation. As a blessing from the Goddess, male Bards recognised the presence of Awen in women, who became their muses.

Of all the Goddesses in Celtic myth, Ceridwen is the one I relate to most strongly. She is a very witchy Goddess who features in the Story of Taliesin, preserved in a sixteenth-century manuscript, but containing much older material. Lady Charlotte Guest published an English translation of it in *The Mabinogion* (1906: 263ff.). Ceridwen brewed the Cauldron of Awen, or Inspiration, for her son, Afagddu, 'Utter Darkness', a child so ugly that she decided to make him all-wise to compensate. The cauldron brewed for a year and a day, during which time Ceridwen had to go gathering herbs, leaving a blind man named Morda to tend the fire, and a child named Gwion Bach, 'Little Innocent', to stir the cauldron.

And one day, towards the end of the year, as Ceridwen was culling plants and making incantations, it chanced that three drops of the charmed liquor flew out of the cauldron and fell upon the finger of Gwion Bach. And by reason of their great heat he put his finger to his mouth, and the instant he put those marvel-working drops into his mouth, he foresaw everything that was to come, and perceived that his chief care must be to guard against the wiles of Ceridwen, for vast was her skill. And in very great fear he fled towards his own land. And the cauldron burst in two, because all the liquor within it except the three charm-bearing drops was poisonous.

Thereupon came in Ceridwen and saw all the toil of the whole year lost. And she seized a billet of wood and struck the blind Morda on the head until one of his eyes fell out upon his cheek. And he said, 'Wrongfully hast thou disfigured me, for I am innocent. Thy loss was not because of me.' 'Thou speakest truth', said Ceridwen, 'it was Gwion Bach who robbed me.'

And Ceridwen went forth after him, running. And he saw her, and changed himself into a hare and fled. But she changed herself into a greyhound and turned him. And he ran towards a river, and became a fish. And she in the form of an otter-bitch chased him under the water, until he was fain to turn himself into a bird of the air. She, as a hawk, followed him and gave him no rest in the sky. And just as she was about to stoop upon him, and he was in fear of death, he espied a heap of winnowed wheat on the floor of a barn, and he dropped among the wheat, and turned himself into one of the grains. Then she transformed herself into a high-crested black hen, and went to the wheat and scratched at it with her feet, and found him out and swallowed him. And, as the story says, she bore him nine months in her womb, and when she was delivered of him, she could not find it in her heart to kill him, by reason of his beauty. So she wrapped him in a leathern bag, and cast him into the sea to the mercy of God, on the twenty-ninth day of April.

The child was rescued on May morning, and the first person to open the leathern bag cried out 'Behold, a radiant brow!' Hence the child was called Taliesin, 'Radiant Brow', and he became Primary Chief Bard of the Isles of Britain. His initiatory ordeals at the hands of the Goddess, and the wisdom he gained from them, are referred to in several medieval poems attributed to him, as in the following, from my own translation:

I have obtained the Awen from the cauldron of Ceridwen;
I have been Bard of the Harp to Lleon of Lochlin;

I have been teacher to all intelligences,
I am able to instruct the whole universe;
I shall be until the day of doom upon the face of the Earth,
And it is not known whether my body be flesh or fish.
Then I was for nine months
In the womb of the hag Ceridwen.
I was originally little Gwion,
At length I am Taliesin.

Ceridwen is clearly an incarnation of what Celtic scholar Anne Ross has identified as 'the Divine Hag' (1973: 139ff.). Yet this darkly dangerous Goddess was the patroness of medieval British Bards and the source of their inspiration. Clearly she also has her beautiful aspect, if one approaches her with due reverence. This dual nature is borne out by my own experience of the Goddess. She confers great blessings on those who follow her, but cross her and she can wreak havoc.

One means by which the divine spirit is invoked in Druid working is chanting the word Awen three or nine times. This single-word mantra for invoking Goddess energy has no direct equivalent in Wicca. In effect, it is not unlike the experience I had when using the rite of Drawing Down the Moon. I still see the flow of energy as silver-white, although it has become denser over the years and now appears like quicksilver. I have seen a silver bowl hovering over sacred circles, into which Awen in the form of silver liquid pours from a large female hand until it overflows. On other occasions I have seen this fluid flow from sacred circles where rituals have been performed, entering the veins of the Earth, bringing healing energy to the land and its inhabitants.

Now, I revere the Goddess as a being external to myself, persuaded of her reality by the fact that she speaks to me, gives me visions and shows me signs through the natural world. She awakens power within me: the power I need to act as Druid and priest. I draw on her power, the Awen, but when I take on the mantle of divinity myself, I do so as a God. When working with priestesses within Druidry and the broader Pagan community I connect with the Goddess through them, feeding back to them the energy of the God, inspired, evoked or invoked in me by Goddess and priestess. For priest and priestess to weave ritual in sacred space is to experience the primal dance of God and Goddess, from which the universe was created and by which it is constantly renewed. The priestess is Shakti, 'power', or Awen, 'the flowing spirit', the primal creative energy of the Goddess; the priest is Shiva, 'the friend, or kind one', or Taliesin, 'the radiant brow', that which directs the energy.

I do not revere male deities, though I respect the gods of many traditions, for, as well as a pantheist and dualist, I am a polytheist. Reverence I reserve for the Goddess, perhaps because she is other, mysterious, and therefore easier to perceive as divine. She represents separateness and the desire for union. To revere a God would, perhaps, be uncomfortably close to worshipping myself! The character played by Peter O'Toole in the film The Ruling Class was asked why he thought he was God and replied that he had been praying one day when he suddenly realised he was talking to himself. To revere that which I can become would, I think, leave me in a similar position. Tantric tradition responds to this problem by concluding that no man may worship a god unless he himself becomes a god. My most powerful experiences of God energy come when the Anglo-Saxon god, Woden, merges his spirit with mine. Our connection stems partly from our both walking with wolves as spirit companions, but also from memories of a past life as his priest. As I first encountered him, he was about fifty years old, grey-haired and bearded, stockily built, strong and one-eyed. His strength is both inner and outer, resulting from harsh ordeals in search of vision, for which he gave up an eye, hung from the World Tree nine nights, sacrificed by himself to himself, and seduced a giantess. He is grim-faced through having seen the ultimate destruction of humankind and the gods. He knows the secrets of the world through the eyes of the two ravens Hugin and Munin, 'Thought' and 'Memory', who are his companions along with the wolves Gere and Freke, 'Voracious' and 'Greedy'. To feel the wolf-cloaked presence of this powerful deity walk into one's body is to partake of the strength of one who has travelled to the world's rim, walked with gods, fought with giants, and wrested wisdom from the jaws of death. All fear and uncertainty are swept aside.

As well as the wolf, I work with the spirit of the eagle, the serpent and other creatures. This is done partly through shape-shifting, which, as I have indicated, is a skill traditionally possessed by the Druid. This ability came to me through a sweat lodge, a rebirth ritual through which I was guided by two priestesses and by the Grandmother of Lakota Sioux tradition, who told me, among other things, to listen to my instincts more than my head. Shape-shifting features in a number of poems attributed to Taliesin, including the famous 'Battle of the Trees' which, in my translation, contains the lines:

I have been in many shapes
Before I took this congenial form:
I have been a sword, narrow in shape;
I believe, since it is apparent,
I have been a teardrop in the sky,
I have been a glittering star,
I have been a word in a letter,
I have been a book in my origin,
I have been a gleaming ray of light,
I have been a pathway,
I have been an eagle,
I have been a coracle on the brink,
I have been the direction of a staff,
I have been a sword in a yielding cleft,
I have been a shield in open conflict,
I have been a string on a harp,
Shape-shifting nine years,
In water, in foam,
I have been consumed in fire,
I have been passion in a covert.
Am I not he who will sing

Of beauty in what is small;
Beauty in the Battle of the Tree-tops.

Implicit in this and other Taliesin poems is the final gift Ceridwen confers on those who honour her: experience of our own divinity and our identity with all creation.

– V CONCLUSION –

The current resurgence of Goddess spirituality manifests in many ways. In the Christian church, hymnals have been produced in which the deity is female, and some branches of Christianity now recognise women as priests. Goddess-centred Paganism is expanding rapidly. This raises the obvious question, why? There may be many answers, but one that seems viable is that the Goddess who manifests as Mother Nature does not want our species to destroy the planet. While many are experiencing the love of the Goddess through turning to her, others are experiencing her anger through setting themselves against her. The anger of the Goddess finds more ways to express itself as the threat of global ecological disaster grows. To give a few examples: the sperm count is declining rapidly, apparently due to increasing levels of the female hormone, oestrogen, in the environment; global warming is now accepted as fact, even by governments; the polar ice caps are breaking up; floods and hurricanes are becoming more frequent and severe; holes in the ozone layer are causing increased levels of skin cancer; 'new' diseases such as BSE/CJD and AIDS are appearing and old diseases are developing immunity to existing treatments. Of course, these events may be purely random, with no causal link between them and no purpose behind them. Or, if there is a causal link, it is simply humankind: we are destroying our own planet. Personally, I tend to agree with the Native American teacher, John Two Birds, who says that 'Grandmother is pissed off', and that Grandfather is going to start 'smudging' cities. Smudging is a Native American purification ritual in which smoke from burning herbs is blown over the object to be purified. Smudging cities means cleansing the Earth of their presence by destroying them. The gods are turning our own destructive actions against us, warning us of the folly of our actions. This does not align very well with the New Age fluffy-bunny view of Mother Earth as all-nurturing, all-loving, all-forgiving. Instead, we see her as inflicting suffering in order to prevent greater harm being done to her creation. This is entirely compatible with my experience of her.

How should we respond to the challenge? If we look on the destruction of our planet as random or inevitable, then there is nothing we can do. If, however, we accept that the gods have a hand in it, then we can attempt to ascertain what they want us to do, and then do it. Of course, blaming deities can be a way of abnegating our own responsibilities. We need to work through ritual and realignment, but should also take responsibility for our own garbage. I met Two Birds while he was on a world tour, contacting tribal peoples, most of whom shared his view of impending ecological disaster. In Britain, he sought out Druids and Wiccans, recognising us as the medicine people of our tribes. He believes that the medicine people of the world hold the key to averting global catastrophe through the ability to create a realignment of the human spirit. He has a vision of tribal peoples gathering together to make healing rituals. Many are working to bring this vision into reality. Mother Earth needs our help. She has given us so much, how can we ignore her call?

In Celtic myths, goddesses usually drive the action. The gods and heroes would have few adventures and gain little of value were they not spurred on by their desire to pursue, outwit, subdue, woo, bed or wed the Goddess in her myriad forms. Celtic Bards would have wrought no rhymes without the bittersweet draught of her inspiration. Many Celtic goddesses are represented as fearsome figures who must be treated with great respect. The goddesses I work with tend to be just these feisty, spiky ones, in particular, Ceridwen. In my experience, in order to become her priest, it is necessary, like Taliesin, to be devoured by the Goddess in her most fearsome aspect as the black hag of winter and the dark of the moon. Only then can we be reborn into the deep warmth of her loving embrace, the fullness of her nurturing breast. These are powerful metaphors, but awesome realities.

I give thanks to the multifaceted and eternally fascinating Goddess for her many gifts, and I leave you with the words of her Bard, Taliesin, from my translation of his poem, The Cattle-Fold of the Bards':

I am song to the last; I am clear and bright;
I am hard; I am a Druid;
I am a wright; I am well-wrought;
I am a serpent; I am reverence, that is an open receptacle.

May all who revere the Goddess be open receptacles to receive her blissful Spirit of Inspiration. So let it be.

CHAPTER 13

Wicca as Nature Religion
VIVIANNE CROWLEY

– I INTRODUCTION –

Wicca or witchcraft is one branch of modern western Paganism. Its self-image is that of an 'Old Religion'; a reawakening of the religious values, ideas, ideals and practices of our Pagan ancestors. Amongst these religious ideas is the veneration of nature. Nature is considered to be ensouled, alive, 'divine'. The beliefs of most Wiccans include elements of pantheism and animism. The divine is seen as 'force' or 'energy' and as manifest in the world of nature. The divine force is generally represented as two deities – Goddess and God – who appear in different forms in different seasons of the year. The forms include the Corn God, Green Man, Sun God and Great Mother Goddess. The deities are worshipped through group rituals. These enact a seasonal myth cycle in which the processes of nature – conception, birth, mating, parenthood, maturation, death – are portrayed in the dynamic interaction of Goddess and God. Themes and symbols drawn from nature are central therefore to Wiccan belief and practice. How does Wicca view its relationship to the world of nature?

– II WHAT IS WICCA? –

The great Sun, moving in the heavenly houses, has left the House of the Fishes for the House of the Water-Bearer. In the coming age shall humanity be holy, and in the perfection of the human shall we find the humane. Take up the manhood into Godhead, and bring down the Godhead into manhood, and this shall be the day of God with us; for God is made manifest in Nature, and Nature is the self-expression of God. (Fortune 1976: 173)

These words were not written by a Wiccan, but appear in the novel *The Sea Priestess* by the esoteric novelist, psychotherapist and proto-Pagan Dion Fortune (Violet Firth), whose works are frequently read and quoted by Wiccans. A Wiccan might choose to say 'the divine' or 'Goddess' rather than 'God', but would echo the sentiment that the divine is immanent in human beings and in nature.

So what is Wicca? Wicca is the name given by its practitioners to the religion of witchcraft. The word 'Wicca' derives from the Anglo-Saxon word for witch and has been used in its present sense since the 1950s. Within the Wiccan community, the term 'witchcraft' is used in a special sense to mean a Pagan mystery religion and nature religion which worships Goddess and God and is open to both men and women. The words 'witchcraft' and 'witch' are often capitalised by practitioners to distinguish their form of 'witchcraft' from anthropological and other uses of the word.

The 'founding father' of modern Wicca was Gerald Gardner, a colonial administrator with a long-standing interest in folklore and naturism. On his return to England on retirement in the 1930s, Gerald Gardner claimed to have made contact with a group of people practising witchcraft. The witches met in the New Forest in Hampshire in a small group, a coven, with a system of initiation not dissimilar to the three degrees of Freemasonry. The group practised activities traditionally associated with witchcraft such as casting spells, but these were for beneficial and altruistic purposes. The witches also worshipped their gods through seasonal rites. A strong distinction was made between witchcraft and Satanism. The witches did not consider themselves to be Satanists or to be members of an anti-Christian cult; rather they claimed to be Pagans, worshippers of pre-Christian deities, the keepers of the 'Old Religion', whose ancestors had practised Paganism underground and secretly for centuries since its suppression by the Christian church.

The veracity of Gerald Gardner's claim that his group were practising an ancient form of faith handed down in secrecy over generations is a subject of much debate within the Wiccan community. Regardless, however, of whether he was reviving an ancient tradition or launching a new religion, Gerald Gardner's books and in particular *Witchcraft Today* (1954) succeeded in spawning a Wiccan movement which has spread first into other English-speaking countries – the United States, Canada, Australia and New Zealand; second into countries such as the Netherlands and Scandinavia, where his books have been readily accessible because English is widely used as a second language; and more recently, from the early 1980s onwards, into countries such as Germany, where Gardner's works and those of his successors have been translated. Interestingly, Wicca has had little appeal in Catholic countries and few books have been translated into French, Italian, Spanish or Portuguese. There is little interest in Wicca in Ireland, for instance, despite the absence of language barriers and the residence there of two of Wicca's most prolific authors – Janet and Stewart Farrar. The reasons for this are unclear. One could speculate that Wicca's emphasis on the feminine in the form of the Goddess and its use of ritual might be more novel and therefore attractive features to those of a Protestant background. Alternatively, those in Catholic countries who are seeking alternative forms of spirituality may be less likely to experiment with a religion which contains deities such as the Horned God and practices (in some groups at least) of ritual nudity which would be difficult to reconcile with their earlier religious teachings.

How large is this movement? Wicca is the most active branch of the Pagan movement. Extrapolating from the membership figures of the UK-based Pagan Federation, which is the largest European organisation in the field and possibly the largest world-wide, it is likely that over half of all Pagans would describe themselves as practising some kind of Wicca. However, given that most Wiccans do not join membership organisations of any kind but belong to small autonomous groups or are solo practitioners, numbers are difficult to assess. Harvey and Hardman (1996) estimate that there are between 50,000 and 100,000 Pagans (Wiccans, Druids, followers of the Northern Tradition and others) in the UK. Walter Schwartz, in the *Guardian*, gives an estimate of 100,000 Pagans. The *Daily Telegraph* plumps for more – 200,000. The newspaper figures seem inflated, but the Pagan movement as a whole is growing, and within that Wicca.

– III WICCA'S SELF-IMAGE –

– MARGARET MURRAY –

If Gardner's account of the historical continuity of Wicca with ancient Paganism is suspect, where did his information about and images of Wicca originate? Gardner's image draws heavily on that of the controversial folklorist, anthropologist and Egyptologist Dr Margaret Murray of University College London. Two of her books were extremely influential in the formation of modern witchcraft, *The Witch-Cult in Western Europe: A Study in Anthropology*, first published in 1921, and *The God of the Witches*, which followed ten years later in 1931.

Margaret Murray's books are not good history but represent a selective presentation and interpretation of the facts. Her thesis, which Gerald Gardner was later to adopt, was that the witches persecuted in the sixteenth- and seventeenth-century witch trials in Europe and the United States were not devil-worshippers, or the victims of society's hysteria and paranoia, but Pagans who worshipped the Horned God and practised magic. In Murray's view, theirs was a cult which derived directly from an ancient Paganism, which had co-existed secretly with Christianity with little active persecution until the witch trials. Moreover, it was protected by those in high places. Many of the English kings were said by Murray to have been sympathetic to the Pagan cause, if not active leaders of it. William II (William Rufus), hitherto more famous for his homosexuality than his spirituality, was recast by Murray as a sacrificial king in the James Frazer mould and the secret leader of the witch-cult.

For Margaret Murray, witchcraft (she does not use the word 'Wicca') involved rain-making and fertility rituals. It was much like any tribal culture she would have studied as an anthropologist. She writes of familiars, the Horned God, coven leadership and discipline (here seen mainly as male-led), and witches' death and rebirth myths. Witchcraft is a fertility cult which worships a dying and resurrecting God. The focus on a Goddess which Gardner later introduced is not apparent here. Murray's image draws on the Cambridge school of anthropology and in particular on Sir James Frazer's famous study of myth, *The Golden Bough*. For Murray, the witches' God is not only the Horned God of hunt and forest, he is the sacrificial victim, the Corn God of the harvest, the dying and resurrecting God. These ideas permeated from James Frazer into anthropology and literature and can be found not only in Margaret Murray, but in Jessie Weston's understanding of the Grail myth in *From Ritual to Romance* (1921), Naomi Mitchinson's novel *The Corn King and the Spring Queen* (1931) and history teacher Henry Treece's novel *The Golden Strangers* (1956). Murray writes:

> The chants used by the witches, the dances, the burning of the god and the broadcast
> scattering of his ashes, all point to the fact that this was a fertility cult; and this is the view

taken by those contemporary writers who give a more or less comprehensive account of the religion and ritual. (Murray 1921: 169)

– GERALD GARDNER –

Gerald Gardner's books cover similar subject matter to those of Margaret Murray. In fact, his *Witchcraft Today* was introduced by Murray. Murray as an academic had created an historical basis for a Pagan witch-cult and Gardner claimed to have found it still in existence in his day.

In Gerald Gardner's books, Wicca is described as the remnants of northern and western European Paganism with influences from the Classical Mysteries. Its origins were said to lie in the Stone Age, but it had been suppressed by the Christian church, which identified its Horned God, named in different parts of Europe as Pan, Cernunnos or Herne, with the Christian Devil. Wicca was not therefore a 'New Religious Movement' but a 'Revived Religious Tradition'.

Gardner describes witchcraft as a fertility cult, but little mention is made of nature religion *per se*. He is also interested in magical powers and the traditional image of the witch as caster of spells. However, despite Margaret Murray's portrayal of the witch as rain-maker, Gardner comments specifically (Gardner 1954: 126–7) that modern witches do not make rain. There is much discussion about the use of dance within a nine-foot-radius circle as a way of raising magical power. Witches are described as worshipping the gods at four major 'Gaelic' festivals: Hallowe'en, Samhain, or Samhuin (1 November); Brigid (1 February); Bealteine or Beltane (1 May); and Lughnasadh (1 August) (Gardner 1954: 130). The festivals that fall in autumn and winter are described as festivals for the God and the spring and summer festivals are dedicated to the Goddess. The deities are seen in what would now be described as sexually stereotyped ways. The God is described as a protector, the Lord of Death and giver of rebirth; the Goddess is described as 'sweetness and beauty'.

More interestingly, the Goddess is also described as 'the soul of nature'. Below is an excerpt from a text known as the 'Great Mother Charge', which has become a standard part of Wiccan ritual liturgy.

> Hear ye the words of the Star Goddess; she in the dust of whose feet are the hosts of heaven; whose body encircles the universe.
>
> I, who am the beauty of the green earth and the white Moon among the stars, and the mystery of the waters, and the desire of the heart of man, call unto thy soul. Arise, and come unto me. For I am the soul of nature, who gives life to the universe. From me all things proceed, and unto me all things must return; and before my face, beloved of Gods and of men, let thine inmost divine self be enfolded in the rapture of the infinite. (Quoted in Farrar and Farrar 1984: 298)

Here, direct links are made between the Wiccan Goddess and the world of nature. Wicca enjoins the exaltation of women, the Goddess and nature.

Wicca as presented by Gardner is not a world-transforming revolutionary movement. It is 'world-affirming' in the sense that the created world is to be enjoyed, but Gardner's Wicca looks to stability, the preservation of ancient tradition, and the revival of an 'Old Religion' which is in danger of dying out, rather than being a radical new movement seeking social reform. Gerald Gardner's vision of society can be found in *Witchcraft Today*:

> The witch wants quiet, regular, ordinary good government with everyone content and happy, plenty of fun and games when you are alive, all fear of death being taken away; as you grow older, you rather welcome the idea of death, as an abode of peace and rest, where you grow young again, ready to return for another round on earth. (Gardner 1954: 127)

Allthough the emphasis is on this world and on reincarnation to return the believer to it, Wicca is also concerned with the inner world and the 'Otherworld'; presumably because experience of these other dimensions can enhance human enjoyment of life on the material plane. Gardner writes:

> Witchcraft was, and is, not a cult for everybody. Unless you have an attraction to the occult, a sense of wonder, a feeling that you can slip for a few minutes out of the world into the world of faery, it is of no use to you. (Gardner 1954: 29)

– Doreen Valiente –

Gardner's books, magazine articles and radio broadcasts created an interest in Wicca and the beginning of the Wiccan movement. However, there was a major flaw in the image of Wicca as presented by Murray and Gardner – Wicca as a fertility religion. Why would a fertility cult appeal to modern worshippers who, with some exceptions, were more likely to be preoccupied with birth control than fertility? The answer was supplied by an initiate of Gerald Gardner's witch coven who later went on to develop her own form of witchcraft – Doreen Valiente. A prolific writer of formative books, but not an initiator and hence direct creator of other witches, Doreen Valiente recasts the concept of fertility in her own image. She writes in *An ABC of Witchcraft Past and Present* (1973):

> But, the sceptic may say, what place have the rites of an ancient fertility cult in the modern world at all? Do we still need to perform these old rituals in order to make the crops grow? And as for increasing the population, isn't the world grossly over-populated already?
>
> The answer is that all things, including living religions, evolve; and the Craft of the Wise is a living religion. Over the years, we have begun to see a new concept of the idea of fertility; one that is not only material, but also of the mind and the soul.
>
> The creative forces are not only creative in the physical sense; they can also beget and give birth to art, music, poetry and literature. We speak of people's minds being 'fertile' or 'barren'. We talk of 'cultivating' ideas as well as fields; of new 'conceptions' of a better way of living. There is a spiritual as well as a material fertility; and human life is a desert without it. These are the aims towards which sincere and intelligent present-day Pagans, witches, and Nature-worshippers are tending.
>
> The spirit of the old rites, therefore, continues; but in a higher form. The concern is not so much with literal fertility as with vitality, and with finding one's harmony with Nature. In this way, people seek for a philosophy of life which bestows peace of mind, as well as physical satisfaction. (Valiente 1973: 135)

Doreen Valiente had also described her rationale for the practice of Witchcraft some years before in her after-dinner speech at the 1964 annual dinner of *Pentagram*, a witchcraft magazine:

> What witches seek for in celebrating these seasonal festivals is a sense of oneness with Nature, and the exhilaration which comes from contact with the One Universal Life. People today need this because they are aware of the tendency of modern life to cut them off from their kinship with the world of living Nature; until their own individuality is processed away, and they begin to feel as if they are just another cog in a huge, senseless machine.
>
> It is the reaction against this feeling which is attracting people's interest in Witchcraft today. They want to get back to Nature, and be human beings again, as She intended them to be.

Doreen Valiente's Wicca has similar purposes to those of Gardner, 'a philosophy of life which bestows peace of mind, as well as physical satisfaction'. However, it is no longer a fertility religion, but a nature religion.

– IV Eco-Wicca –

A nature religion implies a nature to worship. The idea that nature was being exploited, desouled and desacralised and that our environment was in danger was not new to the 1970s. This was a common theme of artists, writers, poets, philosophers, religious thinkers and others from the eighteenth century onwards. However, with the increased pace of industrialisation throughout the nineteenth and into the twentieth centuries, it was a matter of increasing concern. Here, for instance, is Lord Dunsany's 'The Prayer of the Flowers' which appeared in *Fifty One Tales* (1915) and appealed sufficiently to modern witches and Pagans to be reproduced by Pagans Against Nukes in the Lughnasadh 1984 edition of their magazine *Pipes of Pan*:

> It was the voice of the flowers on the West wind, the loveable, the old, the lazy West wind, blowing ceaselessly, blowing sleepily, going Greecewards.
>
> 'The woods have gone away, they have fallen and left us, men love us no longer, we are lonely by moonlight. Great engines rush over the beautiful fields, their ways lie hard and terrible up and down the land.
>
> 'The cancerous cities spread over the grass, they clatter in their lairs continually, they glitter about us blemishing the night.
>
> 'The woods are gone, O Pan, the woods, the woods. And thou art far, O Pan, and far away.'
>
> I was standing by night between two railway embankments on the edge of a Midland city. On one of them I saw the trains go by, once in every two minutes, and on the other the trains went by twice in every five.
>
> Quite close were the glaring factories, and the sky above them wore the fearful look that it wears in dreams of fever.
>
> The flowers were right in the stride of that advancing city, and thence I heard them sending up their cry. And then I heard, beating musically upwind, the voice of Pan reproving them from Arcady – 'Be patient a little, these things are not for long.'

Concern about environmental issues gathered pace during the twentieth century. Initially, concern focused on access to the environment. Urbanisation, coupled with cheap public transport and later the car, brought a desire for and the possibility of leisure access to the countryside. In the 1920s, the Ramblers' Association led mass trespasses to secure access to the countryside for the urban masses. Later concerns focused on the preservation of the planet and of the environment. In the 1950s young and old marched against nuclear weapons; in the 1970s environmental pollution became the rallying cause. Nature was on the agenda.

During the 1970s, a whole new generation was being drawn into Wicca. These were not middle-class ex-colonials who were part of the 'establishment', as many of Gerald Gardner's generation had been, but younger people influenced by the hippie era of peace, love and student demonstrations. Some were commune dwellers. Here, for instance, is a quotation from an application letter written by a would-be member of a now defunct organisation, the British and Irish Pagan Movement, which was published in the Midsummer 1971 edition of its magazine *Waxing Moon*:

> I'd like to join the Pagan Movement. I'm very glad that something like this exists; I heard about it as you know through the Commune Movement, and the two have a lot linking them together, I think, in many ways. I've been interested in the wica [sic] for several years now, not so much from the ritual magic angle but from the fact that witches seem to be more in harmony with the earth, with nature and with PLACES . . . My interests generally accord with the Commune Movement and an ecological, harmonious, non-violent approach to life in general.

The word 'ecological' is important here. Stimulated by those who had participated in the 'alternative society' of the 1960s and 1970s, the ethos of Wicca and Paganism was beginning to evolve from nature veneration to nature preservation. In 1981, the organisation Pagans Against Nukes (PAN) was formed. Its aims and objectives were displayed prominently in its magazine *Pipes of Pan*, which appeared throughout most of the 1980s:

> Pagans Against Nukes (PAN) is an activist organisation dedicated to the banishment of nuclear technology from our Earth, and the re-establishment of a culture that lives in harmony with Her. We seek to co-ordinate all Pagans, of whatever land and tradition, in political and magical work to achieve this end, that the Earth be Greened Anew.

On the other side of the Atlantic, similar ideas were permeating the US Wiccan community. From the late 1960s onwards, Wicca began a strong period of growth in the United States. Gerald Gardner's books became known and within the United States books began to be written about Wicca by witches such as Sybil Leek and Lady Sheba, who were media-friendly and keen self-publicists. The image presented of Wicca by these early US books was drawn from the British template. In fact, Sybil Leek was English and had started her witch career in the New Forest. However, a more radical interpretation of Wicca was to emerge from the American witch Starhawk, one of the generation who had experienced student life in the 1970s.

Her book *The Spiral Dance* (1979) was to have an enormous impact. Starhawk's description of the history of witchcraft draws on the picture presented by Murray and Gardner:

> Witchcraft is a religion, perhaps the oldest religion, extant in the West. Its origins go back before Christianity, Judaism, Islam – before Buddhism and Hinduism, as well, and it is very different from all the so-called great religions. The Old Religion, as we call it, is closer in spirit to Native American traditions or to the shamanism of the Arctic. It is not based on dogma or a set of beliefs, not on scriptures or a sacred book revealed by a great man. Witchcraft takes its teachings from nature, and reads inspiration in the movements of the sun, moon and stars, the flight of birds, the slow growth of trees, and the cycles of the seasons. (Starhawk 1979: 2–3)

In Starhawk's work, there is, however, much greater emphasis on the 'aliveness' of nature:

> To Witches, as to other peoples who live close to nature, all things – plants, animals, stones, and stars – are alive, are on some level conscious beings. All things are divine, are manifestations of the Goddess. (Starhawk 1979: 20)

For her, Wicca includes the by now standard ritual forms, Goddess and Horned God worship, and magic, but there is also a new element: Wicca as the basis for radical action. Starhawk sees Wicca as encompassing active environmentalism:

> Meditation on the balance of nature might be considered a spiritual act in Witchcraft, but not as much as cleaning up garbage left at a campsite or marching to protest an unsafe nuclear plant. (Starhawk 1979: 12)

The transition is significant. Wicca had moved out of the darkness, the occult world of witchery, to occupy the moral high ground – environmentalism. To be at one with nature in one's inner self is no longer enough; radical action to preserve nature is now important.

Just as the commune and hippie movement brought an influx of people into Wicca in the 1970s, so environmental activism brought in a new generation in the 1980s and 1990s. Many of today's Wiccans belong to environmental groups, some Wiccan and Pagan groups are created specifically to focus on environmental concerns, and many cite environmental concerns as one of their reasons for becoming Wiccan. Here, for instance, is a brief biography of one of the founders of the Dragon organisation:

> [His] environmental campaigning began in the early 1980s while studying philosophy and literature at Essex University. His interest in philosophy and the environment led to Paganism and thence to the formation of the Dragon Environmental Group, a Pagan organisation combining environmental work with eco-magic. He was initiated into Wicca in 1991. (Harvey and Hardman 1996: vii)

Dragon was created to practise 'eco-magic', that is, rituals and spells to oppose road-building programmes and other projects with negative environmental impact, and to stimulate environmental awareness. Its rituals are public and take place at threatened sites.

It can be argued that from nature worship to environmentalism and back again is a logical progression. This idea is explored in *Pantheism: A Non-Theistic Concept of Deity* (1994), by Michael P. Levine of the Philosophy Department of the University of Western Australia, in relation to one approach to the divine which is apparent in Wicca:

> Pantheism gives rational confirmation to the sense of unity with Nature which so many people . . . have experienced. From the most primitive vegetation rites to the most sophisticated poetry there is a vast and varied testimony to the fact that the human mind has a spontaneous tendency to feel oneness with natural phenomena, and to see in them a manifestation of the Spirit in which they too participate. This feeling and this vision constitute a perennial strand in 'natural piety'. (H. P. Owen quoted in Levine 1994: 355)

This 'natural piety' impacts on the pantheist's relationship to the earth. Here, Levine quotes Harold W. Wood Jr, a founder of the Universal Pantheist Society:

> Instead of a 'conquer the Earth' mentality, pantheism teaches that respect and reverence for the Earth demands continuing attempts to understand ecosystems. Therefore, among religious viewpoints, pantheism is uniquely qualified to support a foundation for environmental ethics . . . by learning to celebrate and revere such natural events . . . people would be less likely to permit unfettered pollution to take place . . . acid rain would not be seen as merely an inconvenience, but as a travesty against a holy manifestation . . . Pantheist ethics has as its goal a closeness with nature . . . a relationship with nature equivalent to traditional religion's relationship with God. It is closeness based not upon imitation, but upon reverential communion. (Levine 1994: 227)

In taking to environmental activism, Wicca has not abandoned its magical roots. Today, Wiccans not only campaign against environmental abuse and misuse and engage in physical work to reclaim environmentally damaged sites, they also petition their gods and do acts of magic designed to influence the minds of polluters to change their policies and actions. This is logical in a belief system where the material and the spiritual are often seen as a series of 'levels' (Farrar and Farrar 1984: 106–13). 'As above so below, but after another fashion' often appears in Wiccan writings and is a reworking of the saying attributed to Hermes Trismegistus from the body of Neo-Platonist texts, the *Corpus Hermeticum*. For the Wiccan, if it is to be effective, action on one level (the magical/spiritual) must be backed up by action on the physical plane.

In reinforcing physical action by spiritual activity, and vice versa, contemporary Wiccans are acting in a way not dissimilar to, say, a Christian Socialist or a medical missionary. However, the Christian focus has tended to be primarily on human concerns; although environmentalism is now rapidly entering the Christian agenda. Wiccan altruism is less human-focused. It reflects a world view which sees humankind as one of many species; better endowed intellectually but possibly having no spiritual superiority to other species. The Pagan Federation's first mass activity was to declare an annual Earth Healing Day. Members alone or in groups are encouraged to conduct a public, outdoor ritual which has the aim of healing the earth. This takes place at a certain time on a certain day (overseas members synchronise with GMT). However, the rite is preceded by action on the physical plane. Members are encouraged to conduct rituals at sites that are under environmental threat, such as polluted beaches, and to clean up the site before their rite. Members are also encouraged to take a more long-term environmental stance by joining environmental organisations and through lobbying Members of Parliament about local environmental issues.

– V Conclusion –

Wicca is undergoing a transition from an esoteric occult tradition to a more open exoteric movement with environmentalism high on the agenda. This has implications for the way in which Wiccans lead their everyday lives. 'Founding father' Gerald Gardner's focus was on continuity with the past and on how Wiccans might be in contact with the spiritual/magical realm and hence enhance their everyday lives. Modern Wicca is concerned, like the western Pagan movement as a whole, with the condition of nature and with its future. Open 'Earth Healing' and eco-magic rituals encourage an environmentalist agenda which must have political overtones. Nature exists 'out there' in the world, rather than in the inner, closed and secretive world of the occultist. The transition from fertility cult to nature religion and from secretive rituals to pantheist activism can be expected to change Wicca from an occult tradition to a more mainstream movement broadly in sympathy with the aspirations and concerns of many in the postmodern world.

CHAPTER 14

The Gal–Gael Peoples of Scotland: on Tradition Re-bearing, Recovery of Place and Making Identity Anew

Alastair McIntosh

– Introduction –

How do we overcome that anomie of which Durkheim wrote a century ago – that sense of placelessness, emptiness, rootlessness and meaninglessness which colonisation and the neo-colonialism of advanced industrial society have bequeathed?

This question is daily forced in the face of Europe's poor. And it has emerged in Scotland at the cutting edge of action for social and ecological justice. At its heart is the nature of identity and belonging in communities that are no longer tribal and pre-industrial, but multiethnic and postmodern.

The poetic work and integral notes that follow developed out of Glasgow's M77 motorway protest at Pollok and the confluence that this formed with other events. These included moves towards re-establishing a Scottish parliament, Scottish land reform (especially on the Isle of Eigg) and the campaign to prevent Mount Roineabhal on the Isle of Harris – a National Scenic Area – from being turned into a super-quarry by Redland Aggregates plc to pave Europe with more motorways.

The statement was requested of me by Colin MacLeod, who led the Pollok protest and started a family there. It had been asked of him by Mi'Kmaq warrior chief (now, emeritus) and sacred peace-pipe carrier, Sulian Stone Eagle Herney, in his capacity as director of the First Nations Environmental Network in Canada. Stone Eagle had visited Pollok in 1994 on his way to the Isle of Harris at my invitation. Together with the Rev. Prof. Donald MacLeod of the Free Church College, we presented the government public inquiry with unprecedented theological testimony concerning reverence for the integrity of creation.[1]

On his home territory of Cape Breton Island, Stone Eagle had been mandated by the late Grand Chief Donald Marshall to prevent the super-quarrying of Mount Kluscap by Kelly Rock, a local subsidiary of Readymix Concrete. International publicity over the defending of our Scottish mountain helped in the defence of his.

In defence of the Earth, in striving for native land rights and in search of cultural soul, our respective native peoples are presently coming together after five centuries of tragic colonial history. This calls for new and inclusive understandings of what it means to be 'indigenous'. It means recovering our near-lost traditions so that we can again bear them as a compass. And if the elders are broken, the young, like so many of those at Pollok, must rise to early responsibility. Thus the Mi'Kmaq have made Colin MacLeod into the first ever non-Mi'Kmaq district war chief in recognition of his assumption of responsibility in non-violent defence of mother Earth. And as Barney MacCormack, bard of Craigencalt in Fife, wrote on the wall of my son Adam's tree house:

> Child go break off from the herd
> go beyond the lowlands
> leave the valley of shed antlers
> the elders are sick
> it is your time now

– The Gal–Gael peoples of Scotland –

Written at the request of and dedicated to Tawny, Colin and Gehan MacLeod and other powerful gentle warriors at the Pollok Free State M77 Motorway Protest in Glasgow, whose endeavours for renewal are both ecological and cultural.

We, the Gal–Gael, being a loose association of some native peoples of Scotland, extend our hand to all other indigenous peoples in the world. By invitation of First Nation friends in North America we ask to address you with these words.

– (I) The Shoaling –

Dear fellow creatures, sisters, brothers, children:
for some years now we have been listening
Awakening to hear you speak
in ocean swell across the great Atlantic
in musical rhythms danced from brightest Africa's savannah
in wind's feathered mantras fluttering out from prayer flags
of the high Himalaya
in ancient Aboriginal songlines
waulking even through Precambrian bedrock folds[2]
of overworld high roads
underworld low roads[3]
North South East
West of our own recovering discovering shamanic tradition
By all such ways and more
dear long-lost much-abus'ed friends
we have heard the speaking of your drums
been touch'ed
late if not last
by open waiting of your hearts
And ask you to accept us now
a native peoples
the 'Gal–Gael'[4]
of Scotland, Alba,
these Northern tracts of Albion
by apple fragrant Avalon

When sun's white light streams in through raindrop lens
and rainbows arch the covenant of hope[5]
all colours make all peoples from one source
And so it is we here
and more besides
have wrestled long and hard with what it means
to be a Scottish native peoples
of diversity
What does it mean
to be the black among us like the white
the Pole, Italian, Russian and Pakistani
the Tamil, Sinhalese the Japanese and Chinese
English just as Scot or Welsh, Flemish German Moslem Jew Pagan
Irish – Protestant and Catholic?
What does it mean for us a rainbow spectrum
to be a Peoples of this place?
Fully indigenous. Fully belonging.

By salmon's course
we have arrived
long shoaling at the estuary, waiting, waiting, waiting
but Spate now running So we leap . . .
Protesting motorways in Glasgow
Refuting super-quarry mountain destruction Bride's isle the He-brides[6]
Fighting to heat the dampened love-warm crisis-torn homes
of those of us in urban native reservation housing schemes
(where TV up a tower block offers nature's only window[7]
one fifth of Scotland's people live in poverty)
And (resetting seeds of Eden)[8]
one foot venturing into Eden[9]
with Muir and Burns, MacDiarmid, White and mostly unnamed women's song[10]
pressing down 'wet desert' sod to replant native trees[11]
in Border dale and Highland strath
and on the blighted bing
Struggling to regain
a music, dance and language
once usurped from forebears' cradling embrace
usurped to break the spirit
take our land
and even God and gods and saints of old
and scar the very strata deep
with alcohol soaked nicotine smoked Prozac choked
dysfunctionality
Lateral violence of unresolv'ed angst[12]
unable to engage
with power from above
so sideways striking to and from within and all around
. . . hurting . . . hurting . . . hurting . . .
with intergenerational poverty knocking on from then to now

people disempowered in rent-racked famine days
Half a million Highland folk . . .[13]
(Lowlanders before like English further back in time)
. . . Cleared . . . from kindly providential clachan
. . . Cleared . . . to fact'ory or to emigrant ship
. . . dumped . . . Aotearoa . . . North America[14]
. . . recruited . . . skirling hireling regiments of 'Queen's Owned Highlanders'[15]
Empire stitched from butcher's wounds
opp'ressed turned oppressor sprung from opp'ressed' pain
both sides the Atlantic surging with emotion
Intergenerational Transatlantic Cultural Trauma
a three-way brokenness
native peoples our side, the Ossianic Western edge
native peoples their side, the Eastern oceanic seaboard
and Everywhere that breaking dominant disembedded culture
that is in part
us too

Can you forgive us?
Red woman, man, child, creature
red earth
Can we together mend these bygone on-going murders
of murdered souls murdering bodies filled with soul
cultural genocide Roman Norman Modern Empire
corporate limited liability limited responsibility
IMF, GATT-World Trade Organisation, World Bank
triumvirate idols Mammon Moloch Money[16]
loansharks surfing water gardens of the poor
thrashing around in usurious name of pax prosperity
. . . Trashing all . . . All . . . but that Invincible prophetic Remnant of humanity[17]
that hazel nut-like flotsam coasting oceans of the heart in Exodus
those holograms of wisdom
dropped by tree of life in sacred trout filled limpid pool[18]
swept down of old on mighty streams of righteousness[19]
but cast up fragile yet relentlessly on shore of modern times[20]
there to wait reminding us, reminding us, re-minding us . . .
. . . re-member . . . re-vision . . . re-claim . . .
and with a raindrop soft pre-emptive start
reminding too that 'only forgiveness . . . breaks the law of karma'[21]

– (II) Invocation –

Ohhh . . . friends we call across the seas to you from echo chamber of the soul
we call now stirred by rhythm that you drum
We call upon the triple billion year old songlines of world's oldest rock
'I lift a stone; it is the meaning of life I clasp' – says the bard MacDiarmid[22]
So let us honour stone. Let us call afresh the foundational litany:
The Lewisian Gneiss . . .
. . . Druim Alban's kelson of the Baltic to Canadian Shield[23]
The super-quarry threatened South Harris igneous complex

(surveyed by supine Roineabhal
beholding all Scarista's ancient parish of Kilbride[24]
annunciating Brigh, Bride, Brigit, womanhood of God[25]
from Barra and the South to Clisham and beyond . . . the Holy He-brides
these scattered jewels from God's eighth day
of legen'dary last Creation act)[26]
Ohhh . . . the lithogenic litany . . . 'turn but a stone an angel stirs'[27]
The Cairngorm pegmatites and sparkling Aberdeenshire granite
The Old Red Sandstone
The Durness limestone sequences and Bathgate's forest Carboniferous
The Tertiary radiating basalt dykes from great volcanoes Mull and Raasay
The Sgurr of Eigg and Ailsa Craig
(where seventh century Irish shaman Sweeney roosted)[28]
The Seat of Arthur
(watching over Calton faerie hill[29]
where pending Parliament awaits return of Stone of Destiny)
The Calanais standing stones and Ring of Brora
The high crosses of Iona pulsing Ireland Ireland Southern Hebridean Ireland
The twin menhirs of Muirkirk
(resanctifying desecrated opencast fields ploughed of coal)[30]
The cairns to poets and to the brave land raiders
The idle pebbles tossed
with cosmogenic tanka's spiral winkle shell[31]
tossed to and fro, round and round, inwards outwards
dark moon full moon vortexing on today's high tide at noon
Ohhh . . . the rocks the rocks the rocks
we call on you . . .
Rise up from sleep sunk strata beds!
Giant women, wizened men, totemic creatures once laid down to be our hills[32]
Wake up! Wake up! Wake up and waulk this Earth in us![33]
. . . bring back the land within the people's care
. . . bring back the care to touch from hand to land

– (III) Re-membering –

Aye . . .
and so we have united as strong women
resisting landlord's factor
non-lethal direct action Crofters' War, Timex strike
We have united, men of gentleness
straining back temptation just to be like them
and bomb and bribe and blight
Turning instead the heartwood of their minds
by climbing threatened tree
or gently blocking course of Trident submarine
(seven-hundred two-score-ten Hiroshimas each one)
Aye . . . Aye and three times Aye
three times 'yes' of Holy Trinity . . . Father, Child,
Sophia WomanSpirit Holy Spirit Rising[34]
Three times Aye the Triune Goddess

Maiden Mother Crone
Life Death Rebirth
Her mantle oh so green laid out each spring
to fill the world with milk and flowers
. . . Bri'gh! . . . Bri'gh! . . . Bri'gh! . . .
of the oak Cill-Dara, of Iona and of Bethlehem[35]
And three-times-three – Aye
ring out nine blossom bells afresh from silver bardic bough[36]
Restore once more a Politics of Poetry!
. . . for only such poetics can again renew the face of Earth
inform our ancient people's highest aspiration
and like a rowan arch exclude
a waiting nation's re-awaiting parcelled rogues[37]
We must restore the schools and ways of ancient learning
to stand them proud beside the richness of the new
restore what Lord and Bishop wrecked – cruel Statutes of Iona 1609[38]
. . . twelve most powerful Highland chiefs
. . . kidnapped . . . imprisoned over winter . . .
forced to forfeit friendship, tongue, and Bard's vocation
forced to put out culture's flames
(but done with sacred blessing's triple peat[39]
the embers only smoored so not to chill)
Aye Statutes of an Iona cudgelled into modern time by Whitby's Roman synod
Aye post-Culloden Proscription even of our ancient spirit'ual dress
Aye . . . we now bypass you 664, 1609, 1747[40]
We rise now up on eagle wings
above that colonisation of our lands and minds
. . . as fire in head reheats the sacred salmon's sap[41]
we watch it run . . . a babbling silver stream
anointing wisdom's ninth Proverbial dwelling place the heart
We hear with inner ear ancestral chorus, look, and See,
And Are Again Of Shining Countenance!
We are the Tuatha de Danann[42]
emerged by standing stone from Sithean, faerie hill
emerged to Be again Free again the mother Goddess Danann's people
. . . Holy . . . Holy . . . Holy . . .
No exiled 'metaphor for the imagination' any more[43]
the tree ringed mushroom fringed hollow knowe of light[44]
No fortress mound to house true nature's child
unfree in wider desecrated world to be true nature wild . . . but Reality!
. . . And see! See yon distant mythic Fiann . . .
that once sunk down amongst the stanes became a stane[45]
Awakening now! In us with strength to hurl from shores or catch from air
not mountain boulder there left cleft upon the beach
from some old tribal war of legendary adolescent pique
but phantom intercontinental jet ballistic missile star war supergun exports
to catch them Halt! them take them from the sky
and beat them into railway tracks
and homesteads for the poor[46]

– (IV) RE-VISIONING –

We are become again a people
known or unknown touched
by rose of Scotland little white rose
that smells so sharp and sweet it breaks the heart[47]
by eagle, deer, wild cat and long-gone bear
here in spirit where extinct in flesh
Strong totems for recovery – we need strong totems at this time
Remember . . . that three years before
Culloden massacred gasp from clansfolk's tribal voice
the last wolf was shot extinct in Scotland[48]
Nature's death precursing culture's 'thickest night'[49]
Culloden – last battle mainland British soil 1746
internal colonial conquest
blood mingling inseparably soaked through moss Drumossie moor
friend and foe and which is 'us' and which is 'them' now?
Where the 'Gaeltachd' whither 'Galltachd'
Unavoidably mingled
for a' that and a' that
sacrificing, sanctifying, down to an ice-age cleans'ed strata
that is both cultural and in depth, archaeological[50]
long stinking but now compost-rendered for new growth
Something poised
. . . both psychic and somatic
. . . genetic and prophetic
Remnant sprig from taproot of antiquity
awaiting spring to bud re-formed
and Blossom as is needed in our agitated times
. . . a cultural cultivation . . .
Indeed! Let us observe that
the capacity of nature and of human nature
to be hurt
is exceeded
in the fullness of time
only
by the capacity to heal . . .
And that must be joy's greatest cause for hope

So you . . . our friends to whom this statement is addressed
You, we know, will understand.
Take you, First Nation Peoples, North America
uneasy unasked hosts to our Diaspora[51]
You, Chippewa protest leader challenging Exon's mines, Walter Bresette
says . . . 'We are all native people now. The door is shut. We are all inside.'[52]
You, Mi'Kmaq super-quarry warrior chief Sulian Stone Eagle Herney
says . . . 'Your mountain, your shorelines your rivers and your air
are just as much mine and my grandchildren's
as ours is yours.'[53]
You, great teacher huntress Winona La Duke[54]

walking troubled by the Minnesota lakes
who rejects 'genocide by arithmetic'
that allows 'indigenous' belonging
to be governmentally defined by statutes staturing racial purity
Rejecting thresholds like one-sixteenth blood relationship
to be a Sioux or Cree or Cherokee
for human love will always
mingle, meld, and make of prismed light
a golden melanged mockery of all pretensions
to any presumption
of racial purity
that violates sunlight's loving magic dance
a dance insisting
as it pleases, teases
Equally to be white light, coloured light
or warm absorbing dark that holds all light

– (V) RE-CLAIMING –

Aye . . . aye . . . aye
Scotland understands a thing or two about belonging
We have a Gaelic proverb:
'The Bonds of Milk are Stronger than the Bonds of Blood'[55]
Nurture, kinship, counts for more than mere blood lineage
And so let us propose
an ancient new criterion for belonging here;
All Are Indigenous, Native To This Place. All
Who Are Willing To Cherish
And Be Cherished
By This Place
And Its Peoples

All are indigenous, native to this place. All
who are willing to cherish
and be cherished
by this place
and its peoples

Those whose souls so resonate
All we, known and unknown to us
are troubled claiming for ourselves
the obvious tribal names of indigeneity.
Few if any are 'pure'
Pict, Norse, Flemish, Saxon, Angle,
Indian, Greek, Hispanic, Arab
Scotia's royal lineage to daughter of Pharaoh.
Even Gaelic tongue of Irish forebears
dappled once a Pictish land
with blood as well as milk
So What Choice Have We

But To Embrace Full Spectrum?
What choice want we
save the pleasures so to do?
And to SHINE ON. Oh yes friend. SHINE ON![56]

Once Vikings raped and pillaged here
and then too melded
gentle with the healing power of place and time
Became us!
became 'Gall-Gaidheil,' the Gal–Gael
'emerged as a mixed ethnic group by the middle of the ninth century'[57]
in the Hebrides and south-west Scotland
giving Gall-oway its name
and Isle of Lewis, Harris – 'Innse Gall' – the Isle of Strangers[58]
terrible then, a violated and a violating people
(like us today perhaps?)
but us they were
We're all Gal–Gael now
and only by facing the shadows of history
can sunlight warm our backs
and melt the frozen crust
of ice congeal'ed blood around the heart.

Today eight-tenths of Scotland's private land
is owned by less
than one tenth
of one percent
of Scotland's people[59]
Let's call a spade a spade:
. . . too many of us languish lost
in concrete jungles'
post-indust'rial
redundancy
dumped there by those who see no treasure in each soul
(for that is what distinguishes
their force for life-extinguishing
in sectioning nature off
these men of property)
We've had enough!
We now insist on being heard and standing up and standing out
and coming into Being
speaking as it is our truth to power for what it is
'. . . fur the wains' sake . . . our ane sake . . .'[60]
So we declare . . . identity
a claim of right
a name that mingles, honours
many nations in this place
A bioregional identity defending place
nae force of arms

but power o' reverence
transcending narrow nationalism
so not to bleach out ethnic richness rainbow hues
and not to fight in ways that scar and cannot be undone
but yet to find a focal understanding . . .
some constellation of belonging . . .
of folk and place and wonted work[61]

– (VI) Affirmation –

Well . . . here we are
Round protest hearth in Glasgow's Pollok wood
and we again evoke the name
'Gal–Gael'
Impure. Bitter-sweet. Riddled with contradiction.
But belonging here, now
here and now
to and fro
rocking . . . rocking . . . rocking
Rolling into life and promised life abundant[62]
Cherishing and being cherished
A native peoples
We are indigenous!
We stir our voice in singing back this place!

The song breaks out from deep within
Strathallen's torrent roars anew
The oak to triumph o'er war's din
the world is with a friend now[63]

Aye Rabbie Burns – your passion's won
two hundred years your Vision's come
The Bards like emerald earls returned[64]
no more the people's soul be spurned

– (VII) Homecoming –

Dear fellow creatures
native brothers sisters children
in other heartlands of the real, the reel
We ask from you acceptance
of our peoplehood
We ask you weave our native threads
to fabric of one scintillating cloth
that is the mantle of the world
We pledge to you support
for all work sourced in love
recovering right relation'ship your territories
And ask from you forgiveness
for past injustice, ignorance and spoils of fear or greed
We need your help with Spirit's grace

to find clear paths through tangled modern Waste Land tares
to seed as oaks as Gods each one proclaiming Jubilee[65]
To fly in fair formation as wild geese . . .[66]
To hear afresh that deep poetic story
of magic set in time when place began . . .
To make a life worth living . . .
To save this Earth . . .
. . . And play from down the hollow hill[67]
A hallowed music
Sacred dance
That is our soul . . .
. . . our soil

> Yours, for auld lang sine[68]
> Beltane Full Moon Wolf Festival
> Pollok Free State, Scotland, 3 May 1996
> (narrated by Alastair McIntosh)[69]

– NOTES –

1 These notes are provided to aid interpretation, provide acknowledgements and give background information that might interest the reader. However, there is also a political reason. The text has been written before the Isle of Harris proposed super-quarry public inquiry decision has been made by the Secretary of State for Scotland. Pro-quarry forces are currently (late 1996) lobbying hard in an effort to reverse local opinion. Some are maintaining efforts to damage the character of prominent quarry opponents. Sir John Lister Kaye, former chair of Scottish Natural Heritage North West, lost his job, it is thought, partly because of his robust anti-quarry stance. Rev. Prof. Donald MacLeod, who gave evidence with Chief Stone Eagle and me at the public inquiry, has undergone, but survived, a character assassination attempt through the courts and an attempted heresy trial, linked to his wider efforts to bring radical liberal reform to the Free Church. His quarry testimony and the platform he shared have been cited as part of 'the problem' with him (*Scotsman*, 24 May 1995 and 26 June 1996). And an eminent but conservative Scottish university has now forced out of its walls the Centre for Human Ecology where, for nearly seven years, I was teaching director (see *New Scientist* editorial, 4 May 1996, defending our 'tradition of fearless inquiry'). I have been told privately by senior university management that as a result of involvement with the super-quarry and land reform on Eigg, the university feared losing funding as powerful interests sitting on research funding committees became too upset. In such a general climate I need to protect against this text being misunderstood and misused back home in the Western Isles, at least until after the quarry decision has been made. Accordingly, and at the regrettable risk of alienating some readers, I have therefore included notes to demonstrate compatibility with and to acknowledge imagery drawn from biblical sources, as well as to indicate sources which enable linkage with a pre-Christian continuum. This totality is the richness and hidden strength of our culture. It is a potent key in joining together deep cultural taproots of both social and ecological justice.

The Secretary of State for Scotland should decide the outcome in 1998. For testimonies see McIntosh (1995a: 757–91) and Alesia Malt's commentary on this with special attention to US constitutional reflections, (McIntosh 1995a: 792–833). A summary can be found in McIntosh (1995b).

2 Woven cloth (tweed) was traditionally softened by 'waulking', that is, thick folds along the length being communally and rhythmically pounded to the accompaniment of waulking songs. Margaret Fay Shaw (1986: 7) remarks: 'Those were the days when a wearer could regard his homespun from the Hebrides with the thought of the songs and gaiety that went into the making of it.'

3 In the 'Loch Lomond' song, the lover to be executed expects to reach Scotland first because, after death, the soul was believed rapidly to travel home under the surface of the earth – the 'low road'.

4 Normally spelt 'Gall' in English, but 'Gal' is how it has been carved in wood and stone at Pollok which, being a 'free state', is permitted a measure of distinctive anarchy.

5 Here a social connotation, but cf. Genesis 9.9–17 where the rainbow signifies ecological covenant.

6 The name, 'Hebrides', may result from scribal errors. The earliest written reference was to 'Ebudae'. However, as n. 24 about Kilbride implies, it is eminently appropriate and the Hebridean scholar, John MacAulay (1996: 6), points out that an ancient name for the Outer Isles was Innis Bhrighde, meaning the isles of Brigh/Brigit/Bride/Bridey, etc.

7 On the relation between ecology and Scotland's urban poor, see MSc human ecology dissertation work of O'Leary (1996: 62–80).

8 Mike Collard, Future Forests, Bantry, Ireland.

9 Edwin Muir, 'One Foot in Eden' in Dunn (1992: 29–30).

10 I.e. Kenneth White, Scots-born professor of twentieth-century poetics at the Sorbonne. His work has greatly influenced this piece. Inspired partly by Walt Whitman, he proposes 'poetics, geography – and a higher unity – geopoetics' (1992: 163–78). Through Tony McMahon (1990: 5–14, 1991: 2–3), Kenneth alerted me to the shamanic nature of Burns's work.

11 Frank Fraser-Darling, author of the famous study in human ecology, *West Highland Survey*.

12 Jane Middleton-Moz, American therapist, whose talk at the International Transpersonal Association conference in Killarney, 1994, inspired my thinking about the need for cultural psychotherapies – a notion I now see that Paulo Freire was also effectively aware of.

13 No accurate estimate exists that I know of. This figure has been cited, but would appear to be a guesstimate. Half a million would certainly not be an exaggerated ballpark for the sum of mid-eighteenth to late nineteenth-century clearances if indirect clearance through imposed economic pressure is included, as it ought to be.

14 Aotearoa – indigenous people's name for New Zealand.

15 Lewis poet Mary Montgomery – poem by this name.

16 Moloch was an Old Testament god into whose fire-filled stone arms the children were sacrificed to secure present prosperity. American theologian Walter Wink advocates new ways of 'naming, unmasking and engaging the powers' in order to transform and redeem power. In this sense Moloch can be seen to have many contemporary incarnations, not least nuclear weapons.

17 In the Old Testament the 'Remnant' are the few remaining people of God (e.g. Isaiah 11.21–2, 1 Kings 19). A role of the prophets – visionaries who 'speak truth to power' especially on issues of social and ecological justice – was to 'gather' the Remnant to restore society.

Moses in Numbers 11, like Jesus later, recognised prophesy as a universal vocation of the faithful. When he leads his people away from the treasure houses of Egypt towards an ecologically sound (though politically usurped) land of milk and honey, he declares, 'would God that all the Lord's people were prophets' (11.29). In the spirit of contextual theology I have rewritten Numbers 11 as a metaphor for the work of anti-motorway protestors, likening them to a prophetic Remnant living off manna, speaking to the ills of our times, and holding out an alternative wholesome ecological vision (1996: 18–20). In ecology, the concept of the remnant is similarly used for those remaining few areas of native flora – remnant pinewoods, etc. – which if saved will provide seedstock of local provenance to restore ecosystems.

Shamanic understanding opens a whole new realm of biblical hermeneutical exegesis. The shamanic nature of the prophetic role is clear if cross-cultural shamanic understanding is applied to scripture. Prophets and shamans alike are women and men who step outside normal constructs of society to see better its ills, in order, when they return, to facilitate Spirit in healing these. In so doing they often had a special relationship to the natural world. Moses, for instance speaks to God (identified as 'I AM') in a bush (Exodus 3); each of the four apostles is totemically represented, John being the eagle (Revelation 4.7); Elijah was fed by ravens (1 Kings 17.4–6) and used his mantle for changing the state of reality (1 Kings 19.13; 2 Kings 2.7–15); Daniel had command over lions in the den (Daniel 6); Joseph had a coat of many colours and dreamed prophetic visions (Genesis 37), and Elisha was aided by two she-bears when the double dose of power he inherited at his own request through Elijah's mantle went to his head.

Indeed, Elisha's arrogance on being teased about having a bald head by children on his way to Mount Carmel tragically resulted in forty-two of them being torn apart by the bears (2 Kings 2.23–4). Jungian theologians might consider that these represented his feminine side, out of control because of not being integrated into his psyche on account of a power-crazed male ego (baldness signified mourning and thus loss in Old Testament culture – cf. Isaiah 15.2). Transpersonal psychology recognises such ego inflation as a common dysfunction of new-found spiritual power (cf. Grof and Grof 1989).

18 In Celtic folklore, hazel nuts contained the knowledge of poetry and art. Eaten by the salmon (or 'trout') on falling into sacred wells or streams they caused the red spots on the fish's belly, and conveyed wisdom to whoever first tasted juice from its cooked flesh – hence the 'salmon of wisdom' and my reference to 'by salmon's course' (see McNeill 1989: 74–5; NB W. B. Yeats' Celtic shamanic lyric, 'The Song of Wandering Aengus').

19 Amos 5.21–7.

20 While writing this, inspiration was fuelled by finding a perfectly preserved, small, hazelnut half-shell. It lay in mud, packed hard inside with peat, amongst ancient forest detritus washed out of a sea-eroded peat bank at a remote location on Great Bernera, Isle of Lewis, where I had gone with the antiquarian Jim Crawford to see an historic lobster pend wall he had rebuilt and to read him a draft of this work. Such ancient forest detritus in Scotland usually radio-carbon dates at 4,000 to 6,000 years old.

21 Panikkar (1991: 49–56). This paper by a remarkable Hindu-Catholic cross-cultural scholar also points to rhythm as being central to Being, and therefore to peace-making.

22 'On a Raised Beach' – Scotland's finest work of mystical geology (in Dunn 1992: 56–68).

23 Gaelic name going back to ancient times for 'the spine of Britain' Highland massif.

24 Jim Crawford (n. 20) has recently discovered foliated grave slabs at Scarista including one of the Iona School. He believes part of the original St Bride's church foundation is still

apparent, most of it having disappeared when the pre-Reformation church was pulled down to build what is now the Church of Scotland. He informs me that Kilbride (Cill(e) Bride – the cell (church or parish) of St Bride) was an old name for Harris, marked on a map as late as the eighteenth century. The pre-Reformation parish of Kilbride extended from Harris down to Barra. Christianised as St Bride or Bridgit, Brigh was originally a pan-European Celtic goddess. Ancient Irish tracts associate her veneration not just with the cow and milk (thus with shieling transhumance), but also with the long-extinct bear, thereby suggesting links going back to early human settlement. The Irish name MacMahon and the Scots Matheson both have the bear as their meaning and totem. Use was made of this by us to draw on strength of gentleness at Pollok Free State at times when violence threatened.

25 Cf. Song of Songs, the femininity of Sophia (Woman Wisdom), identified with the Holy Spirit in Proverbs 8–9, and reference to Creation pouring out of the womb of God in Job 38.8, 29. Note the trenchant warning in Proverbs 8.36, that everyone who neglects this feminine face of God 'wrongeth his own soul' and 'love[s] death'.

26 Rev. Alistair MacLean, *Hebridean Altars* (1937: 12–13): ' "The world was finished and the Good One was mighty tired and took a rest and, while He was resting, He thought 'Well, I have let my earth-children see the power of my mind, in rock and mountain and tree and wind and flower. And I have shown them the likeness of my mind, for I have made theirs like my own. And I have shown them the love of my mind, for I have made them happy. But halt,' says the Good One to Himself, 'I have not shown them the beauty of my mind.' So the next day, and that was the eighth day, He takes up a handful of jewels and opens a window in the sky and throws them down into the sea. And those jewels are the Hebrides. I had the story of it from my father's father," he went on. "An extra fine man, and terrible strong for the truth." – "John of the Cattle" of the Isle of Mull'.

27 George MacLeod, Iona Community.

28 Seamus Heaney (1984). This remarkable Celtic shamanic text presents a deep ecology rooted in the first millennium.

29 The Royal High School, symbolic if not the actual site for a future Scottish Parliament, lies on the side of Calton Hill known for the 'Fairy Boy of Leith' legend – McNeill (1989).

30 As a result of local resident Ian Michael Ramsay's negotiations with the Coal Board. Hopefully a wood is to be planted around them to make a special site. Each boulder stands some twelve feet high and would otherwise have been blasted and bulldozed as part of site landscaping.

31 The winkle is associated with Brigh (O'Cathain 1995: xi, and see n. 44). In Tibetan Buddhist tankas (religious art) and in Hindu depictions of Krishna, the conch shell symbolises the call to spiritual awakening. Spirals symbolise life.

32 A Lewis legend has it that the mountains were once giant women who lay down to sleep.

33 For more information on waulking cloth and waulking songs, see Carmichael (1992: 443–70 and notes). Carmichael's material is from the second half of the nineteenth century and is also relevant to many other parts of this text, such as faerie lore.

34 See n. 25.

35 The Irish St Bride is said to have established her convent at Kildare (Cill-Dara/Doire – the church of the oak). The Scots Gaelic equivalent was St Bride of the Isles or Brigdhe-nam-Brat, Bride of the Mantles, or Plaid. Traditionally this was woven by Bride herself on Iona. There she lived (Fiona Macleod's perhaps inspired fiction suggesting that she learned from Druids), until she was taken up in a dark-blue mantle (the colour of her own eyes) by two

angels and transported to Bethlehem to be foster-mother to the newborn Jesus (McNeill (1990: 63–72; Carmichael 1992: 237–40). A splendid painting resplendent with Celtic symbols, *St Bride*, by John Duncan (1913), depicts her transportation. It rests in the National Gallery of Scotland at the Mound, Edinburgh.

The mantle plays a crucial role in shamanic practice (cf. both Joseph and Elijah). It can be seen to represent shape-shifting, consciousness change, transformation of the world and other aspects of liminality. In Celtic lore Bride rolls out her green mantle on Bride's day, 1 February, each spring to restore life to the world. An Irish tune, 'Her Mantle so Green' captures the beauty of this spirit. Burns uses the mantle as an image for consciousness change in 'The Vision' (see n. 64). Adamnan, Columba's biographer, recounts that between the conception and birth of St Columba of Iona an angel appeared to his mother in sleep with 'a certain mantle of marvellous beauty, in which lovely colours of all flowers were depicted'. As the vision drew to a close, 'the woman saw the afore-mentioned mantle gradually receding from her in its flight, and increasing in size so as to exceed the width of the plains, and to overtop the mountains and forests' (extract in McNeill 19, translating Adamnan section 3:1).

In the gender construction of these Christian accounts, woman is no longer Goddess, but nursemaid to God incarnate or to the carrier of a male-gendered God's message. For those of us to whom this is a problem when taken out of the context of the totality of womanhood, such construction requires attention if we still want to draw on the best from ancient traditions in shaping spiritual understandings for today. Such work is being undertaken by some feminist Celtic theologians and hagiographers (for instance, Condren, 1989). Prof. Murdo MacDonald, formerly editor of the *Edinburgh Review*, suggests that the transformation of Brigh from Celtic goddess to foster-mother of Christ might imply an astonishingly 'harmonious negotiation' between old and new faiths (pers. com.).

36 The Silver Bough (Celtic equivalent of the Golden Bough) is the bough of apple blossom gifted by the faeries as passport into the musical/poetic realms. The bard's silver bough with nine bells symbolises the 'apples' of the heavenly realm of Avalon that this gives fruit to (McNeill 1989: 105–6; Evans Wentz [1911] 1977: 336–44).

37 Burns dubbed the mercantile MPs who sold out Scotland's parliament in 1707 'Sic (such) a parcel o' rogues in a nation!'

38 For a summary of Scottish and some Irish history on this crucial period and its bardic tradition, see the introduction to O'Baoill (1994: 1–39). For discussion of Bardic schools see Corkery (1967).

39 Alistair MacLean (1937: 142–3) describes how at night in the Isles the fire would be smoored with three peats in the name of the Holy Trinity, to the rune, 'The Sacred Three, My fortress be, Encircling me. Come and be round, My hearth, my home . . . Through mid of night, To light's release.'

40 It has been suggested that too much has been made of the 664 Synod of Whitby's merging of the Celtic church of Columba with that of Rome. However, the psychological impact of a change of calendar (concerning the date of Easter) is perhaps underestimated by the modern mind.

Fr Dara Molloy of the Aran Isles, County Clare, is attempting to re-establish the Celtic Church. See Molloy (1996: 5–13), where he writes: 'The Roman model of Church is hierarchical, patriarchal and clerical. At all levels of Church life the priest, bishop or Pope is in charge. The Celtic model of Church is communitarian, inclusive, and locally controlled. In this model, the people are the Church, and look after it themselves while drawing on the services of the priest, bishop and Pope'.

41 Yeats 'Song of Wandering Aengus' (in most Yeats anthologies; see too his splendid but sadly maligned book, *The Celtic Twilight*, (1990 [1893]): 'I went out to the hazel wood, because a fire was in my head . . . I dropped the berry in a stream, and caught a little silver trout'). 'Wandering Aengus' has got to be our finest contemporary Celtic shamanic lyric. Fire in the head is a shamanic experience widespread in the world, the word 'shaman' meaning 'to heat'. The dwelling place of wisdom, according to some interpretations of Proverbs 9.1 (Raimon Panikkar), is the human heart.

42 According to the Irish Book of Invasions, the 'de Danann' were driven underground by the invading Milesians some 4,000 years ago. Many legends say they became the *sidth*, the people of peace, the faeries, living in the 'Sithean' or faerie mounds. When I asked Mike Collard of Bantry 'who are the faeries?' he replied that we are they. The old nature consciousness is coming alive in us now. Our 'Milesian' iron-based ways have damaged the Earth to such an extent that we are learning to listen again to the sounds from inside the hill.

One of my 1994–5 MSc students, Patrick Laviolette, has undertaken research with me and done his human ecology dissertation into Scottish faerie hills as reservoirs of biodiversity. The folklore and taboos surrounding wooded ones helps maintain habitat remnants not unlike sacred groves elsewhere in the world. See Laviolette and McIntosh (forthcoming).

43 John MacInnes, School of Scottish Studies, Edinburgh University, St Bride's Day lecture, February 1996. John described how a Uist man would say to him, 'my mind was away in the Hill', the realm of faerie being an imaginal (not imaginary) realm. Another expression is to be 'away with the faeries' (cf. Synge, 1992: 284). To the modern 'Gall', metaphor is often little understood and the imaginal realm of symbols, myth and poetic/musical upwelling often dismissed as unreal. The converse is commonly true of the 'Gael'. Imaginal metaphoric reality is the foundation of reality in mythopoetic societies. Future dignified human survival, 'sustainable development', will depend upon choosing understandings of reality that best accord with deep truth.

Increasingly I believe this to be musical, poetic, and that we must rethink Plato's elevation of the rational and denigration of rhetoric and poetics. The word 'poetic', derives from the Greek *poesis* and means 'the making'. Mythopoesis is the insight that poetics form the ultimate basis of reality, usually expressed in story; legend. The 'west' needs a new mythopoesis to live sustainably – new stories that more closely accord with the deep reality of nature and the human soul. In the past the Bards structured this and held political power, exerted, not least, through panegyric (praise poetry/song). It is pleasing that when the Scottish Constitutional Convention launched their parliamentary proposals in November 1995, the Bards were present – political speeches being interspersed with harp music, folk song and Sheboom – a troupe of women drummers. The spiritual significance of this had not escaped some of the Convention's senior organisers.

44 After completing early drafts of this text I was thrilled, following his lecture on Brigh and shieling transhumance at Edinburgh University's Celtic Department, to discover O'Cathain's (1995) work. Professor Seamas O'Cathain, dean of Celtic Studies at University College, Dublin, uses Nordic and Celtic (including ancient Germanic) folkloric material to propose links between Brigh and prehistoric bear cults (NB my section IV). In a remarkable conclusion he also presents evidence to suggest that the

colour-coding of Brigh's feast day (1 February) into 'speckled' and 'white' pertains to ancient shamanic use of the fly agaric mushroom (*Amanita muscaria*). This grows in association with birch or pine. 'Punk' from the birch bracket fungus makes tinder, thus creating fire of both wood and, by metaphor, the spirit. O'Cathain refers to the 'fitting and wonderful harmony' of this with aspects of the festival of Brigh, noting that, 'Wasson describes this combination of birch, punk and fly-agaric as "nature's triangle", fly-agaric holding "the place of honour in this Trinity"' (1995: 158). He cites the noted ethnobotanist, Wasson, as saying, 'I suggest that the "toadstool" was the fly-agaric of the Celtic world: that the toadstool in its shamanic role had aroused such awe and fear and adoration that it came under a powerful tabu' (1995: 159). O'Cathain's scholarly exegesis is partly linked to Wasson's view that the fly-agaric's cap suggested an udder to the Rigveda poets, to whom it was probably the sacred *soma*. *Soma* has links with the Hindu fire god Agni and possibly with his Celtic counterpart, Aed meic Brecc – the 'flying master-physician' of Sliabh Liag in County Donegal. Aed means 'fire', and he is linked to Brigh's feast-day. Brigh's connection with the udder or breast is that she was also goddess of pastures and milk, the white cow being especially sacred to her (cf. Hinduism's sacred cow; also, some species of the mushroom *Psilocobe* grow in cow dung).

O'Cathain even speculates on a link with St Columba of Iona. Noting that milk is a powerful detoxicant to counteract the impact of fly-agaric, he says, 'We may well wonder whether some such consideration lies behind *Aed meic Brecc's* chaffing of Colm Cille (Columba) about . . . the adulteration of his daily sustenance with watered down milk' (1995: 161). The milk was secretly added by the saint's cook to improve his physical condition. The implication of O'Cathain's speculation might be considered unthinkable had it derived from a lesser authority in the field.

Murdo MacDonald, professor of Scottish Art History at Dundee University, has pointed out to me that John Duncan, who is mentioned in n. 35 for having painted the transportation of St Bride, produced a remarkable 1960s-like picture for the summer 1896 edition of *The Evergreen*, edited by Patrick Geddes. Called *Surface Water*, the painting depicts a youth leaning into a pond, surrounded by mushrooms. These are hard to identify, but certainly have an appearance as magical as that of the youth's countenance is 'spaced'.

Surprisingly, O'Cathain does not discuss the 'liberty cap' or 'magic mushroom', *Psilocybe semilanceata*. These grow in profusion in the British Isles from September to November, favouring unimproved pasture. I have noticed particular association with eyebright – in visual terms a fire-herb if ever there was one. Some thirty to sixty such mushrooms, fresh or dried, are said to induce powerful experiences, often of nature and sometimes mystical. These can include literally 'seeing the light', the fire of God, and developing totemic relationships with spirit animals, etc. The beautiful little mushroom, usually about 1 cm across the cap, assumes a perfect breast shape complete with an often pronounced nipple. I have interviewed occasional eco-activists who consider that the divine or consciousness in nature speaks through the mushroom. This is one factor present in the resurgence of neo-shamanism, but not one to be taken out of proportion and used to caricature the whole movement.

Presumably it would be going too far, on purely morphological observation, to speculate that faerie knowes or raths were Druidic groves, earth piled up or natural locations chosen to be shaped as breast-cum-mushroom temples. However, it is intriguing, to say the least, that O'Cathain's building on Wasson's work gives ground for speculation that Brigh's feastday, perhaps especially its eve, 31 January, may originally have been the magic mushroom festival of our ancient peoples, celebrated on the first day of Celtic spring when life bursts out anew across the face of the earth.

May I suggest, as was pointed out to me by Murdo MacDonald when discussing the various spellings of 'fairy', that diverse spellings of Brigit might be seen as part of a shape-changing veil to be delighted in. I mostly choose 'Brigh' in this text because it most approximates an Irish pronunciation that I find pleasing in a mantric way – 'Breeee-jah'.

45 The 19-foot-tall standing stone Clach an Truisei is said to be the tallest monolith in Britain and believed to be a Fiann left behind by the Irish warriors, the Fianna, after they had come to Lewis to free the people from oppression by giants (Donald Macdonald 1990: 14–16). It was Macdonald's paragraph on the Gal–Gael that prompted Colin MacLeod, who started the Pollok protest, to reinvoke the concept. Colin's father is a Gaelic speaker with roots in Gravir, Lewis. Colin grew up in Govan and Australia. He attended the secondary school immediately beside the Free State protest site. The name Pollok may derive from a Celtic word *Pollach*, meaning 'muddy place'.

46 Isaiah 2.4.

47 MacDiarmid, 'The Little White Rose' in Bruce and Rennie (1991: 213). The Burnett rose (*Rosa spinosissima*) has been a totem for our original work with the Isle of Eigg Trust. As Neil Gunn noted, it grows on (what is almost certainly from his description) Eigg 'in greater abundance than anywhere else I know. It is the genius of this place . . . For me it has a fragrance more exquisite than that of any other rose' (1949). Mention here is included at the request of, and in honour of, the Trust's founder, Tom Forsyth. The Isle of Eigg's 7,400 acres were restored to community ownership after seven generations of landlordism on 12 June 1997. It previously represented fully 1 per cent of privately owned land in the Scottish Highlands (see 'They're All Lairds Now!', *New York Times*, 6 June 1997).

48 Martin Mathers of Worldwide Fund for Nature (Scotland) pointed this out to me.

49 Burns, 'Strathallan's Lament' (see n. 63).

50 Acknowledgement to Seamus Heaney for the concept of the bog as the unconscious.

51 My friend and mentor in some of the issues discussed in these notes, Michael Newton of the Celtic Department, Edinburgh University, strenuously points out that the Gael did not in the first instance choose to be a coloniser, but became perforce a party to others' colonising aspirations. A rightly proud claim of modern Irish people is: 'We were colonised, but never colonised anybody else.' Residual Pictish voices might think otherwise . . . but with no hard feelings any longer, especially as incursions between like tribes make poor comparison with the principles of Romanesque *colonia*.

52 During a joint ceremony that we conducted at a University of Wisconsin conference on spirituality and ecological resistance, 1995 (see discussion of this and other issues relevant to this work in Bron Taylor's paper (1997: 183–215)). The similarities between Native American and Celtic shamanic practice become more striking the more closely they are researched. For example, in northern parts of Ireland such as Inishmurray there were *tigh 'n alluis*, or sweat lodges, which prepared the participant for *dercad* meditation, in which several mystics together would seek a state of *sitchain* or transcendent peace (Hennessy 1885–6).

53 Sulian Stone Eagle Herney, super-quarry public inquiry precognition statement.

54 At International Transpersonal Association conference, Killarney, 1994.

55 Cited in Nicholson's *Gaelic Proverbs*.

56 This line is prompted not just by Pink Floyd's famous 'shine on you crazy diamond', but also by the way in which 'Glasgow Two' hunger striker Tommy Campbell ends his letters from Shotts prison. Tommy's and Joseph Steele's campaign for judicial review is not just personal, but concerns the quality of Scottish justice generally. Shine on! Tommy. Your captors may or may not be dead, but you're certainly not. (Since first writing this, Campbell and Steele have been released and reimprisoned.)

57 Smythe (1984: 156–7).

58 It is a paradox that the Long Island, Lewis and Harris together, became known by the Gael of the past by this name because mainly Viking settlement meant that so many strangers (Gall) lived there; but now it has become the Remnant heartland of the Gael. This resonates richly with the philosophy of cultural renewal behind Pollok's 'Gal–Gael' concept.

59 From the Scottish Landowners' Federation's own, perhaps exaggerated claim, that their 4,000 members control 80 per cent of Scotland's private (non-government) land. A 1976 study showed that just thirty-five families or companies possessed one-third of the Highlands' 7.39 million acres of private land. See McIntosh et al. (1994: 64–70). A more recent study by Wightman (1996 figures extrapolated as cited in ECOS 17:(3/4) indicates that nearly two-thirds of Scottish private land is owned by just 1,000 people, representative (were they all resident) of one fiftieth of one percent of the Scottish population.

60 Braendam women interviewed by O'Leary (1996) – wains = children.

61 I.e. the Patrick Geddes human ecology trilogy of folk, work, place. The pun on 'wonted' is deliberate. Something is 'wonted' if it is habitual, belonging to a place or custom. cf. 'as is her wont'. Michael Newton points to the similarity of the Gaelic word *duth* (pers. com.)

62 John 10.10.

63 Robert Burns. In 'Strathallan's Lament', Burns portrays the psychic collapse of Strathallan, who can no longer enjoy nature (the river's torrent, etc.) and sees the wide world before him reduced to 'but a world without a friend'. In 'The Tree o' Liberty', Burns, sounding like a Rastafarian hippie, uses the oak as a symbol of national strength and freedom: 'Wi' plenty o' sic trees I trow / the world would live in peace, Man / the sword would help to mak a plough / the din o' war would cease, Man.'

64 Colin MacLeod started the Pollok Free State M77 motorway protest site by planting an eagle totem pole, after having experienced an eagle vision quest and protesting alone up a tree for two weeks with a copy of Burns' poetry. This then intermingled with the culture of his surrounding native Pollok and Govan, also drawing in Gehan Ibrahim's peace-protest insights from the Faslane nuclear submarine base, and ideas from English road protesters such as the Dongas Tribe. Colin drew my attention to Burns' remarkable call to restore the Bardic basis of culture in 'The Vision'. In this, Burns is given a vision quest by the Celtic muse who appears as a woman. Her mantle transforms to reveal the whole cosmos and sends Burns off into shamanic rapture. Her mission is: 'To give my counsels all in one / Thy tuneful flame still careful fan / Preserve the dignity of Man / With soul erect / and trust the Universal Plan / will all protect.' This might be taken as a manifesto for Scottish education. It might entail a triple confluence between the Bardic schools, the monastic schools and modern schools, especially those embodying feminist epistemology. Our Peoples' Free University of Pollok, which taught 'degrees in living' to striking school children and other M77 protesters, was one such experiment (see 'Children's Crusade', *Scotsman*, 4 March 1995).

My reference to reversing the flight of the Irish earls should be taken as metaphoric. I mean that we need to replenish the psychic vacuum left when the traditional leadership took flight in Ireland's 'saddest day'; not a wish to see restoration *per se* of the traditional patriarchal military leadership forms of the clans of the Scots–Irish Gaelic continuum. Incidentally, it should be noted that that continuum was split as a result of deliberate colonial policy by King James VI and I, who instituted the Plantation of Ulster, as well as the Statutes of Iona and the colonisation of the eastern American seaboard. As Malcolm MacLean of the Gaelic Arts Project on Lewis says, the Irish peace process is also helping now to remake links between Irish and Scottish identity (pers. com.; see also MacInnes 1981).

Many of us who grew up in Presbyterian homes on Lewis now deeply resent the conditioning then often imposed on us to the effect that the Irish (and Southern Hebrideans) are 'Papist' and therefore 'Antichrist worshippers'. It was a conditioning not just of ignorance, but of long-standing manipulation by internal British colonial policy that divided us against our own people and contributed to a subtle Anglophobia which we must also wrestle to overcome – especially as many English, themselves, wake up to what it means to honour soul instead of pretending that it has no place in the brilliant rational techno-sunlight of modernity. I do not want such comments to be interpreted as a total refutation of the twentieth century. As Papua New Guineans recognise with their concept of the 'Melanesian Way', the future lies in our choosing what we want to meld from tradition and modernity. This means economy and technology serving community, and not vice versa as is the case with the triumvirate of institutions derived from Bretton Woods (IMF, World Bank and the GATT/WTO) to which I earlier alluded (see McIntosh 1994: 52–67, 1996a: 3–30).

Canon Angus MacQueen of Barra is one of my inspirers in thinking about the bardic schools. Douglas Fraser interviewing him for *The Scotsman* (Weekend, 1 October 1994: 2–3) quotes him as saying, 'All we want is the privilege of remaining poor and being crofters. Crofting is about poverty with dignity. If you stand on your own four or eight acres, you are monarch of all you survey, and it gives you a natural dignity which you are without the moment you walk on to the mainland.' Fraser goes on to say, 'But MacQueen has faced criticism for extending his views to education, for many Hebrideans, the only way out of poverty. Schools, he says, should be teaching them the bardic traditions of an oral culture, not encouraging them to leave the island for college. "Education now in the Hebrides is rubbish", says the Canon. "These schools should be in the middle of England. The 80% of them who want to be fishermen should be encouraged to do what they want. But the younger people now want to get on. Education has ruined them, and made parents ambitious for their children to get on, when they should be enjoying life. I don't blame them for wanting to get on, but I feel more at home with the lad or the girl who leaves school at 16 to become a fisherman or whatever. For those who have to go through the rough world of colleges and university, it's very unbalancing. So many of them are packing in half way through their courses. A Hebridean will find a quality of life, or else become an alcoholic or drug addict. He will cave in completely." '

Having myself left Lewis to go to university and 'get on and get out', I could not have appreciated the significance of Canon MacQueen's words until reflecting on my own background after serving as deputy-head of a school for 'drop-out' children in Papua New Guinea, where the same issues apply.

65 Partly allusion to Burns 'Tree of Liberty'; also Isaiah 61.3. Note that when Jesus launches

his ministry in Luke 4 by reading from Isaiah 61 he stops and closes the book half way through the second verse: that is, he is selective in his use of scripture. He associates himself with being in solidarity with the poor and freeing the oppressed, he continues up to the point of proclaiming the 'acceptable year of the Lord'. This is probably reference to the remarkable 'Jubilee' land ethic of Leviticus 25, whereby the land is rested every seventh year, and every fiftieth year (i.e. after seven times seven) all debts are cancelled and land that had been traded is returned to its original owners. Social and ecological justice would thereby have been regularly re-established (though there is no actual historical record of this being carried out). The excellent *HarperCollins Study Bible* (NRSV) commentary on the 'acceptable year' or 'time of favour' (61.2; 49.8) suggests that a better translation would be, 'establishing the land, apportioning the desolate heritages'. As such, Jesus' words are deeply relevant to land reform. What he significantly avoids is to continue reading from the Isaiah text after the first part of 61.2. If he had done so, he would have got straight into 'the day of vengeance of our God' and 'the sons of the alien shall be your plowmen' etc. Might this suggest that he would have sympathised with the Palestinian political cause?

Jesus' avoidance or reformation of parts of Old Testament theology is always striking. Carl Jung, in his brilliant *Answer to Job* (1984), suggests that Old Testament and some New Testament scripture can be read as a process of God's growing up into being humanised as God, through interaction with humankind within the constraints of time. Thus it is not only humankind that is evolving spiritually. How else, Jung asks, do we account for a supposedly omniscient God's infantile behaviour in making pacts with the Devil to torment poor Job? Was incarnation not as much a necessity for God as for humankind? And one might add, in a culture where mythopoetic narrative runs that we are made in God's image, is not the reciprocal that, in a sense, God is also in our image? Nowhere is the sometime moral superiority of humankind better drawn out than in the hilarious pleading of Abraham with God in Genesis 18.16–33. Here God is about to destroy Sodom. Abraham admonishes him, saying, 'Far be it from you to do such a thing, to slay the righteous with the wicked, so that the righteous fare as the wicked! Far be that from you!' He asks if God would spare the city if just fifty righteous men could be found there. God agrees. Abraham then progressively beats him down until God says he will spare the city if there are just ten such men.

Genesis 18.22 has it that Abraham remained standing before the Lord during this dialogue. However, the ancient Hebrew rendition was that 'the Lord remained standing before Abraham' (*HarperCollins Study Bible*, 28). I am advised by an Old Testament scholar friend that the conventional scripture translators could not bring themselves to use a rendition that showed God in the subordinate position, so they changed it. The radically orthodox St Athanasius (1953: 93) says of God that, through Christ, 'He, indeed, assumed humanity that we might become God.' However, the profound implications of the heresy I am here supporting is that through such figures as Abraham and Job, and doubtless many unsung women, the converse was also true. Humankind assumed God-like status in order that God might become more deeply humanised. This is better understood from the insight of Hindu Atman-Brahman metaphysics. Here individual soul is universal soul, thus dissolving any sharp God–human dichotomy. Such theology is in fact also buried in Christian scripture; for instance, in Jesus' parable of the vine (John 15) and, most profoundly, in a text that conventional biblical commentaries and clergy generally overlook because it fails to fit with the dogma of Jesus being the unique son of

God: namely, John 10.34–6. Here Jesus draws upon Psalms 82.6 for authority in claiming that, effectively, all who heed God are sons and daughters of God; indeed, all such are Gods, albeit are mortal. This might cast some light on the enigmatic plurality of the godhead in the early chapters of Genesis.

66 This is a Celtic symbol of the Holy Spirit, though when George MacLeod, founder of the Iona Community, was asked by his biographer Ron Fergusson what was his source, he replied, 'I have no idea. I probably made it up' (pers. com.).

As for standing stones, any Christian critique of new-found veneration for such 'sacred sites' must start by taking account of what might be learned of their purpose from scripture. As always, scripture is deeply ambivalent on such matters (cf. the smashing of standing stones in Exodus 34.10–15; note that the 'sacred poles' denounced by the jealous patriarchal representation of God in this text were emblems of Asherah (Astarte, Ashteroth), goddess of love and fecundity – *Jerusalem Bible* footnote and *HarperCollins* commentary). Nevertheless, we might reflect that the Book of Joshua (24.26–7) closes with Joshua setting up a standing stone to mark the new-found monotheism of his people: 'and [Joshua] took a great stone, and set it up there under an oak, that was by the sanctuary of the Lord. And Joshua said unto all the people, Behold, this stone shall be a witness unto us: for it hath heard all the words of the Lord which he spake unto us: it shall be therefore a witness unto you, lest ye deny your God'. Jacob, after his dream nearly four millennia ago of a ladder reaching into heaven, declared (Genesis 29.11–22): 'Surely the Lord is in this place; and I knew it not.' He then erected the stone that had been his pillow, saying, 'And this stone, which I have set for a pillar, shall be God's house.' In Scottish legend (which is psychologically true if factually open to question) this stone was a meteorite that had fallen to earth. In the sixth century BCE, Phoenicians brought it to Ireland's Hill of Tara. Around 500 CE the Dal Riata tribe brought it to Scotland, where it became St Columba's pillow. After this text was completed, it was returned from exile in England, to which it had been taken in 1296 by Edward I. This 'Pillow of the Community' yet awaits a more appropriate resting place than that military stronghold of the imperial British army, Edinburgh Castle.

67 Again, there is possible contradiction but no necessary contradiction between such 'pagan' imagery and Scotland's Christian tradition. In tradition, the faeries are all parts of the realms of God. Gaelic Bible translator the Rev. Robert Kirk of Aberfoyle (1691 [1990]), gives extensive scriptural analysis and justification of traditional faerie beliefs. North America's most prophetic white male Protestant theologian, Walter Wink (1992), effectively updates this in volume two of his powerful trilogy on naming, unmasking and engaging the powers in a world of domination; but for general reading see especially his remarkable, multiple-award-winning *Engaging the Powers* (1984). Fr. Dara Molloy of the Aran Islands, Ireland, sees pre-Christian beliefs as simply being 'our Old Testament' (1996).

The centrality of forgiveness to Christianity at its best is of key concern to this piece on the Gal–Gael (cf. William Blake, 'The Everlasting Gospel'). That is why, quite apart from defending myself from being discredited by super-quarry supporters, I have made such a point of weaving together Christian and pre-Christian traditions in this text. I believe we must hold as our touchstone an understanding of forgiveness if we are to avoid falling into nationalistic fascism; if we are to be with MacDiarmid whilst not succumbing to his excesses; if we are to refute the use of vestigial Scottish warriorship material in under-pinning certain American (and Scottish) racist cults such as the KKK and what I dub the

CCC – Celtic Culture Cops (cf. K. Scott, 'Marching as to War', *Herald*, 19 April 1996: 15). Forgiveness is simply acceptance – of others and, most importantly, of self. Only with such acceptance can the grip of the past release us into new growth; can the bonds of karma be broken to allow liberation from the potentially brutal cycle of cause and effect. It has been suggested that this is why our Druidic tradition needed Christianity. But too often 'Churchianity' has emphasised a transcendent 'otherworldly' 'pie-in-the-sky-when-you-die' type of Christianity. This has contributed towards the death of nature. Such travesty is violation of the saying of Luke 17.21, that the realm of God is here and now, and a violation of the very concept of incarnation, be it metaphorical or otherwise. Many of the churches increasingly recognise this as they come to terms with 'creation-centred' (as distinct from 'creationist') theology, which emphasises original blessing in counterpoint to original sin. Reconnection with our own 'Old Testament' in a Celtic spirituality of God and nature offers restoration of the face of the earth as well as good news to the poor.

68 'Old long ago' – for old times' sake.

69 This text grew out of many sessions round the fire at Pollok. Multiple events and people contributed ideas, which is why I would see myself as more narrator than sole author. The protest camp at Pollok ceremonially closed on 14 November 1996, the motorway driven through but a new consciousness opened up of spiritual, cultural, ecological and social renewal. The insight of 'Nature Religion Today' developed there is being taken forward under a newly constituted Gal–Gael Trust, aimed at self-help empowerment, cultural, ecological and employment projects and training.

My thanks go out to all who have commented on this text, especially Tessa Ransford, Scottish Poetry Library. The commentary to this text is dedicated to my great-great-grandfather, Murdo MacLennan (d. 1899), inspirational Free Church precentor (of spiritual song) and tradition bearer of Jamestown, Contin, Highlands.

Bibliography

Adams, Carol J. (1993), *Ecofeminism and the Sacred*, New York: Continuum

Adler, Margot (1986), *Drawing Down the Moon: Witches, Druids, Goddess-Worshippers and Other Pagans in America Today*, rev. and expanded edn, Boston: Beacon Press

Adorno, T. W. (1976), 'Alienated Masterpiece: The *Missa Solemnis*', *Telos* 28

Africa, T. W. (1991), 'Aunt Glegg Amongst the Dons', in W. M. Calder III (ed.), *The Cambridge Ritualists Reconsidered*, Atlanta: Illinois Classical Studies, pp. 21–35

Albanese, Catherine L. (1990), *Nature Religion in America: From the American Indians to the New Age*, Chicago: University of Chicago Press

Alexander, Kay (1992), 'Roots of the New Age', in Lewis, J. R. and J. G. Melton (eds), *Perspectives on the New Age*, Albany, NY: SUNY Press, pp. 30–47

Anand, Margo (1989), *The Art of Sexual Ecstasy*, Los Angeles: Tarcher

Andersen, Benedict (1991), *Imagined Communities: Reflections on the Origin and Spread of Nationalism*, rev. edn, London: Verso

Anderson, Cora (1994), *Fifty Years in the Faeri Tradition*, San Leandro, CA: Cora Anderson

Andresen, Karl (ed.) (1985ff.), *Handbuch der Dogmen- und Theologiegeschichte*, 3 vols, Berlin: de Gruyter

Apuleius, L. (1950), *The Golden Ass*, trans. R. Graves, Harmondsworth: Penguin

Ardener, S. (ed.) (1975), *Perceiving Women*, London: Malaby

Athanasius, St (1953), *On the Incarnation*, London: Mowbray

Atkinson, J. (1992), 'Shamanisms Today', *Annual Review of Anthropology* 21, pp. 307–30

Attfield, Robin (1991), *The Ethics of Environmental Concern*, London: University of Georgia Press

Augustine, St (1908), *The Confessions of Saint Augustine*, Cambridge: Cambridge University Press

Avalon, Arthur (1952), *The Great Liberation*, 5th edn, reprinted Madras: Ganeshan

Avalon, Arthur (1956), *Shākti and Shākta*, reprinted Madras: Ganeshan

Bachofen, J. J. (1967), *Myth, Religion and the Mother Right: Selected Writings of J. J. Bachofen*, London: Routledge and Kegan Paul

Bailey, Alice (1983), *The Soul, the Quality of Life: A Compilation*, London: Lucis Press

Balch, Robert W. and Taylor, David (1977), 'Seekers and Saucers: The Role of the Cultic Milieu in Joining a UFO Cult', *American Behavioral Scientist* 20 (6), pp. 839–60

Barker, E. (1989), *New Religious Movements: A Practical Introduction*, London: HMSO

Batchelor, Stephen (1994), *The Awakening of the West: The Encounter of Buddhism and Western Culture*, London: Aquarian

Baur, F. C. (1835), *Die christliche Gnosis: oder die christliche Religions-Philosophie in ihrer geschichlichen Entwicklung*, Tübingen

Beauvoir, Simone de (1972), *The Second Sex*, Harmondsworth: Penguin

Beck, Ulrich (1992), *The Risk Society*, London: Sage

Bednarowski, Mary (1992), 'The New Age and Feminist Spirituality', in J. R. Lewis and J. G. Melton (eds), *Perspectives on the New Age*, Albany, NY SUNY Press

Bem, Sandra (1974), 'The Measurement of Psychological Androgyny', *Journal of Consulting and Clinical Psychology*, 42(4), pp. 155–62

Bem, Sandra (1979), 'The Theory and Measurement of Androgyny', *Journal of Personality and Social Psychology*, 37(6), pp. 1047–54

Berger, P. (1970), *A Rumour of Angels*, New York: Doubleday

Berger, P. (1980), *The Heretical Imperative*, New York: Anchor Books

Berlin, I. (1955), 'The Counter Enlightenment', in *Against the Current: Essays in the History of Ideas*, Harmondsworth: Penguin

Beth, Rae (1992), *Hedge Witch: A Guide to Solitary Witchcraft*, London: Robert Hale

Beyer, Peter (1994), *Religion and Globalization*, London: Sage

Beyer, Peter (1996), 'World Views and Moralities: Constructing Effective Identities in a Globalising Society', paper presented to an international conference on the Study of World Views, Sigtuna, Sweden, March 1996

Bharati, Agehananda (1965), *The Tantric Tradition*, London: Rider

Bharati, Agehananda (1976), *The Light at the Centre*, Santa Barbara, CA: Ross-Erikson

Blonsky, Marshall (1985), *On Signs*, Baltimore: Johns Hopkins University Press

Bloom, William (ed.) (1991), *The New Age: An Anthology of Essential Writings*, London: Rider

Blumenberg, H. (1961), 'Die Vorbereitung der Neuzeit', *Philosophische Rundschau* 9, pp. 81–133

Bly, Robert (1990), *Iron John: A Book About Men*, Shaftesbury: Element

Boddy, J. (1994), 'Spirit Possession Revisited: Beyond Instrumentality', *Annual Review of Anthropology* 23, pp. 407–34

Boff, Leonardo ([1987] 1998), *The Maternal Face of God: The Feminine and its Religious Expressions*, London: Collins

Boucher, Sandy (1988), *Turning the Wheel: American Women Creating the New Buddhism*, Boston: Beacon Press

Bourguignon, E. (1973), *Religion, Altered States of Consciousness and Social Change*, Columbus: Ohio State University Press

Bourguignon, E. (1979), *Psychological Anthropology: An Introduction to Human Nature and Cultural Differences*, New York: Holt, Rinehart and Winston

Bradley, Stephen P., Hausman, Jerry A. and Nolan, Richard L. (eds) (1993), *Globalization, Technology, and Competition: The Fusion of Computers and Telecommunications in the 1990s*, Boston: Harvard Business School

Brooke, Anthony (1976), *Towards Human Unity*, London: Mitre Press

Brown, Peter (1990), *The Body and Sexuality: Men, Women and Sexual Renunciation in Early Christianity*, London: Faber

Bruce, S. (1995), *Religion in Modern Britain*, Oxford: Oxford University Press

Bruce, A. and Rennie, F. (1991), *The Land Out There: A Scottish Land Anthology*, Aberdeen: Aberdeen University Press

Burkert, W. (1979), *Structure and History in Greek Mythology and Ritual*, Berkeley CA: University of California Press

Burkert, W. (1985), *Greek Religion*, Cambridge, MA: Harvard University Press

Butler, Judith (1990), *Gender Trouble: Feminism and the Subversion of Identity*, London: Routledge

Butler, Judith (1993), *Bodies that Matter: On the Discursive Limits of Sex*, London: Routledge

Butterfield, Stephen (1992), 'Accusing the Tiger: Sexual Ethics and Buddhist Teachers', *Tricycle*, Summer, pp. 46–51

Butterfield, Stephen (1994), *The Double Mirror: A Skeptical Journey into Buddhist Tantra*, Berkeley, CA: North Atlantic

Caddy, Eileen (1988), *Flight into Freedom*, Shaftesbury: Element

Caddy, Peter (1996), *In Perfect Timing: Memoirs of a Man for the New Millennium*, Forres: Findhorn Press

Campbell, June (1996), *Traveller in Space: In Search of Female Identity in Tibetan Buddhism*, London: Athlone Press

Cantwell, Cathy (1995), 'The Dance of the Guru's Eight Aspects', *Tibet Journal* 20 (4), pp. 47–63

Carmichael, A. (1992), *Carmina Gadelica: Hymns and Incantations*, Edinburgh: Floris

Carr, Anne and Fiorenza, Elizabeth Schussler (eds) ([1991] 1996), *The Special Nature of Women?*, London: SCM Press pp. 75–84

Carson, Rachel (1965), *Silent Spring*, Harmondsworth: Penguin

Chabpel Tseten Phuntsok (1991), 'The Deity Invocation Ritual and the Purification Rite of Incense Burning in Tibet', *Tibet Journal* 16(3), pp. 3–27

Chambers (1992), *Dictionary of Beliefs and Religions*, Edinburgh: W. and R. Chambers

Champion, Françoise (1993), 'Religieux flottant, éclectisme et syncrétismes', in Jean Delumeau (ed.), *Le fait religieux*, Paris: Fayard, pp. 741–2

Chögyam [Rinpoche], Ngakpa (1990), 'Shamanic Practices in Tibetan Buddhism: An Interview with Ngakpa Chögyam Rinpoche', *Shaman's Drum* 20, pp. 44–52

Chorafas, Dimitris N. (1992), *The Globalization of Money and Securities: The New Products, Players, and Markets*, Chicago: Probus

Christ, Carol P. (1987), *Laughter of Aphrodite: Reflections on a Journey to the Goddess*, San Francisco: Harper & Row

Christ, Carol and Judith, Plaskow (1992), *WomanSpirit Rising*, 2nd edn, San Francisco: HarperSanFrancisco

Church of All Worlds (1995), Statement about the Church on the CAW World Wide Web Page (http://www.caw.org/)

Clark, E. A. (1983), *Women in the Early Church*, Washington, DE: Michael Glazer

Clark, G. (1940), *Prehistoric England*, London: Batsford

Clark, Jerome (1990), 'UFOs in the New Age', in J. G. Melton, J. Clark and A. Kelly (eds), *New Age Encyclopedia*, Detroit: Gale Research, pp. 476–80

Clatterbaugh, Kenneth (1990), *Contemporary Perspectives on Masculinity: Men, Women and Politics in Modern Society*, Boulder CO/Oxford: Westview Press

Cohn, Norman (1978), *The Pursuit of the Millennium*, St Albans: Paladin/Granada

Condren, M. (1989), *The Serpent and the Goddess: Women, Religion and Power in Celtic Ireland*, San Francisco: HarperSanFrancisco

Conley, Verena Andermatt (1997), *Ecopolitics: The Environment in Poststructuralist Thought*, London: Routledge

Cooper, David E. (1992), 'The Idea of Environment', in David E. Cooper and Joy A. Palmer (eds), *The Environment in Question: Ethics and Global Issues*, London: Routledge, pp. 165–80

Corkery, D. (1967), *The Hidden Ireland*, Dublin: Gill and Macmillan

Coward, Rosalind (1989), *The Whole Truth: The Myth of Alternative Health*, London: Faber

Crawford, O. G. S. (1925), *The Long Barrows of the Cotswolds*, Gloucester: John Bellows

Crawford, O. G. S. (1957), *The Eye Goddess*, London: Phoenix

Crowley, A. (1929 [1970], *Moonchild*, York Beach, ME: Samuel Weiser

Crowley, Vivianne ([1989] 1996), *Wicca: The Old Religion in the New Millennium*, London: Thorsons

Crowley, Vivianne (1990), 'Priestess and Witch', in Caitlín Matthews (ed.), *Voices of the Goddess: A Chorus of Sibyls*, Wellingborough: Aquarian Press, pp. 45–65

Crowley, Vivianne (1994), *Phoenix from the Flame: Pagan Spirituality in the Western World*, London: Aquarian

Dalai Lama, H. H. the 14th (1994), 'The Sheltering Tree of Interdependence', reprinted in *Snow Lion Newsletter and Catalog*, Spring, pp. 6–7

Daly, Mary ([1973] 1986), *Beyond God the Father: Toward a Philosophy of Women's Liberation*, London: Women's Press

Daly, Mary (1979), *Gyn/Ecology: The Metaethics of Radical Feminism*, London: Women's Press

Daly, Mary (1984), *Pure Lust: Elemental Feminist Philosophy*, London: Women's Press

Daly, Mary (1991), *Ecofeminism: Sacred Matter/Sacred Mother*, Chambersburg, PA: Anima Books

Dames, M. (1976), *The Silbury Treasure*, London: Thames and Hudson

Daniel, G. (1958), *The Megalith Builders of Western Europe*, London: Hutchinson

Daniel, G. and Renfrew, C. (1988), *The Idea of Prehistory*, Edinburgh: Edinburgh University Press

Daniel, Stephen L. (1986), 'The Patient as Text: A Model of Clinical Hermeneutics', *Theoretical Medicine*, 7

Deghage, Pierre (1985), *La naissance de Dieu, ou la doctrine de Jacob Boehme*, Paris: Albin Michel

Deghage, Pierre (1992) 'Jacob Boehme and his Followers', in A. Faivre and J. Needleman (eds), *Modern Esoteric Spirituality*, New York: Crossroad

Dehejia, Vidya (1986), *Yogini Cult and Temples: A Tantric Tradition*, New Delhi: National Museum

Delaney, C. (1988), 'Mortal Flow: Menstruation in Turkish Village Society', in T. Buckley and A. Gottlieb (eds), *Blood Magic*, Berkeley, CA: University of California Press

Denton, L. T. (1992), 'Varieties of Hindu Female Asceticism', in J. Leslie (ed.), *Roles and Rituals for Hindu Women*, Delhi: Motilal Banarsidass, pp. 211–31

Dillard, A. (1974), *Pilgrim at Tinker Creek*, New York: HarperCollins

Dillard, A. (1982), *Teaching a Stone to Talk: Expeditions and Encounters*, New York: HarperCollins

Douglas, Ann (1977), *The Feminization of American Culture*, New York: Knopf

Dunn, D. (ed.) (1992), *Twentieth-Century Scottish Poetry*, London: Faber

Dunning, John H., Kogut, Bruce and Blomstrom, Magnus (1990), *Globalization of Firms and the Competitiveness of Nations*, Lund: Institute of Economic Research, Lund University

Eder, Klaus (1996), *The Social Construction of Nature*, London: Sage

Eliade, M. ([1951] 1974), *Shamanism*, New York: Princeton University Press

Elliott, D. and Elliott, J. (eds) (1982), *Gods of the Byways*, Oxford: Museum of Modern Art

English-Lueck, J. A. (1990), *Health in the New Age: A Study in California Holistic Practices*, Albuquerque, NM: University of New Mexico Press

Evans, Sir A. (1901), 'The Neolithic Settlement at Knossos and its Place in the History of Early Aegean Culture', *Man* 1, pp. 184–6

Evans, Sir A. (1921), *The Palace of Minos*, London: Macmillan

Evans, Donald D. (1993), *Spirituality and Human Nature*, Albany, NY: SUNY Press

Evans Wentz, W. (1977), *The Fairy Faith in Celtic Countries*, Atlantic Highlands: Humanities Press

Faivre, A. (1994), *Access to Western Esotericism*, Albany, NY: SUNY Press

Faivre, A. and Needleman, J. (eds) (1992), *Modern Esoteric Spirituality*, New York: Crossroad

Faivre, A. and Voss, K. (1995), 'Western Esotericism and the Science of Religions', *Numen* 42 (1) pp. 48–77

Farrar, J. and Farrar, S. ([1981] 1989), *Eight Sabbats for Witches*, London: Robert Hale

Farrar, J. and Farrar, S. (1984), *The Witches' Way: Principles, Rituals and Beliefs of Modern Witchcraft*, London: Robert Hale

Farrar, J. and Farrar, S. (1991), *A Witches' Bible Compleat*, New York: Magickal Childe

Farrow, G. W. and Menon, I. (1992), *The Concealed Essence of the Hevajra Tantra*, Delhi: Motilal Banarsidass

Featherstone, M., Lash, S. and Robertson, R. (eds) (1995), *Global Modernities*, London: Sage

Fewell, Darner Nolan and Gunn, David M. (1993), *Gender, Power and Promise*, Nashville: Abingdon Press

Fields, Rick (1986), *How the Swans Came to the Lake: A Narrative History of Buddhism in America*, Boston: Shambhala

Findhorn Community (1978), *The Findhorn Garden*, London: Turnstone/Wildwood House

Fiorenza, Elizabeth Schussler (1983), *In Memory of Her: A Feminist Theological Reconstruction of Christian Origins*, London: SCM

Fleming, A. (1969), 'The Myth of the Mother Goddess', *World Archaeology* 1, pp. 247–61

Fludd, R. (1617), *Utriusque Cosmi Historia*, Oppenheim

Fortune, Dion (1935), *The Winged Bull*, London: Aquarian

Fortune, Dion (1976), *The Sea Priestess*, London: Wyndham

Foucault, Michel (1990), *The Order of Things: An Archeology of the Human Sciences*, London: Tavistock

Fox, Matthew (1990), *The Coming of the Cosmic Christ: The Healing of Mother Earth and the Birth of a Global Resource*, New York: Harper and Row

Fox, Robin Lane (1986a), 'Living Like Angels', in *Pagans and Christians in the Mediterranean World from the Second Century to the Conversion of Constantine*, London: Penguin, ch. 7

Fox, Robin Lane (1986b), *Pagans and Christians*, Oxford: Oxford University Press

Fox, Selena (1995), 'Sacred Forests, Sacred Trees of Circle Sanctuary', *Circle Network News* 17 (1) (1995), p. 4

Fox, Selena (1996), 'Sacred Land and Sacred Web: Circle Sanctuary', paper presented to the international conference on Nature Religion Today, Ambleside, April 1996

Gardner, Gerald B. ([1954] 1988), *Witchcraft Today*, London: Rider & Co., reprinted (1988), New York: Magickal Childe

Gardner, Gerald B. (1994), *High Magic's Aid*, London: Pentacle Enterprises

Gardner, G. B. (1959), *The Meaning of Witchcraft*, London: Aquarian

Gellner, David N. (1992), *Monk, Householder and Tantric Priest: Newar Buddhism and its Hierarchy of Ritual*, Cambridge: Cambridge University Press

Giddens, Anthony (1990), *The Consequences of Modernity*, Stanford, CA: Stanford University Press

Gilbert, Sandra and Gubar, Susan (1988), *No Man's Land: The Place of the Woman Writer in the Twentieth Century*, Newhaven, CI: Yale University Press

Gilley, S. and Shiels, W. J. [eds] (1994), *A History of Religion in Britain*, Oxford: Blackwell

Gimbutas, Marija (1982), *The Civilization of the Goddess: The World of Old Europe*, San Francisco: Harper and Row

Gimbutas, Marija (1989), *The Language of the Goddess*, San Francisco: Harper and Row

Ginzburg, C. (1992), *Ecstasies: Deciphering the Witches' Sabbat*, New York: Penguin

Godwin, J. (1994), *The Theosophical Enlightenment*, Albany, NY: SUNY Press

Goldenberg, Naomi (1979), *Changing of the Gods: Feminism and the End of Traditional Religions*, Boston, Beacon Press

Goodman, Felicitas D. (1988), *Ecstasy, Ritual and Alternate Reality*, Bloomington: Indiana University Press

Gordon-Brown, Ian and Somers, B. (1988), 'Transpersonal Psychotherapy', in John Rowan and W. Dryden (eds), *Innovative Therapy in Britain*, Milton Keynes: Open University Press, pp. 225–49

Gossman, Elizabeth (1991), 'The Construction of Women's Difference in the Christian Theological Tradition', in Anne Carr and Elizabeth Schussler Fiorenza (eds), *The Special Nature of Women?*, London: SCM Press, pp. 50–9

Gottlieb, Roger S. (ed.) (1996), *This Sacred Earth: Religion, Nature, Environment*, London: Routledge

Graham, E. (1995), *Making the Difference: Gender, Personhood and Theology*, London: Mowbray

Graves, Robert ([1948, 1952] 1961), *The White Goddess: A Historical Grammar of Poetic Myth*, London: Faber

Greenfield, Allen (1992), 'A True History of Witchcraft', e-text incorporated in *Book of Shadows of the Riders of the Crystal Wind*, on Lysator Pagan Archives, ftp.lysator.liu.se

Greenwood, S. (1995), 'Wake the Flame Inside Us: Magic, Healing and the Enterprise Culture in Contemporary Britain', *Etnofoor* VII (1), pp. 47–62

Greenwood, S. (1996a), 'Feminist Witchcraft: A Transformatory Politics', in N. Charles and F. Hughes-Freeland (eds), *Practising Feminism: Identity, Difference and Power*, London: Routledge, pp. 109–34

Greenwood, S. (1996b), 'The Magical Will: Gender and Power in Magical Practices', in G. Harvey and C. Hardman (eds), *Paganism Today*, London: Thorsons, pp. 191–203

Grey, Mary (1989), *Redeeming the Dream: Feminism, Redemption and Christian Tradition*, London: SPCK

Grof, S. and Grof, C. (eds) (1989), *Spiritual Emergency: When Personal Transformation Becomes a Crisis*, New York: Tarcher/Putnam

Grove-White, Robin (1993), 'Environmentalism: A New Moral Discourse?', in K. Milton (ed.) *Environmentalism: The View from Anthropology*, London: Routledge, pp. 18–30

Guest, C. (trans.) (1906), *The Mabinogion*, London: Dent

Dunn, N. (1949), *Highland Pack*, London: Faber

Gupta, Sanjukta, Hoens, D. J. and Goudriaan, T. (1979), *Hindu Tantrism*, Handbuch der Orientalistik, pt 2 vol. 4, Leiden: Brill

Hables Gray, Chris (ed.) (1995), *The Cyborg Handbook*, London: Routledge

Hamilton, Malcolm *et al.* (1995), 'Eat, Drink and Be Saved: The Spiritual Significance of Alternative Diets', *Social Compass* (4), pp. 497–511

Hampson, M. D. (1990), *Theology and Feminism*, Oxford: Blackwell

Hanegraaff, Wouter (1993), 'In den beginne was de toorn: Het demonische bij Jacob Böhme', in Ab de Jong and Aleid de Jong (eds), *Kleine Encyclopedie van de Toorn*, Utrechtse Theologische Reeks 21, Utrecht

Hanegraaff, Wouter (1995), 'From the Devil's Gateway to the Goddess Within: The Image of the Witch in Neopaganism', in R. Kloppenborg and W. J. Hanegraaff (eds), *Female Stereotypes in Religious Traditions*, Leiden: Brill, pp. 213–42

Hanegraaf, Wouter (forthcoming), 'A Woman Alone: The Beatification of Friederika Hauffe née Wanner (1801–1829)', in Anne-Marie Korte (ed.)

Harner, M. (1980), *The Way of the Shaman*, San Francisco: Harper

Harraway, Donna J. (1991), *Simians, Cyborgs and Women: The Reinvention of Nature*, New York: Free Association Books

Harris, Ian (1995), 'Getting to Grips with Buddhist Environmentalism: A Provisional Typology', *Journal of Buddhist Ethics* 2, pp. 173–90

Harrison, J. E. (1903), *Prolegomena to the Study of Greek Religion*, 2nd edn, Cambridge: Cambridge University Press

Harrison, J. E. (1912), *Themis: A Study of the Origins of Greek Religion*, Cambridge: Cambridge University Press

Harrison, J. E. (1913), *Ancient Art and Ritual*, London: Williams Norgate

Harvey, Graham (1996), 'Handfastings, Funerals and other Druid Rites of Passage', in P. Carr-Gomm (ed.), *The Druid Renaissance*, London: Thorsons, pp. 202–17

Harvey, Graham (1997), *Listening People, Speaking Earth: Contemporary Paganism*, London: Hurst

Harvey, Graham and Hardman, Charlotte (eds) (1996), *Paganism Today: Wiccans, Druids, the Goddess and Ancient Earth Traditions for the Twenty-First Century*, London: Thorsons

Hawkes, J. (1951), *A Land*, London: Cresset

Hawkes, J. (1954a), *A Guide to the Prehistoric and Roman Monuments of England and Wales*, London: Chatto and Windus

Hawkes, J. (1954b), *Man on Earth*, London: Cresset

Hawkes, J. (1962), *Man and the Sun*, London: Cresset

Hawkes, J. (1963) UNESCO *History of Mankind: Volume 1, Part 1*, New York: UNESCO

Hawkes, J. (1967), 'God in the Machine', *Antiquity* 41, pp. 174–80

Hawkes, J. (1968a), 'The Proper Study of Mankind', *Antiquity* 42, pp. 255–62

Hawkes, J. (1968b), *Dawn of the Gods*, London: Chatto and Windus

Hawkes, J. and Priestley, J. B. (1955) *Journey Down a Rainbow*, London: Heinemann-Cresset

Heaney, S. (trans.) (1984), *Sweeney Astray*, London: Faber

Heckman, S. J. (1990), *Gender and Knowledge: Elements of a Postmodern Feminism*, Cambridge: Polity Press

Heelas, Paul (1996), *The New Age Movement*, Oxford: Blackwell

Hennessy (1885–6), *Kilkenny Archaeological Journal*, cited in P. B. Ellis (1995), *Celtic Women*, London: Constable

Hinnells, John R. (ed. 1995), *A New Dictionary of Religions*, Oxford: Blackwell

Hobsbawm, E. and Ranger, T. (eds) (1983), *The Invention of Tradition*, Cambridge: Cambridge University Press

Holm, Hans-Henrik and Sensen, Georg (1995), *Whose World Order? Uneven Globalization and the End of the Cold War*, Boulder, CO: Westview Press

Huber, Toni (1991), 'Traditional Environmental Protectionism in Tibet Reconsidered', *Tibet Journal* 16(3), pp. 63–77

Huntington, Samuel P. (1992), 'The Clash of Civilizations?', *Foreign Affairs* 72, pp. 22–49

Hutton, R. (1991), *Pagan Religions of the Ancient British Isles*, Oxford: Blackwell

Hutton, R. (1996a), 'The Roots of Modern Paganism', in G. Harvey and C. Hardman (eds), *Paganism Today*, London: Thorsons, pp. 3–15

Hutton, R. (1996b) 'The Discovery of the Modern Goddess', paper presented to the international conference on Nature Religion Today, Ambleside, April 1996 (in this volume)

Hutton, R. (1996c), *The Stations of the Sun: A History of the Ritual Year in Britain*, Oxford/New York: Oxford University Press

Jacobs, Janet (1984), 'The Economy of Love in Religious Commitment: the Deconversion of Women from Non-Traditional Religious Movements', *Journal for the Scientific Study of Religion*, 23(2), pp. 155–71

James, E. O. (1959), *The Cult of the Mother Goddess*, London: Thames and Hudson

John Paul II, Pope (1988), *Mulieris Dignitatem*, London: CTS

John Paul II, Pope (1990), 'The Ecological Crisis: A Common Responsibility', London: CTS

Jonas, Hans (1963), *The Gnostic Religion: The Message of the Alien God and the Beginnings of Christianity*, Boston: Beacon Press

Jones, Cheslyn, Wainwright, Geoffrey and Yarnold, Edward (eds) (1986), *The Study of Spirituality*, London: SPCK

Jones, Prudence (1992), *The Path to the Centre: The Grail Initiations in Wicca*, 2nd edn, London: Pagan Federation

Jones, P. (1996), 'The European Native Tradition', paper presented to the international conference on Nature Religion Today, Ambleside, April 1996 (in this volume)

Jones, P. and Pennick, N. (1995), *A History of Pagan Europe*, London: Routledge

Joy, M. (1995), 'God and Gender: Some Reflections on Women's Invocations of the Divine', in U. King (ed.), *Religion and Gender*, Oxford: Blackwell, pp. 121–43

Jung, C. G. (1959), *Collected Works. Volume 9, Part 1: The Archetypes and the Collective Unconscious*, London: Routledge

Jung, C. G. (1984), *Answer to Job*, London: Ark

Jung, C G (1986), *Aspects of the Feminine*, London: Ark

Kapferer, B. ([1983] 1991), *A Celebration of Demons*, Oxford: Berg

Kelly, Aidan A. (1991), *Crafting the Art of Magic, Book I*, St Paul, MN: Llewellyn

Kelly, J. N. D. (1968), 'From Nicaea to Chalcedon', in *Early Christian Doctrines*, London: Adam & Charles Black, pt III

Kendrick, T. D. (1927), *The Druids*, London: Methuen

Keyes, Charles F. (1984), 'Mother or Mistress but Never a Monk: Buddhist Notions of Female Gender in Rural Thailand', *American Ethnologist* 11, pp. 223–4

King, Ursula ([1989] 1993), *Women and Spirituality: Voices of Protest and Promise*, London: Macmillan

King, Ursula (1995), *Religion and Gender*, Oxford: Blackwell

Kircher, A. (1652), *Oepidus Aegyptiacus*, Rome

Kirk, Rev. R. of Aberfoyle ([1691] 1990), 'The Secret Commonwealth of Elves, Fauns and Fairies', in R. J. Stewart, *Robert Kirk: Walker Between Worlds*, Longmead: Elements

Kirsch, A. Thomas (1985), 'Text and Context: Buddhist Sex Roles/Culture of Gender Revisited', *American Ethnologist* 12, pp. 302–20

Klein, Anne Carolyn (1995), *Meeting the Great Bliss Queen: Buddhists, Feminists, and the Art of the Self*, Boston: Beacon Press

Knott, Kim (1995), 'The Debate about Women in the Hare Krishna Movement', *Journal of Vaishnava Studies* 3(4), pp. 85–109

Kuhn, H. (1963), 'Natur', in H. Fries (ed.), *Handbuch Theologischer Grundbegriffe*, Munich: Kosel Verlag, vol. 1, pp. 211–17

Lalou, Marcelle (1965), 'Préliminaires d'une étude des Ganacakra', in Yukei Matsunaga (ed). *Studies of Esoteric Buddhism and Tantrism in Commemoration of the 1150th Anniversary of the Founding of Koyasan*, Koyasan: Koyasan University Press

Lau, D. C. (trans.) (1963), *Tao Te Ching*, Harmondsworth: Penguin

Laviolette, P. and MacIntosh, A. (forthcoming), 'Fairy Hills: Merging Heritage and Conservation', *ECOS: Journal of the British Association for Nature Conservationists*

Laxer, James (1993), *False God: How the Globalization Myth has Impoverished Canada*, Toronto: Lester

Leach, E. (1976), *Culture and Communication*, Cambridge: Cambridge University Press

Leech, Kenneth (1986), *Soul Friend*, London: Sheldon Press

Lethbridge, T. C. (1961), *Ghost and Ghoul*, London: Routledge and Kegan Paul

Levenson, Joseph R. (1967), *European Expansion and the Counter-Example of Asia 1300–1600*, Englewood Cliffs, NJ: Prentice-Hall

Levine, Michael P. (1994), *Pantheism: A Non-theistic Concept of Deity*, London/New York: Routledge

Lewis, J. R. and Melton, J. G. (eds) (1992), *Perspectives on the New Age*, Albany, NY: SUNY Press

Loades, Ann (1990), *Feminist Theology: A Reader*, London: SPCK

Lovelock, James E. (1979), *Gaia: A New Look at Life on Earth*, Oxford: Oxford University Press

Luhrmann, Tanya H. (1989), *Persuasions of the Witch's Craft*, Boston: Harvard University Press

MacAulay, J. (1996), *Birlinn: Longships of the Hebrides*, Harris: White Horse

MacCormack, Carol P. (1980), 'Nature Culture, and Gender: a Critique', in Carol P. MacCormack and M. Strathern (eds), *Nature, Culture and Gender*, Cambridge: Cambridge University Press

Macdonald, D. (1990), *Lewis: A History of the Island*, Edinburgh: Gordon Wright

MacInnes, J. (1981), 'The Gaelic Continuum in Scotland', in R. O'Driscoll (ed.), *The Celtic Consciousness*, Edinburgh: Canongate, pp. 269–81

MacLean, Rev. A. (1937), *Hebridean Altars*, Edinburgh: Moray Press

Maclean, Dorothy (1980), *To Hear the Angels Sing*, Forres: Findhorn Press

Mann, Michael (1986), *The Sources of Social Power*, vol. 1, *A History of Power from the Beginning to AD 1760*, Cambridge: Cambridge University Press

Mann, T. ([1924] 1967), *Der Zauberberg*, Frankfurt: S. Fischer

Mann, T. (1972), *The Magic Mountain*, trans. H. T. Lowe-Porter, New York

Marglin, F. A. (1985), *Wives of the God-King: The Rituals of the Devadasis of Puri*, Delhi: Oxford University Press

Maringer, J. (1960), *The Gods of Prehistoric Man*, London: Weidenfeld and Nicolson

Massingham, H. J. (1932), *World Without End*, London: Cobden-Sanderson

Massingham, H. J. (1943), *The Tree of Life*, London: Chapman and Hall

Massingham, H. J. (1944), *Remembrance: An Autobiography*, London: Batsford

Matthews, Caitlín (1989), *The Elements of the Goddess*, Shaftesbury: Element

Matthews, Caitlín (ed.) (1990), *Voices of the Goddess*, London: Aquarian Press

McDaniel, June (1989), *The Madness of the Saints: Ecstatic Religion in Bengal*, Chicago: University of Chicago Press

McDaniel, June (1992), 'The Embodiment of God among the Bauls of Bengal', *Journal of Feminist Studies in Religion* 8, (2), pp. 27–39

McGaa, Ed (Eagleman) (1990), *Mother Earth Spirituality*, San Francisco: HarperSanFrancisco

McIntosh, A. (1994), 'Journey to the Hebrides', *Scottish Affairs* 6, pp. 52–67

McIntosh, A. (1995a), 'Public Inquiry on the Proposed Harris Superquarry: Witness on the Theological Considerations Concerning Superquarrying and the Integrity of Creation', *Journal of Law and Religion*, Hamline University Law School, XI (2), pp. 757–91, 792–833

McIntosh, A. (1995b), 'Theology Rocks Superquarry Scheme', in ECOS: *Journal of the British Association for Nature Conservationists* 16 (1), pp. 18–20

McIntosh, A. (1996a), 'The Emperor has no Clothes . . . Let us Paint our Loincloths Rainbow: A Classical and Feminist Critique of Contemporary Science Policy', *Environmental Values* 5 (1), pp. 3–30

McIntosh, A. (1966b), 'MacMoses Motorway', *Lady Godiva* 97

McIntosh, A., Wightman, A and Morgan, D. (1994), 'Reclaiming the Scottish Highlands: Clearance, Conflict and Crofting', *Ecologist* 24 (2), pp. 64–70

McKay, George (1996), *Senseless Acts of Beauty: Cultures of Resistance since the Sixties*, London/ New York: Verso

McMahon, T. (1990) 'Tam o' Shanter': An Interpretation', *Scottish Literary Journal*, 17 (2), pp. 5–14

McMahon, T. (1991), 'Shaman Dancing on a Glacier: Bruns, Beuys and Beyond', *Supplement to ArtWork* 50, pp. 2–3

McNeill, F. M. (1989), *The Silver Bough*, Edinburgh: Canongate

McNeill, F. M. (ed.) (1990), *An Iona Anthology*, Iona: Iona Community

Melton, J. Gordon (1994), 'Sexuality and the Maturation of "The Family"', unpublished paper presented at Federal University of Pernambuco, Brazil

Melton, J. Gordon (1993), *The Encyclopedia of American Religions*, 3rd edn, Detroit: Gale Research

Melton, J. G., Clark, J. and Kelly, A. (1990), *New Age Encyclopedia*, 1st edn, Detroit: Gale Research

Merchant, C. (1980), *The Death of Nature*, San Francisco: Harper Row

Meszaros, Istvan ([1972] 1975), *Marx's Theory of Alienation*, London: Merlin

Metz, J. B. (ed.), *God as Father?*, special issue of *Concilium* 143

Mind Body Spirit (1996), *20th Anniversary Festival Programme*, London: New Life Promotions

Mitchinson, N. (1931), *The Corn King and the Spring Queen*, London: Jonathan Cape

Molloy, Fr Dara (1996), 'Refounding the Celtic Church', *Aisling* 18, pp. 5–13

Moltmann-Wendel, Elizabeth (1986), *A Land Flowing with Milk and Honey*, London: SCM

Moltmann-Wendel, Elizabeth and Moltmann, Jürgen (1983), *Humanity in God*, London: SCM

Murray, Margaret A. (1921), *The Witch-Cult in Western Europe: A Study in Anthropology*, Oxford: Clarendon Press

Murray, Margaret A. ([1931] 1971), *The God of the Witches*, New York: Oxford University Press; London: Faber

Nasr, Seyyed Hossein (1968), *Man and Nature: The Spiritual Crisis in Modern Man*, London: George Allen and Unwin

Nasr, Seyyed Hossein (1996), *Religion and the Order of Nature*, Oxford: Oxford University Press

Nederven Pieterse, Jan (1993), *Globalization as Hybridization*, The Hague: Institute of Social Studies

Needleman, J. (1970), *The New Religions*, Garden City, NY: Doubleday

Needleman, J. (1993), 'Introduction II', in Antoine Faivre and J. Needleman (eds), *Modern Esoteric Spirituality*, London: SCM, pp. xxiii–xxx

Neitz, Mary-Jo (1990), 'In Goddess We Trust', in Robbins and Anthony (eds), *In Gods We Trust*, 2nd edn, New Brunswick NJ: Transaction Publishers

Nelson, James (1992), *The Intimate Connection: Male Sexuality, Masculine Spirituality*, London: SPCK

Neumann, Erich (1963), *The Great Mother: An Analysis of an Archetype*, Princeton, NJ: Princeton University Press

Neumann, Erich (1964), *The Origins and History of Consciousness*, Princeton, NJ: Princeton University Press

Nicolescu, B. (1991), *Science, Meaning & Evolution: The Cosmology of Jacob Boehme*, New York: Parabola Books

Noble, V. (1989), 'Marija Gimbutas Reclaiming the Great Goddess', *Snake Power* 1, pp. 5–7

Noble, V. (1991), *Shakti Woman*, San Francisco: HarperSanFrancisco

Noll, R. (1985), 'Mental Imagery Cultivation as a Cultural Phenomenon: The Role of Visions in Shamanism', *Current Anthropology* 26 (4)

Norbu, Namkhai (1986), *The Crystal and the Way of Light: Sutra, Tantra and Dzogchen*, ed. J. Shane (ed.) New York/London: Routledge and Kegan Paul

Northcott, Michael (1996), *The Environment and Christian Ethics*, Cambridge: Cambridge University Press

O'Baoill, C. (1994), *Gair nan Clarsach, The Harp's Cry*, Edinburgh: Birlinn

O'Cathain, S. (1995), *The Festival of Brigit: Celtic Goddess and Holy Woman*, Dublin: DBS Publishing

Odum, Eugene P. (1953), *The Fundamentals of Ecology*, Philadelphia: W. B. Saunders

O'Leary, T. (1996), 'Nae fur the Likes O' Us: Poverty, Agenda 21 and Scotland's Non-Governmental Organisations', *Scottish Affairs* 16, pp. 62–80

Orion, Loretta (1995), *Never Again the Burning Times: Paganism Revived*, Prospect Heights, IL: Waveland Press

Ortner, S. B. (1974), 'Is Female to Nature as Nature is to Culture?', in M. Z. Rosaldo and L. Lanphere (eds), *Women, Culture and Society*, Stanford, Stanford University Press

Otto, Rudolf (1919), *Das Heilige: Über das Irrationale in der Idee des Göttlichen und sein Verhältnis zum Rationalen*, 3rd edn, Breslau: Trewendt & Granier

Pagels, Elaine (1982), *The Gnostic Gospels*, Harmondsworth: Penguin

Palmer, S. (1994), *Moon Sisters, Krishna Mothers, Rajneesh Lovers*, New York: Syracuse

Panikkar, R. (1991), 'Nine Sutras on Peace', *Interculture* 24 (1), pp. 49–56

Peacock, S. J. (1998), *Jane Ellen Harrison: The Mask and the Self*, New Haven, CT: Yale University Press

Pendderwen, Gwydion (1995), *Wheel of the Year: The Music of Gwydion Pendderwen*, Ukiah, CA: Nemeton

Phillips, Julia (1991), 'History of Wicca in England: 1939–Present Day', e-text, incorporated in *Book of Shadows of the Riders of the Crystal Wind*, on Lysator Pagan Archives, ftp.lysator.liu.se

Piggott, S. (1986), 'Ancient British Craftsmen', *Antiquity* 60

Plaskow, Judith (1983), *Sex, Sin and Grace: Women's Experience and the Theologies of Reinhold Niebuhr and Paul Tillich*, Washington, DC: University Press of America

Plaskow, J. and Christ, C. P. (eds) (1989), *Weaving the Visions: New Patterns in Feminist Spirituality*, New York: Harper and Row

Plumwood, V. (1993), *Feminism and the Mastery of Nature*, London: Routledge

Ponting, Clive (1988), *The Green History of the World*, London: Penguin

Porterfield, Amanda (1990), 'American Indian Spirituality as a Counter-Cultural Movement', in C. Vecsey (ed.), *Religion in Native North America*, Moscow, ID: University of Idaho, pp. 152–64

Primavesi, A. (1991), *From Apocalypse to Genesis: Ecology, Feminism and Christianity*, London: Burns and Oates

Puttick, Elizabeth (1997), *Women in New Religions*, London: Macmillan

Qualls-Corbett, Nancy (1988), *The Sacred Prostitute*, Toronto: Inner City Books

Ranke-Heinemann, U. ([1990] 1991), *Eunuchs for Heaven: The Catholic Church and Sexuality*, London: Deutsch

Redfield, James (1994), *The Celestine Prophecy*, London: Bantam

Regardie, I. (1971), *The Golden Dawn*, St Paul, MN: Llewellyn Publications

Restall Orr, Emma (forthcoming a), *Principles of Druidry*, London: Thorsons

Restall Orr, Emma (forthcoming b), *Spirits of the Sacred Grove*, London: Thorsons

Reuter, O. S. (1934), *Germanische Himmelskunde*, Munich: Lehmann

Ricoeur, Paul (1988), *Från text till handling*, Stockholm: Symposion Bokförlag

Riesebrodt, M. (1993), *Pious Passion: The Emergence of Modern Fundamentalism in the United States and Iran*, Berkeley, CA: University of California Press

Riordan, Suzanne (1992), 'Channeling: A New Revelation?', in James R. Lewis and J. G. Melton (eds), *Perspectives on the New Age*, Albany, NY: SUNY Press, pp. 105–26

Ritzer, George (1996), *The McDonaldization of Society: An Investigation into the Changing Character of Contemporary Life*, rev. edn, Thousand Oaks, CA: Pine Forge

Roberts, R. H. (1990), *Hope and its Hieroglyph: A Critical Decipherment of Ernst Bloch's 'Principle of Hope'*, Atlanta: Scholars Press

Roberts, R. H. (1992), *A Theology on Its Way: Essays on Karl Barth*, Edinburgh: T. & T. Clark

Roberts, R. H. (1993), 'The Spirit of Democratic Capitalism: A Critique of Michael Novak', in Jon Davies and David Green (eds), *God and the Marketplace: Essays on the Morality of Wealth Creation*, London: Institute of Economic Affairs, pp. 64–81

Roberts, R. H. (1995), 'Identity and Belonging', in Theo van Willigenberg, Robert Heeger and Wibren van der Burg (eds), *Nation, State, and the Coexistence of Different Communities*, Kampen: Kok Pharos Publishing House, pp. 25–56

Roberts, R. H. (1996a), 'Like Glist'ring Phaethon: Male Self-Identity in an Era of Diminishing Expectations', unpublished lecture delivered in the Universities of Durham and Bristol

Roberts, R. H. (1996b), 'Theology and Social Science', in David Ford (ed.), *The Modern Theologians*, 2nd rev. edn, Oxford: Blackwell, pp. 700–19

Roberts, R. H. (forthcoming), 'Masculinity', in Adrian Hastings (ed.), *The Oxford Companion to Christian Thought*, Oxford: Oxford University Press

Robertson, Roland (1987), 'Globalization and Societal Modernization: A Note on Japan and Japanese Religion', *Sociological Analysis* 47(S), pp. 35–42

Robertson, Roland (1992), *Globalization: Social Theory and Global Culture*, London: Sage

Robertson, Roland and Garrett, R. William (1991), *Religion and Global Order*, New York: Paragon House

Rodd, R. (1892), *The Customs and Love of Modern Greece*, London: David Stott

Roper, L. (1994), *Oedipus and the Devil*, London: Routledge

Rose, Stuart (1996), 'Transforming the World: An Examination of the Roles Played by Spirituality and Healing in the New Age Movement "The Aquarian Conspiracy Revisited" ', Lancaster, unpublished doctoral thesis

Ross, A. (1973), 'The Divine Hag of the Pagan Celts', in V. Newell (ed.), *The Witch Figure*, London: Routledge and Kegan Paul

Rowan, John (1976), *Ordinary Ecstasy: Humanistic Psychology in Action*, London: Routledge and Kegan Paul

Ruether, Rosemary Radford (1975), *New Woman, New Earth*, New York: Seabury

Ruether, Rosemary Radford (1983), *Sexism and God-Talk: Towards a Feminist Theology*, London: SMC

Russell, Peter (1988), *The Earth Awakening: The Global Brain*, Harmondsworth: Arkana

Rutter, Peter (1990), *Sex in the Forbidden Zone*, London: Mandala

Sachs, Wolfgang (ed.) (1993), *Global Ecology: A New Arena of Conflict*, London: Zed Books

Salomonsen, Jone (1996), ' "I am a Witch – a Healer and a Bender": An Expression of Women's Religiosity in Contemporary USA', Oslo, unpublished doctoral dissertation

Samuel, Geoffrey (1989), 'The Body in Buddhist and Hindu Tantra', *Religion* 19, pp. 197–210

Samuel, Geoffrey (1993), *Civilized Shamans: Buddhism in Tibetan Societies*, Washington, DC: Smithsonian Institution Press

Samuel, Geoffrey (1994), 'Auspiciousness and the Goddesses of India', paper for Department of Religious Studies, Lancaster University, March 1994

Samuel, Geoffrey (1995a), 'Tibetan Buddhism as a World Religion: Global Networking and its Consequences', paper for workshop at the Department of Theology and Religious Studies, King's College, University of London, December 1995

Samuel, Geoffrey (1995b), 'Vajrayāna Buddhism in Tibet as a Dissenting Tradition and its Partial Hegemonization in Tibet', paper for the South Asian Anthropology Group conference, London School of Economics, September 1995

Sanderson, Alexis (1988), 'Śaivism and the Tantric Traditions', in Stewart Sutherland, L. Houldern, P. Clarke and F. Hardy (eds), *The World's Religions*, London: Routledge, pp. 660–704

Sawyer, D. F. (1992), 'Resurrecting Eve? Feminist Critique of the Garden of Eden', in P. M. Morris and D. F. Sawyer (eds), *A Walk in the Garden: Biblical, Iconographical and Literary Images of Eden*, Sheffield: Sheffield Academic Press, pp. 273–89

Seed, John, Macy, Joanna, Fleming, Pat and Naess, Arne (1988), *Thinking Like a Mountain: Towards a Council of All Beings*, Philadelphia: New Society

Segal, Lynne (1990), *Slow Motion: Changing Masculinities, Changing Men*, London: Virago

Shallcrass, Philip (1996a), 'A Priest of the Goddess', *Druid's Voice* 7, pp. 9–18

Shallcrass, Philip (1996b), 'Awen: Holy Spirit of Druidry', in *Druidry: Native Spirituality in Britain*, St Leonards-on-Sea: British Druid Order, pp. 24–38

Shallcrass, Philip (1997), *The Story of Taliesin*, St Leonards-on-Sea: British Druid Order

Shaw, M. F. (1986), *Folksongs and Folklore of South Uist*, Aberdeen: Aberdeen University Press

Shaw, Miranda (1994), *Passionate Enlightenment: Women in Tantric Buddhism*, Princeton, NJ: Princeton University Press

Sjöö, Monica (1992), *New Age and Armageddon: The Goddess or the Gurus? Towards a Feminist Vision of the Future*, London: Women's Press

Sjöö, M. and Mor, B. ([1987] 1991), *The Great Cosmic Mother: Rediscovering the Religion of the Earth*, San Francisco: Harper and Row

Smith, Anthony D. (1991), *The Age of Behemoths: The Globalization of Mass Media Firms*, New York: Priority

Smith, David (1996), 'Kali East and West', paper presented to the international conference on Nature Religion Today, April 1996

Smith, E. (1984), *A Dictionary of Classical Reference in English Poetry*, Cambridge: D. S. Brewer

Smythe, A. D. (1984), *Warlords and Holy Men*, Edinburgh: Edinburgh University Press

Snellgrove, David L. (1987), *Indo-Tibetan Buddhism: Indian Buddhists and Their Tibetan Successors*, 2 vols, Boston: Shambhala

Spangler, D. (1977), *Revelation: The Birth of a New Age*, Forres: Findhorn Foundation

Spangler, D. (1984), *Emergence: The Rebirth of the Sacred*, New York: Dell

Spiro, Melford E. (1967), *Burmese Supernaturalism: A Study in the Explanation and Reduction of Suffering*, Englewood Cliffs, NJ: Prentice-Hall, [expanded edn (1978), Philadelphia: Institute for the Study of Human Issues.

Sponberg, Alan (1992), 'Attitudes towards Women and the Feminine in Early Buddhism', in José Cabezón (ed.), *Buddhism, Sexuality and Gender*, Albany, NY: SUNY Press

Spretnak, C. (1982), *The Politics of Christian Spirituality: Essays on the Rise of Spiritual Power in the Feminist Movement*, Garden City, NY: Anchor Books

St John, John (1977), *Travels in Inner Space: One Man's Exploration of Encounter Groups, Meditation and Altered States of Consciousness*, London: Victor Gollancz

Starhawk ([1979], 1989), *The Spiral Dance: A Rebirth of the Ancient Religion of the Great Goddess*, 10th anniversary edn, San Francisco: HarperSanFrancisco

Starhawk (1990a), *Dreaming the Dark: Magic, Sex and Politics*, new edn, London: Mandala (Unwin Paperbacks)

Starhawk (1990b), *Truth or Dare: Encounters with Power, Authority, and Mystery*, San Francisco: Harper and Row

Starhawk (1993), *The Fifth Sacred Thing*, New York: Bantam

Stevens, John (1990), *Lust for Enlightenment*, Boston: Shambhala

Steyn, Chrissie (1994), *Worldviews in Transition: An Investigation into the New Age Movement in South Africa*, Pretoria: Unisa Press

Stone, Donald (1976), The Human Potential Movement', in Charles Glock and R. Bellah (eds), *The New Religious Consciousness*, Berkeley, CA: University of California Press, pp. 93–115

Storm, Rachel (1991), *In Search of Heaven on Earth*, London: Bloomsbury Press

Synge, J. M. (1992), 'The Aran Islands', in J. M. Synge, *Plays, Poems and Prose*

Tambiah, Stanley J. (1970), *Buddhism and the Spirit Cults in North-East Thailand*, Cambridge: Cambridge University Press

Taylor, B. (1997), 'Earthen Spirituality or Cultural Genocide? Radical Environmentalism's Appropriation of Native American Spirituality', *Religion* 27, pp. 183–215

Templeman, David (1994), 'Dohā, Vajragīti and Caryā Songs', in G. Samuel, H. Gregor and E. Stutchbury (eds), *Tantra and Popular Religion in Tibet*, New Delhi: Aditya Prakashan, pp. 15–38

Thompson, Keith (1991), *To Be a Man: In Search of the Deep Masculine*, Los Angeles: Jeremy B. Tarcher

Thompson, William Irwin (1981), *The Time Falling Bodies Take to Light: Mythology, Sexuality, and the Origins of Culture*, New York: St Martin's Press

Tillich, P. (1951), *Systematic Theology*, Vol. 1, Chicago: Chicago University Press

Tiryakian, Edward A. (1996), 'Three Metacultures of Modernity: Christian, Gnostic and Chthonic', *Theory, Culture and Society*, 13(1), pp. 99–118

Torrance, T. F. (1965), 'The Place of Christology in Biblical and Dogmatic Theology', *Theology in Reconstruction*, London: SCM, ch. 8

Treece, H. (1956), *The Golden Strangers*, London: Bodley Head

Trevelyan, George (1986), *Summons to a High Crusade*, Forres: Findhorn Press

Trible, Phyllis (1978), *God and the Rhetoric of Sexuality*, Philadelphia: Fortress Press

Tringham, R. (1993), 'Review of "Civilization of the Goddess" ', *American Anthropologist* 95, pp. 196–7

Troeltsch, E. (1931), *The Social Teachings of the Christian Churches*, 2 vols, London: George Allen and Unwin

Trungpa, Chögyam (1978), 'Some Aspects of Pön', in J. F. Fisher (ed.), *Himalayan Anthropology: The Indo-Tibetan Interface*, The Hague: Mouton, pp. 299–308

Trungpa, Chögyam (1982), *The Life of Marpa the Translator*, by Tsang Nyön Heruka, trans. from the Tibetan by the Nalanda Translation Committee under the direction of Chögyam Trungpa, Boulder, CO: Prajña

Turner, Bryan S. (1984), *The Body and Society: Explorations in Social Theory*, Oxford: Blackwell

Turner, Victor W. (1969), *The Ritual Process: Structure and Anti-Structure*, Chicago: Aldine

Twigg, Julia (1979), 'Food for Thought: Purity and Vegetarianism', *Religion* 9 (1) pp. 13–35

Ucko, P. (1962), 'The Interpretation of Prehistoric Athropomorphic Figurines', *Journal of the Royal Anthropological Institute* 92, pp. 38–54

Ucko, P. (1968), *Anthropomorphic Figurines of Predynastic Egypt and Neolithic Crete with Comparative Material from the Prehistoric Near East and Mainland Greece*, Royal Anthropological Institute Occasional Paper

Valiente, D. ([1973] 1986), *An ABC of Witchcraft Past and Present*, London: Robert Hale

Valiente, Doreen (1978), *Witchcraft for Tomorrow*, Custer, WA: Phoenix

Valiente, Doreen (1984), 'Appendix A: The Search for Old Dorothy', in J. Farrar and S. Farrar (eds), *The Witches' Way: Principles, Rituals and Beliefs of Modern Witchcraft*, London: Robert Hale, pp. 283–293

Valiente, Doreen (1989), *The Rebirth of Witchcraft*, Custer, WA: Phoenix

Valiente, Doreen (1995), 'Interview with Doreen Valiente', *Pagan Dawn* 117, pp. 18–22

Varndell, G. (1991), 'The Ritual Finds', in I. Longworth *et al.*, *Excavations at Grimes Graves, Norfolk 1972–1976: Fascicule 3*, London: British Museum, pp. 103–6

Velius, N. ([1981] 1989), *The World Outlook of the Ancient Balts*, Vilnius: Minters

Volkmann, Rosemarie (1995), 'Female Stereotypes in Tibetan Religion and Art: The Genitrix/Progenitress as the Exponent of the Underworld', in R. Kloppenborg and W. J. Hanegraaff (eds), *Female Stereotypes in Religious Traditions*, Leiden: Brill, pp. 171–211

Wadsworth, D. S. M. (1997), 'On Being a Priestess', unpublished material

Wakefield, G. S. (ed.) (1983), *A Dictionary of Christian Spirituality*, London: SCM

Wales, Roxana (1996), 'San Francisco Witches: Transformation and Personal Psychology in Harmony with a Living World', paper presented to the international conference on Nature Religion Today, Ambleside, April 1996

Walker, Alex (ed.) (1994), *The Kingdom Within: A Guide to the Spiritual Work of the Findhorn Community*, Forres: Findhorn Press

Wallerstein, Immanuel (1974), *The Modern World-System: Capitalist Agriculture and the Origins of the European World-Economy in the Sixteenth Century*, New York: Academic

Wallerstein, Immanuel (1979), *The Capitalist World-Economy*, Cambridge: Cambridge University Press

Wallis, Roy (1974), 'The Aetherius Society: A Case Study in the Formation of a Mystagogic Congregation', *Sociological Review* 22 (1), pp. 27–44

Webb, James (1991), *The Occult Establishment*, La Salle, IL: Open Court

Weber, Max (1979), *Economy and Society: An Outline of Interpretative Sociology*, 2 vols, Berkeley, CA: University of California Press

Webster, Sam (1996), 'Pagan Dharma', *Gnosis* 39 pp. 54–8

Weeks, Andrew (1991), *Boehme: An Intellectual Biography of the Seventeenth Century Philosopher and Mystic*, Albany, NY: SUNY Press

Weir, Allison (1996), *Sacrificial Logics: Feminist Theory and the Critique of Identity*, London: Routledge

Weiss, Brian (1988), *Many Lives, Many Masters*, London: Piatkus

Weston, J. ([1921] 1957), *From Ritual to Romance*, New York: Doubleday Anchor

White, Harlan (Moonstorm) (n.d.), 'Three Liberal Religious Traditions: Unitarian Universalism, Siddha Yoga, Church of All Worlds', CAW World Wide Web Page (http://www.caw.org/)

White, Hayden (1987), 'The Absurdist Movement in Literary Criticism', in Hayden White (ed.), *Tropics of Discourse*, Baltimore: Johns Hopkins University Press

White, Lynn (1967), 'The Historical Roots of our Ecological Crisis', *Science* 155, pp. 1203–7

Wightman, A. (1996), *Who Owns Scotland*, Edinburgh: Canongate

Williams, Raymond (1976), *Keywords: A Vocabulary of Culture and Society*, Glasgow: Fontana

Williams, Rowan (1979), *The Wound of Knowledge: Christian Spirituality from the New Testament to St John of the Cross*, London: Darton, Longman and Todd

Wilson, Steve and Medway, Gareth J. (1995), 'The New Forest Papers', *Aisling* (Magazine of the Druid Clan of Dana) 8, pp. 5–16

Wink, W. (1984), *Engaging the Powers: Discernment and Resistance in a World of Domination*, Minneapolis: Fortress Press

Wink, W. (1992), *Unmasking the Powers*, Minneapolis: Fortress Press

Wissowa, G. (1912), *Religion und Kultus der Römer*, Munich: Beck

Woodhead, Linda (1996), 'Untangling the Historical Roots of Alternative Spirituality', paper presented to the international conference on Nature Religion Today, Ambleside, April 1996

Worster, Donald (1993), *The Wealth of Nature: Environmental History and the Ecological Imagination*, New York: Oxford University Press

Wren, Brian (1989), *What Language Shall I Borrow? God-Talk in Worship: A Male Response to Feminist Theology*, London: SCM

Yeats, W. B. ([1893] 1990), *The Celtic Twilight*, Bridport: Prism Press

York, M. (1994), 'New Age in Britain: An Overview', *Religion Today* 9 (3), pp. 14–22

York, M. (1995), *The Emerging Network: A Sociology of the New Age and Neo-Pagan Movements*, Lanham, MD: Rowman and Littlefield

Zappone, K. (1991), *Hope for Wholeness: A Spirituality for Feminists*, Mystic, CT: Twenty-Third Publications

Index